Birds of
Nepal

OM FIELD GUIDES

Birds of Nepal

Richard Grimmett,
Carol Inskipp & Tim Inskipp

Illustrated by Clive Byers, Daniel Cole, John Cox,
Gerald Driessens, Carl D'Silva, Martin Elliott, Kim Franklin,
Alan Harris, Peter Hayman, Craig Robson, Jan Wilczur
and Tim Worfolk

OM
Om Books International

With special thanks to Hem Sagar Baral for the section on bird conservation.

To Helen, Ella and George with love and appreciation.
Richard Grimmett

To all those who generously sent us information about birds in Nepal, especially the Nepalis for their important contribution.
Carol and Tim Inskipp

THE COLOUR PLATES
Clive Byers 81-87, 97, 100-110
Daniel Cole 1-4, 20-22, 27, 58 (part), 75
John Cox 23-25
Gerald Driessens 19, 79,
Carl D'Silva 9-18, 26, 50-62, 80, 98, 99
Martin Elliott 34, 35
Kim Franklin 38 (part), 39
Alan Harris 36, 38 (part), 40 (part)-42, 47, 48, 64-74
Peter Hayman 28-33
Craig Robson 76-78, 88-96
Jan Wilczur 5-8, 49
Tim Worfolk 37, 40 (part), 43-46

Cover illustrations by John Cox

Published in 2009 by Om Books International
4379/4B, Prakash House, Ansari Road, Darya Ganj, New Delhi – 110002
Tel: +91 11 23263363 / 23265303
Fax: +91 11 23278091
Email: sales@ombooks.com
Web: www.ombooks.com

Photographs by Carol and Tim Inskipp

ISBN 978-81-87108-58-0

Published 2000 by Christopher Helm, an imprint of A & C Black Publishers Ltd.,
36 Soho Square, London W1D 3QY

Edited and designed by D&N Publishing, Unit 3c Lowesden Business Park, Lambourn Woodlands, Hungerford, Berkshire, UK

Printed in Thailand by Imago

10 9 8 7 6 5 4 3 2

CONTENTS

PAIR OF CHEER PHEASANTS CATREUS WALLICHII, BY DANIEL COLE

INTRODUCTION

Nepal is renowned for its high diversity of bird species, spectacular mountains and rich culture. Here you can enjoy birdwatching in one of the most beautiful places on Earth. This guide aims to help observers identify all of the bird species currently recorded in Nepal.

HOW TO USE THIS BOOK

Nomenclature

Taxonomy and nomenclature follow *An Annotated Checklist of the Birds of the Oriental Region* by Tim Inskipp, Nigel Lindsey and William Duckworth (1996). The sequence generally follows the same reference, although some species have been grouped out of this systematic order to enable useful comparisons to be made. In cases where differences in taxonomic opinion exist in the literature, the species limits are fully discussed in that work, to which readers requiring further information should initially refer.

Colour Plates and Plate Captions

Species that occur regularly in Nepal are illustrated in colour and described in the plate captions. Vagrant species are described in Appendix 1, with reference to distinguishing features from other more regularly recorded species where appropriate. The illustrations show distinctive sexual variation whenever possible. Some distinctive races as well as immature plumages are also depicted.

The captions identify the figures illustrated, very briefly summarise the species's distribution, status, altitudinal range and habitats, and provide information on the most important identification characters, including voice where this is an important feature, and approximate body length of the species, including bill and tail, in centimetres. Length is expressed as a range when there is marked variation within the species (e.g. as a result of sexual dimorphism or racial differences).

A general description is given of the species's status as a resident, winter visitor, summer visitor, passage migrant or altitudinal migrant. Data on actual breeding records and non-breeding ranges are very few, so it has not been possible to give comprehensive details. In addition, space limitations have meant that the simple terms, 'summers' and 'winters' are used to describe altitudinal ranges and habitats for many species. Note that many Himalayan species are recorded in summer over a wider altitudinal range than that within which they actually breed. Altitudes given are those for which the species have been recorded in Nepal unless otherwise stated. Altitudes thought to be outside the normal range are given in brackets. The identification texts are based on *Birds of the Indian Subcontinent*, by R. Grimmett, C. Inskipp and T. Inskipp. The vast majority of the illustrations have been taken from the same work and, wherever possible, the correct races for Nepal have been depicted. A small number of additional illustrations of races occurring in Nepal were executed for this book. Preparation of the text and plates for that work included extensive reference to museum specimens combined with considerable work in the field.

Plumage Terminology

The figures on p.8 illustrate the main plumage tracts and bare-part features, and are based on Grant and Mullarney (1988–1989). This terminology for bird topography has been used in the captions. Other terms have been used and are defined in the Glossary (*see* p.31). Juvenile plumage is the first plumage on fledging, and in many species it is looser, more

DESCRIPTIVE PARTS OF A BIRD

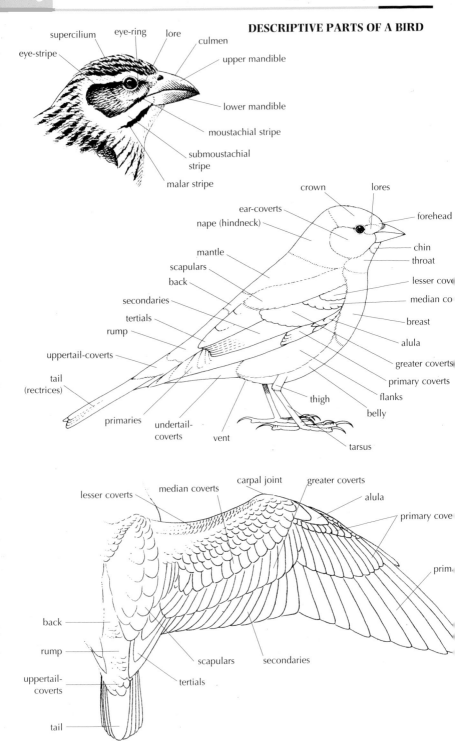

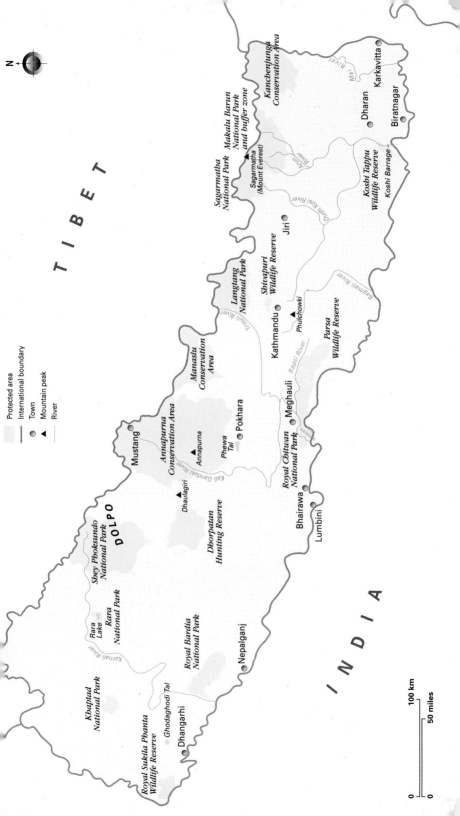

KALI GANDAKI VALLEY, LOOKING SOUTH FROM MARPHA.

fluffy, than subsequent plumages. In some families, juvenile plumage is retained only briefly after leaving the nest (e.g. pigeons), or hardly differs from adult plumage (e.g. many babblers), while in other groups it may be retained for the duration of long migrations or for many months (e.g. many waders). In some species (e.g. *Aquila* eagles), it may be several years before all juvenile feathers are finally moulted. The relevance of the juvenile plumage to field identification therefore varies considerably. Some species reach adult plumage after their first post-juvenile moult (e.g. larks), whereas others go through a series of immature plumages. The term 'immature' has been employed more generally to denote plumages other than adult, and is used either where a more exact terminology has not been possible or where more precision would give rise to unnecessary complexity. Terms such as 'first-winter' (resulting from a partial moult from juvenile plumage) or 'first-summer' (plumage acquired prior to the breeding season of the year after hatching) have, however, been used where it was felt that this would be useful.

Many species assume a more colourful breeding plumage, which is often more striking in the male compared with the female. This can be realised either through a partial (or in some species complete) body moult (e.g. waders) or results from the wearing-off of pale or dark feather fringes (e.g. redstarts and buntings).

GEOGRAPHICAL SETTING

Most of Nepal lies in the central Himalayas and includes eight of the highest peaks in the world, each over 8000 m. Nepal is surrounded by the world's two most populous countries, India and China, but is one of the smallest nations. The country covers an area of 147,181 km^2, little more than England and Wales combined, and averages about 870 km from east to west. Nepal has more contrasts of landscape and culture than in most other countries many times its size. There is a narrow strip of lowlands, known as the terai in the south that differs sharply from the rugged terrain of the rest of the country. Slightly higher up lies the dry bhabar zone that extends to about 300 m. Beyond the bhabar are the first Himalayan foothills known as the Siwalik hills, rising to 1220 m. To the north lies the Mahabharat Lekh climbing to 2740 m. Between these two ranges are the dun valleys or inner terai. Until recently the terai and inner terai were malaria-ridden jungle and rich in wildlife, but today they hold almost all of Nepal's industry and are highly cultivated. Beyond the Mahabharat Lekh lies a broad complex of midland hills and valleys including the Kathmandu Valley, the traditional heartland of Nepal. North of the midland regions lies the main Himalayan range including Sagarmatha (Mount Everest), 8848 m, which is no more than 160 km as the crow flies from the terai at 75m. Some of the world's deepest river gorges, notably the Kali Gandaki, cut through the Himalayan range. In the north-west of the country, a trans-Himalayan range marks the boundary between Nepal and Tibet. These peaks of 6000 to 7000 m are less rugged and wind-eroded landforms are dominant.

CLIMATE

Nepal has extremes of climate varying from tropical in the lowlands to arctic in the high peaks. At Meghauli near Chitwan, maximum temperatures reach 23 to 33°C between October and March and 37°C between April and early June. In sharp contrast, maximum temperatures in Namche Bazaar in Khumbu (Everest region) vary from 6 to 8°C from October to March and 11 to 15°C between April and June. Nepal's capital, Kathmandu which lies at 1330 m, has a mild climate however. From October to March skies are clear and there is little rain. Maximum temperatures are 17 to 25°C and may drop to near freezing at night. In April maximum temperatures average 27°C and 30°C in June and rain falls more frequently.

Nepal's climate is dominated by the monsoon of south Asia. About 90 % of the rain falls between June and September. The region north of the Himalayan range including Mustang, Manang and Dolpo districts, lies in the rain shadow and has very low rainfall. Western Nepal is generally drier than the east as the monsoon rains reach there later and last for a shorter period than in the east. However, there are pockets of high rainfall in the west caused by the topography, notably the area south of Annapurna, which is the wettest in the country. Rainfall also increases with altitude until the clouds have lost most of their moisture and then it decreases again. The direction a slope faces has a marked influence on climate; southern slopes are significantly warmer and sunnier than those facing north.

MAIN HABITATS AND BIRD SPECIES

The vegetation is classified following J.F. Dobremez (1976) *Le Nepal ecologie et biogéographie.*

Nepal's bird habitats can be roughly divided into forest, scrub, alpine habitats, wetlands, grasslands, agricultural land and around human habitation.

Forests and Scrub

Nepal has a very rich diversity of forest types. Forests and bushes hold the high proportion of 77% of Nepal's breeding birds.

FOREST IN THE MODI KHOLA WATERSHED, ANNAPURNA CONSERVATION AREA.

Tropical forest lies between approximately 75 m and 1000 m. Tropical forest is the richest in bird species. It includes Sal *Shorea robusta*, which is by far the most extensive forest, and tropical evergreen forest which is restricted to narrow belts in damp shady sites in the centre and east, often within sal forest. The restricted-range species Wedge-billed Wren Babbler *Sphenocichla humei* has recently been recorded in the east. Yellow-vented Warbler *Phylloscopus cantator* is the only other restricted range species that occurs. It is probably mainly a winter visitor to Nepal, but has bred in dense, moist broadleaved evergreen forest in the east. Spot-bellied Eagle Owl *Bubo nipalensis*, Lesser Fish Eagle *Ichthyophaga humilis* and Grey-headed Fish Eagle *I. ichthyaetus* are rare and local specialities.

Subtropical forest lies between approximately 1000 m and 2000 m in the west and 1000 m and 1700 m in the east.

Broadleaved subtropical forest is second in species-richness to tropical forest. *Schima-Castanopsis* is a moist broadleaved forest that once covered much of subtropical central and eastern Nepal, but now only small patches remain in most places. Riverine forest grows along water courses within *Schima-Castanopsis*. Alder *Alnus nepalensis* also grows along streams and often colonises abandoned cultivation. Three restricted-range species breed: White-naped Yuhina *Yuhina bakeri* and Yellow-vented Warbler, which are both rare and local in the east, and Hoary-throated Barwing *Actinodura nipalensis*, Spot-bellied Eagle Owl, Pied Thrush *Zoothera wardii* and Purple Cochoa *Cochoa purpurea* are other breeding specialities.

Chir Pine *Pinus roxburghii* forest is widespread in the west, but in the centre and east is confined to drier situations. These forests are typically open with little or no understorey because of frequent fires. They are poor in bird species and hold no specialities. Breeding birds include Blue-capped Rock Thrush *Monticola cinclorhynchus*.

Lower temperate forest lies between approximately 2000 m and 2700 m in the west and 1700 m and 2400 m in the east.

Moist broadleaved lower temperate forest grows in central and eastern Nepal and mainly comprises species of oaks *Quercus* with laurels Lauraceae. This habitat is important for the restricted-range species Broad-billed Warbler *Tickellia hodgsoni*, Rufous-throated Wren Babbler *Spelaeornis caudatus* and White-naped Yuhina, which are very local and rare in the east; the more widespread Hoary-throated Barwing; Nepal Wren Babbler *Pnoepyga immaculata*, whose breeding season records have all been from Nepal, Satyr Tragopan *Tragopan satyra*, Spot-bellied Eagle Owl, Yellow-rumped Honeyguide *Indicator xanthonotus*, Pied Thrush, Long-billed Thrush *Zoothera monticola*, Purple Cochoa, Slender-billed Scimitar Babbler *Xiphirhynchus superciliaris*, Fire-tailed Myzornis *Myzornis pyrrhoura* and Black-headed Shrike Babbler *Pteruthius rufiventer* are other breeding specialities.

Dry broadleaved lower temperate forest occurs in the west and on drier slopes in the centre. Most remaining forest is degraded and supports a low number of bird species compared to the moist forest. Brown-fronted Woodpecker *Dendrocopos auriceps* is characteristic of this dry forest.

Blue Pine *Pinus wallichiana* forest has a large altitudinal range, from 1800 m to 4000 m. It is widespread in the west and on dry slopes in the centre and east and is species-poor for birds. Breeding birds include Yellow-billed Blue Magpie *Urocissa flavirostris*.

Upper temperate forest occurs between about 2700 m and 3100 m in the west and centre and from 2400 m to 2800 m in the east. It is much less disturbed than forests lower down.

Broadleaved upper temperate forest Oak and mixed broadleaved forests grow in the centre and east. Rhododendrons are most widespread in high-rainfall areas where they are dominant in many areas. They are also common in forests of fir *Abies*, hemlock *Tsuga* and birch *Betula*.

RHODODENDRON SHRUBBERIES, LANGTANG NATIONAL PARK.

Broadleaved upper temperate forest is relatively rich in birds. Hoary-throated Barwing is fairly common and widespread in the mossy oak forests. Nepal Wren Babbler, Satyr Tragopan, Yellow-rumped Honeyguide, Long-billed Thrush, Slender-billed Scimitar Babbler and Fire-tailed Myzornis all occur in the breeding season.

Upper temperate coniferous forest Blue Pine is the most common and widespread conifer in the upper temperate zone. In moister areas it is mixed with other conifers, such as spruce *Picea smithiana* and *Abies pindrow*, which sometimes also form pure stands. In drier regions it is associated with juniper *Juniperus indica*. Characteristic species include White-throated Tit *Aegithalos niveogularis*, White-cheeked Nuthatch *Sitta leucopsis* and Kashmir Nuthatch *S. cashmirensis*.

Subalpine forest lies between 3000 m and 4200 m in the west, and 3000 m to 3800 m in the east. This includes some of the least disturbed forest, especially that of fir *Abies spectabilis*. Fir usually forms a continuous belt between 3000 m and 3500 m on the southern slopes of the main ranges in central Nepal. Birch *Betula utilis* forest is found between 3300 m and the tree line and both fir and birch usually have a rhododendron understorey. On very wet sites *Rhododendron* spp. forest often replaces other forest types and forms shrubberies at higher altitudes. In drier areas juniper *Juniperus* spp. forest occurs both as a tree and a small shrub. Specialities include Satyr Tragopan, Gould's Shortwing *Brachypteryx stellata* and Rufous-breasted Bush Robin *Tarsiger hyperythrus*, Slender-billed Scimitar Babbler and Fire-tailed Myzornis.

Bamboo flourishes in very high rainfall areas and in a few places, such as the Modi Khola valley, south of Annapurna, it forms pure dense stands. Bamboo is an important component of forests for many birds. These include Broad-billed Warbler, Golden-breasted Fulvetta *Alcippe chrysotis* in temperate forests and Fulvous Parrotbill *Paradoxornis fulvifrons* and Great Parrotbill *Conostoma oemodium* in subalpine forest.

Alpine Habitats
Alpine habitats lie between the tree line (3800 m in the east and 4200 m in the west) and the region of permanent snow. Alpine scrub, including rhododendron and juniper, grows up to as high as 4870 m in places. Only a small number of bird species breed,

notably the internationally threatened Wood Snipe *Gallinago nemoricola*, which occurs in alpine meadows with scattered bushes and a few streams. Other breeding species include Tibetan Snowcock *Tetraogallus tibetanus*, Robin Accentor *Prunella rubeculoides* and Grandala *Grandala coelicolor* which occur as high as 5500 m.

Tibetan Steppe Zone

North and northwest of Dhaulagiri and Annapurna the country is almost treeless with a climate and flora of Tibetan character. The dominant vegetation is of shrubs, especially *Caragana*, grasses and alpine flora. Characteristic species include White-browed Tit Warbler *Leptopoecile sophiae* and Fire-fronted Serin *Serinus pusillus* and, in summer, Desert Wheatear *Oenanthe deserti* and Blue Rock Thrush *Monticola solitarius*.

Wetlands

The Koshi Barrage area in the southeast terai is by far the most significant of Nepal's wetlands and in 1987 it was designated a Ramsar Site of international importance for migrating wildfowl, waders, gulls and terns. It comprises a large expanse of open water, marshes, grassland and scrub. As many as nine globally threatened wetland species all occur regularly: Baer's Pochard *Aythya baeri*, Pallas's Fish Eagle *Haliaeetus leucoryphus*, Greater Spotted Eagle *Aquila clanga*, Imperial Eagle *Aquila heliaca*, Indian Skimmer *Rynchops albicollis*, Spot-billed Pelican *Pelecanus philippensis*, Greater Adjutant *Leptoptilos dubius* and Lesser Adjutant *L. javanicus* and Swamp Francolin *Francolinus gularis* (which inhabits tall grasses and swamps).

Large lakes include Rara Lake (3050 m) in the northwest, Phewa Tal (915 m) near Pokhara and Ghodaghodi Tal in the western terai. In addition, small lakes are scattered at all altitudes throughout the country. These act as staging posts for small numbers of

ALPINE ZONE, SAGARMATHA NATIONAL PARK.

migrating wetland birds; those in the lowlands and foothills also support resident and wintering species.

Rivers and streams are generally fast-flowing and support a good variety of breeding species including kingfishers, forktails, dippers, wagtails, redstarts and Blue Whistling Thrush *Myophonus caeruleus*.

There are numerous small ponds and marshes, often in cultivation and around habitation, throughout Nepal. The internationally threatened Sarus Crane *Grus antigone* occurs in open cultivation in well-watered country with marshes and pools in the western terai.

Grasslands

Only small grassland areas remain and these are almost all within protected areas in the lowlands. These are important for several globally threatened species that breed or probably breed: Swamp Francolin, Bengal Florican *Houbaropsis bengalensis*, Lesser Florican *Sypheotides indica* (rare), Jerdon's Babbler *Chrysomma altirostre*, Slender-billed Babbler *Turdoides longirostris*, Grey-crowned Prinia *Prinia cinereocapilla*, Bristled Grassbird *Chaetornis striatus* and Finn's Weaver *Ploceus megarhynchus* (very local). Hodgson's Bushchat *Saxicola insignis* is a regular local winter visitor.

Agricultural Land

Only a small number of species inhabit agricultural land compared to the natural habitats of forests, wetlands and grasslands that it replaced. Most of them are widespread and common, either in Nepal or in the plains of India south of the border. Exceptions are the internationally threatened Sarus Crane *Grus antigone*, White-rumped Vulture *Gyps bengalensis* and Long-billed Vulture *G. indicus*. Typical breeding species of agricultural land in the tropical and subtropical zones are Spotted Dove *Streptopelia chinensis* and Paddyfield Pipit *Anthus rufulus*. Oriental Turtle Dove *S. orientalis* and Grey Bushchat *Saxicola ferrea* are common in the temperate zone.

Villages and Towns

A small number of species are especially associated with human habitation including White-rumped Vulture, Long-billed Vulture, Spotted Owlet *Athene brama*, House Crow *Corvus splendens*, Asian Pied Starling *Sturnus contra*, Common Myna *Acridotheres tristis* and *Passer* sparrows, House Sparrow *Passer domesticus*, Eurasian Tree Sparrow *P. montanus* and Russet Sparrow *P. rutilans*. Three aerial species commonly nest under the eaves of houses: House Swift *Apus affinis*, Red-rumped Swallow *Hirundo daurica* and Barn Swallow *H. rustica*. The last species even nests in some streets of Kathmandu.

IMPORTANCE FOR BIRDS

Nepal's avifauna is highly diverse considering the size of the country. A total of 852 species has been recorded, including about 600 that probably breed or have bred.

Vagrants

A total of 61 vagrant species has so far been recorded. These are listed and described, together with habitat details, in Appendix 1.

Extinct Species

The following species were all recorded in the nineteenth century by Brian Hodgson, but are now extirpated in Nepal: Jungle Bush Quail *Perdicula asiatica*, Rufous-necked

Hornbill *Aceros nipalensis*, White-bellied Heron *Ardea insignis*, Silver-breasted Broadbill *Serilophus lunatus*, Green Cochoa *Cochoa viridis*, Red-faced Liocichla *Liocichla phoenicea* and Black-breasted Parrotbill *Paradoxornis flavirostris*. Hodgson also collected Pink-headed Duck *Rhodonessa caryophyllacea* from Nepal, but this species is now considered extinct worldwide. These species are also described in Appendix 1.

Additional Species
An additional 15 species collected in the nineteenth century by Hodgson were listed for Nepal by Gray (1863), but may have originated from forests in India close to the Nepalese border (Inskipp and Inskipp 1991). These species are listed in Appendix 2.

Endemic Species
Spiny Babbler *Turdoides nipalensis* is the only endemic species. It has been found from east to west Nepal and may occur west into India, but there are no definite records. Nepal Wren Babbler, which was only recently described for science (Martens and Eck 1991), was previously thought to be endemic, but several birds were found near Corbett National Park in Uttar Pradesh, India in November 1998 (Robson 1999).

Reasons for Species-richness
Nepal's species-richness can be partly explained by the wide range of altitude in the country, from 75 m above sea level in the terai up to the summit of the Himalayas, the world's highest mountains. Other factors are Nepal's highly varied topography and climate and associated diverse vegetation. Also important is the country's geographical position in a region of overlap between two biogeographical provinces: the Indomalayan (South and Southeast Asia) and Palearctic. As a result, species typical of both realms occur.

Restricted-range Species
There are two areas of especially high biological diversity in Nepal which are of global importance. These are known as the Central Himalayas and Eastern Himalayas 'conservation hotspots' and are two of eight such areas identified in the Indian subcontinent. BirdLife International identified 'conservation hotspots' throughout the world. First, BirdLife analysed the distribution patterns of birds with restricted ranges, that is landbird species which have, throughout historical times (i.e. post-1800), had a total global breeding range of below 50,000 km^2 (about the size of Sri Lanka) (Stattersfield *et al.* 1998). BirdLife analysis showed that restricted-range species often tend to occur on islands or in isolated patches of a particular habitat. These are known as centres of endemism and are often called Endemic Bird Areas.

The Central Himalayas Endemic Bird Area lies entirely within Nepal. Its key habitats are moist temperate forest, and dense secondary forest and scrub. It supports three restricted-range species: Nepal Wren Babbler, Hoary-throated Barwing (also found in the eastern Himalayas) and Spiny Babbler.

The Eastern Himalayas Endemic Bird Area is important because of its wet forests. It encompasses southern and eastern Bhutan and extends into northeastern India, eastern Nepal, southeastern Tibet autonomous region, the Chittagong hills in southeastern Bangladesh, Chin hills in western Myanmar and northeastern Myanmar to southwestern China. Six of the 22 restricted-range species in this Endemic Bird Area are recorded from Nepal: Rufous-throated Wren Babbler, Wedge-billed Wren Babbler, Hoary-throated Barwing, White-naped Yuhina, Yellow-vented Warbler and Broad-billed Warbler. All are forest species.

Globally Threatened Species

A total of 29 species recorded in Nepal were identified as globally threatened by BirdLife International in 1999 (BirdLife International in prep.). These are Swamp Francolin, Cheer Pheasant *Catreus wallichii*, Bengal Florican, Lesser Florican, Sarus Crane, Wood Snipe, White-rumped Vulture, Long-billed Vulture, Lesser Adjutant, Grey-crowned Prinia, Bristled Grassbird, Jerdon's Babbler, Slender-billed Babbler and Finn's Weaver which currently breed or probably breed. Baer's Pochard, Imperial Eagle *Aquila heliaca*, Pallas's Fish Eagle, Greater Spotted Eagle *Aquila clanga* and Hodgson's Bushchat are rare, but regular winter visitors and passage migrants. Lesser Kestrel *Falco naumanni* and Kashmir Flycatcher *Ficedula subrubra* are uncommon passage migrants. Spot-billed Pelican is a very local, non-breeding visitor, mainly in spring, while Indian Skimmer and Greater Adjutant now visit Nepal rarely and irregularly. Black-necked Crane *Grus nigricollis* is a vagrant. Rufous-necked Hornbill, White-bellied Heron and Black-breasted Parrotbill have been extirpated in Nepal and Pink-headed Duck is now extinct.

MIGRATION

Many Himalayan residents are altitudinal migrants, the level to which they descend in winter frequently depending on weather conditions. For instance, the Red-billed Chough *Pyrrhocorax pyrrhocorax*, which has been found as high as 7950 m, and usually remains above 2440 m in winter, has been noted as low as 1450 m in cold weather. Some residents are sedentary throughout the year, while others undertake irregular movements, either locally or more widely in the region, depending on food supply, for example the Speckled Wood Pigeon *Columba hodgsonii*.

About 62 species are summer visitors or partial migrants and include species of cuckoos, swifts, bee-eaters, *Phylloscopus* warblers, flycatchers and drongos. Many species winter further south in the subcontinent, including Common Hoopoe *Upupa epops*, Blue-tailed Bee-eater *Merops philippinus*, Asian Brown Flycatcher *Muscicapa dauurica* and Asian Paradise-flycatcher *Terpsiphone paradisi*. The winter quarters of some of these summer visitors are poorly known, for example Oriental Cuckoo *Cuculus saturatus*, Fork-tailed Swift *Apus pacificus* and Dark-sided Flycatcher *Muscicapa sibirica*. Other species move southeastwards, perhaps as far as Malaysia and Indonesia: Crow-billed Drongo *Dicrurus annectans* and Hooded Pitta *Pitta sordida*, Lesser Cuckoo *Cuculus poliocephalus* and Common Swift *Apus apus* winter in Africa.

Nepal attracts about 150 winter visitors, originating mainly in northern and central Asia, and some of these are also passage migrants. These include ducks, waders, birds of prey, gulls, terns, thrushes, bush warblers, *Acrocephalus*, *Locustella* and *Phylloscopus* warblers, pipits, wagtails, finches and buntings.

Increasing evidence suggests that some birds breeding in the Palearctic, mainly non-passerines, migrate directly across the Himalayas to winter in the subcontinent. Birds have been seen flying over the highest regions of these ranges; for example a flock of Bar-headed Geese *Anser indicus* was recorded flying as high as 9375 m over Sagarmatha. Other birds follow the main valleys, such as those of the Kali Gandaki, Dudh Kosi and Arun. Birds of prey, especially *Aquila* eagles, have also been found to use the Himalayas as an east–west pathway when migrating from their breeding grounds; the wintering area of these birds is unknown. The Spot-winged Starling *Saroglossa spiloptera* also undertakes east–west movements along the Himalayas, and it is possible that other species perform similar migrations.

RIVER NARAYANI, ROYAL CHITWAN NATIONAL PARK.

BIRDWATCHING AREAS

s = spring and summer; w = winter.

Royal Chitwan National Park
Location: Southcentral Nepal.
Habitat: Grasslands, sal and riverain forests on low ground, sal forest on hills and sal/Chir Pine on ridges, rivers and small lakes.
Best time to visit: October to May, especially late April.
Birds: Oriental Pied and Great Hornbills, Red-headed Trogon, Blue-eared Kingfisher (rare), White-rumped Needletail, Spot-bellied and Dusky Eagle Owls (rare), Bengal Florican, Lesser Fish and Grey-headed Fish Eagles (rare), Pallid and Pied Harriers (w), Greater Spotted Eagle (w), Darter, Lesser Adjutant, Hooded Pitta (s), Indian Pitta (s), Bright-capped Cisticola, Pale-footed Bush Warbler, Chestnut-crowned Bush Warbler (w), Grey-crowned Prinia, Dusky and Smoky Warblers (w), Bristled Grassbird (s), Rufous-rumped Grassbird, Jerdon's Babbler (rare), Slender-billed Babbler.

Phulchowki Mountain (2760 m)
Location: Edge of Kathmandu Valley, eastcentral Nepal.
Habitat: Subtropical broadleaved and moist broadleaved lower temperate forests.
Best time to visit: October to early May
Birds: Long-billed Thrush (w, rare), Pied Thrush (s), Black-faced Warbler, Rufous-chinned Laughingthrush, Grey-sided Laughingthrush (rare), Spiny Babbler, Cutia, Black-throated Parrotbill (rare), Yellow-bellied Flowerpecker (w), Gold-naped Finch, Spot-winged Grosbeak.

Sheopuri Wildlife Reserve (2730 m)
Location: Edge of Kathmandu Valley, eastcentral Nepal.
Habitat: Dense scrub on lower slopes, temperate broadleaved forest higher up.
Best time to visit: October to early May.
Birds: Yellowish-bellied Bush Warbler, Black-faced Warbler, Spiny Babbler (good locality), Scarlet Finch, Gold-naped Finch.

Kosi Tappu Wildlife Reserve and Kosi Barrage

Location: Southeast lowlands.

Habitat: Marshes, impounded rivers, wet grasslands, scrub and riverine forest.

Best time to visit: Late January to late May.

Birds: Largest numbers and diversity of passage migrant and wintering wildfowl and waders in Nepal including Bar-headed Goose, Baer's Pochard, Falcated Duck, Pacific Golden Plover, Lesser Sand Plover and Oriental Pratincole; also a good variety of mainly passage migrant or wintering gulls, terns and birds of prey including Pallas's Fish Eagle, White-tailed Eagle, Cinereous Vulture, Pallid and Pied Harriers, Greater Spotted Eagle, Imperial Eagle, and Red-necked Falcon. Regular winter visitors and passage migrants include Baillon's Crake, Spot-billed Pelican, Spotted Bush Warbler, Clamorous Reed, Dusky and Smoky Warblers and Black-faced Bunting. Yellow and Cinnamon Bitterns and Watercock are summer visitors. Residents include Swamp Francolin, Indian Courser (rare), Black-bellied Tern, Black-necked Stork (rare), Lesser Adjutant and White-tailed Stonechat. Greater Adjutant, Hodgson's Bushchat and Bristled Grassbird are rare visitors.

Royal Bardia National Park

Location: Western Nepal.

Habitats: Sal forest, deciduous hill forest and Chir pine; grasslands, river and riverine habitats.

Best time to visit: October to April, especially from December onwards.

Birds: White-naped and Great Slaty Woodpeckers, Oriental Pied Hornbill, Bengal Florican, passage migrant wetland birds including Bar-headed Goose, Pallas's Gull and waders, Great Thick-knee, Cinereous Vulture, Grey-headed Fish Eagle, White-tailed Eagle, Darter, Indian Pitta, Grey-crowned Prinia.

Trekking in Langtang National Park – Gosainkund and Langtang Valley

Both treks can easily be combined.

Location: Eastcentral Nepal.

Habitats: Lower temperate and upper temperate broadleaved forests; subalpine forests of fir, rhododendron, birch and juniper; alpine scrub of rhododendron and juniper, and alpine grasslands.

Best time for treks: late April to early June.

Recommended time: 3 to 4 weeks.

Gosainkund

Sundarijal, Kathmandu Valley (1265 m) – Pati Bhanjyang (1770 m) – Khutumsang (2470 m) – Thare Pati (3505 m) – Gapte Cave (3565 m) – Laurebina Pass (4600 m) – Gosainkund lakes (4380 m) – Sing Gomba (3255 m) – Dhunche (1965 m).

Birds: Snow Partridge (Gosainkund lakes), Blood Pheasant, Himalayan Monal, Long-billed Thrush, Gould's Shortwing (s, above Gapte), Rufous-breasted Bush Robin, Grandala, Smoky Warbler (above Gapte), Spotted Laughingthrush, Fire-tailed Myzornis (near Gapte), Spot-winged Rosefinch, Red-fronted Rosefinch (Laurebina Pass).

Langtang Valley

Dhunche (1965 m) – Syabru (2120 m) – Kyanjin, upper Langtang valley (3750 m).

Birds: Blood Pheasant, Satyr Tragopan (Syabru, rare), Himalayan Monal, Yellow-rumped Honeyguide, Wood Snipe, Ibisbill (Kyanjin), Pied Thrush (s), Nepal Wren

Babbler (Dhunche – Syabru), Mrs Gould's Sunbird, Yellow-bellied Flowerpecker, Spot-winged Rosefinch, Scarlet Finch.

Trekking in Annapurna Conservation Area
Location: Westcentral Nepal.

Thak Khola Trek
Pokhara (915 m) – Birethante (1065 m) (mainly by bus) – Tirkedhungha (1525 m) – Ghorepani (2775 m) – side trips to Poon Hill and along trail to Ghandrung – Tatopani (1190 m) – Ghasa (2000 m) – Jomosom (2715 m) – Kagbeni (2805 m) – Muktinath (3800 m).

This trek can easily be linked to the Annapurna Sanctuary trek by using the trail from Ghorepani to Ghandrung.

Habitats: Broadleaved subtropical forest, Chir pine forest, broadleaved lower and upper temperate forests, coniferous upper temperate, subalpine forests of fir, birch and *Caragana* scrub in the Tibetan steppe zone.

Best time for trek: December to March; also October (for migrants).

Recommended time: 17 days.

Birds: Cinereous Vulture (w) and Greater Spotted Eagle (w) (Pokhara – Ghorepani); Crested Kingfisher, Little, Slaty-backed and Spotted Forktails (especially between Birethante and Tirkedhungha); Koklass Pheasant (Ghorepani and Ghasa); White-browed and Rufous-breasted Bush Robins, Yellowish-bellied Bush Warbler, Great, Brown and Black-throated Parrotbills (Ghorepani, Ghorepani – Ghandrung), Spotted Laughingthrush, Spot-winged Rosefinch (Ghorepani and Ghasa), Variegated Laughingthrush (Ghasa), Crimson-browed Finch (Ghorepani); White-throated and White-winged Redstarts, White-browed Tit Warbler, Brown, Robin, Altai and Alpine Accentors, Fire-fronted Serin, Streaked and Great Rosefinches (Tukche – Muktinath); Solitary Snipe (Muktinath and nearby Jharkhot), Tibetan and Himalayan Snowcocks (above Muktinath on trail to Thorang La).

TERRACES, ANNAPURNA CONSERVATION AREA.

Annapurna Sanctuary Trek

Pokhara – Phedi (bus), Phedi – Pothana (2035 m) – Landrung (1715 m) – Chomro (2050 m) – Khuldi (2550 m) – Bagar (3300 m) – Annapurna Base Camp (4130 m).
Best time for trek: March, April, October, early November.
Recommended time: 14 days.
Habitats: Moist broadleaved lower temperate forest; upper temperate forest of oak and rhododendron, bamboo jungles, subalpine birch and rhododendron; alpine scrub and grasslands.
Birds: Cinereous Vulture (w), Yellow-rumped Honeyguide, Rufous-breasted Bush Robin, Grandala, Slender-billed Scimitar Babbler, Golden Babbler, Black-headed Shrike Babbler (scarce), Golden-breasted Fulvetta, Great and Fulvous Parrotbills, Yellow-bellied Flowerpecker, Spot-winged, Streaked and Red-fronted Rosefinch.

Trekking in Arun and Barun Valleys

Location: Eastern Nepal.
Best time for trek: April and May.
Habitats: Moist broadleaved subtropical, lower temperate and upper temperate forests, subalpine forests of rhododendron, fir and birch, rhododendron shrubberies and alpine meadows.

Arun Valley

Kathmandu – Tumlingtar (550 m) (flight) – Khandbari (900 m) – Bhotebas (1900 m) – Num (1700 m) – Seduwa (1500 m) – Navagaon (2200 m) – Tashigaon (2300 m) – Shunin Oral (3300 m) – Khangma (3800 m) – return by same route.
Recommended time for trek: 19 days.

Barun Valley Extension

Khangma – Makalu Base Camp – Khangma.
Recommended time for trek: 6 days.
Birds: Blood Pheasant, Himalayan Monal, Orange-rumped Honeyguide, Solitary Snipe, Wood Snipe (Barun Valley), Gould's Shortwing (Barun Valley), White-browed and Rufous-breasted Bush Robins, Grandala, Purple Cochoa, Sultan Tit, Yellow-vented Warbler, Broad-billed Warbler, Rufous-chinned, Spotted, Grey-sided and Blue-winged Laughingthrushes, Slender-billed Scimitar Babbler, Rufous-throated and Nepal Wren Babblers, Fire-tailed Myzornis, White-naped Yuhina, Great, Fulvous and Black-throated Parrotbills, Yellow-bellied Flowerpecker, Maroon-backed Accentor, Crimson-browed and Gold-naped Finches.

WHAT BIRDWATCHERS CAN DO

By recording the observations that they make, birdwatchers can play a valuable role by increasing the knowledge of the country's birds and helping to conserve them. Studies of globally threatened species would be especially useful. Much is still to be learned and discovered about the breeding behaviour of many of Nepal's birds. Tape recordings of calls and songs are currently available for relatively few species to date. Future fieldwork in western Nepal, which is still poorly known, will undoubtedly lead to new information being gathered. Please send any information that corrects or adds to that presented here to Bird Conservation Nepal, the leading national non-governmental bird organisation in the country, which compiles and publishes significant new bird records.

JUST NORTH OF POKHARA.

BIRD CONSERVATION

BY HEM SAGAR BARAL, PRESIDENT, BIRD CONSERVATION NEPAL

This magnificent picture of thine is very charming indeed, O Lord
of the forest, when these birds are happily enjoying themselves upon trees,
Oh! And their sweet musical notes are heard distinctly as they sing
beautifully during the season of fragrant flowers (the Spring).

Mahâbhârat 12.150. 14–15

Religious Attitudes and Traditional Protection

Attitudes to wildlife that stem from the teachings of Hinduism and Buddhism have
undoubtedly helped to conserve Nepal's rich natural diversity. Nepal's birds are abundant and tame, at least outside heavily disturbed areas.

Wildlife, forests and water are viewed primarily as important resources and so people have traditionally created many ways to preserve, manage and use them. In every
aspect of communal interest, such as forestry and pasture, local people established
unwritten laws that have become a way of life. Special permission was required to cut
down trees in community forests, for example. Defaulters were fined and the revenue
collected was used in community welfare. Forests protected for religious reasons, for
example in Pashupatinath, Swayambhunath, Dakshinkali and Chapagaon, are important wildlife habitats. These traditional conservation methods are effective but, unfor-
tunately, many have broken down in more recent times, giving rise to increasing
deforestation and environmental degradation (Basnet 1992).

Current Threats

As many as 130 breeding and wintering species (15% of Nepal's birds) are now considered nationally threatened. To date, eight species are believed to have been recently
extirpated from Nepal. Habitat loss is the major threat to 86% of the birds at risk (Baral
et al. 1996). The root causes of loss and damage to habitats are complex, interlinked and
often controversial. Most of Nepal's environmental problems have been attributed to

poverty and a rapidly growing population, but other factors, including national debt (which encourages countries to overexploit their natural resources for export), insecurity of tenure, and tourism are also important. There is general lack of awareness amongst the poorer people on the importance and conservation of wildlife.

The large proportion (16.2% and 18.2% including buffer zones) of Nepal designated as protected areas illustrates the country's enlightened attitude to biodiversity conservation, but threats nevertheless extend even to these areas. All protected areas face pressure from livestock grazing, fodder collection and fuelwood gathering by local villagers whose basic needs have not always been met. Park staff often lack sufficient resources to implement regulations and their own management skills.

Threats to Forest Birds

At one time Nepal was extensively forested, but now only 29% of the country is forest land (Ravi Bista in WWF Nepal Program/International Centre for Integrated Mountain Development 1999 Workshop on Biodiversity Vision for the Eastern Himalaya) that is partially covered by trees and shrubs. Forest decline has been attributed partly to the breakdown of traditional management. All forest areas were nationalised in 1957 in an attempt to protect them, but in many areas this accelerated deforestation as people felt they had lost ownership. Illegal logging is now common and legal measures have failed to control it. The vast majority of Nepalis depend on forests for their essential requirements of fuel, animal fodder and other basic materials; fuelwood, for example, providing 87% of Nepal's domestic energy (CBS 1998). Overgrazing by domestic animals frequently prevents forest regeneration. The number of domestic animals that need grazing lands increased from 13 million in 1981 to more than 16 million in 1991 (CBS 1998).

With 68% of nationally threatened birds depending on forests, loss and deterioration of the latter are major threats to the country's birds. Many of the threatened species require plenty of undergrowth, moist conditions or trees covered in epiphytes. Hornbills and the Great Slaty Woodpecker *Mulleripicus pulverulentus* depend on mature trees (Inskipp and Inskipp 1991, Baral *et al.* 1996). Only 16% of Nepal's bird species have adapted to habitats heavily modified or created by people, such as groves, gardens, scrub and trees and bushes at the edges of cultivation (Inskipp 1989). Nearly all of these are widespread and common, and presumably they once bred in forest edges, gaps and clearings.

Construction of hydroelectric dams brings substantial threats to wildlife and people. They inundate important habitats, act as barriers to migration, lead to associated development, displace people into new sensitive habitats, and can also alter local microclimates. Nepal's large annual precipitation and dense river networks provide high potential for hydroelectricity so that several dams are planned to meet the increasing electricity demand. Problems of erosion, damage to turbines and siltation caused by heavy sediment loads are often overlooked. The World Bank's Operation Evaluation Department has recognised by its own analysis that the Kulekhani Hydroelectric Dam should not have been built (Dharmadhikary 1998). Although the controversial Arun III project has been cancelled, threats are again posed by proposals for new dams on the Karnali and Koshi.

Threats to Wetland Birds

Nepal's wetlands face threats from drainage, diversion, abstraction, siltation, over-enrichment, pollution and poisons used to kill fish. Many observers have noted a decline in wetland birds, although data are currently lacking to illustrate trends on a national level. Figures available over a ten-year period from 1989 to 1999 for three wetlands in Royal Chitwan National Park reveal a decline in wetland dependent birds (Baral 1999).

The internationally important wetland at Koshi is one of the sites at risk, and noticeable declines in the numbers and variety of birds have occurred from 1990 to 1997. Heavy grazing and grass-cutting on the reserve are destroying important wetland bird habitats (Giri 1997). Lakes near Pokhara which support a good variety of wildlife are also threatened, for example by fish-farming, agriculture, increasing urbanisation, recreational activities and siltation (Karki and Thapa 1999). Phewa Tal, the largest of the lakes in Pokhara, suffers from uncontrolled urbanisation, solid waste disposal, sewage input, encroachment, noise pollution, and ownership and demarcation problems. The natural condition of the lake has now deteriorated markedly, making it increasingly unsuitable for both tourist recreation and wildlife (Oli 1995). There is no wetland legislation as such, although four Acts deal with water and water resources in Nepal (Bhandari 1998).

Threats to Grassland Birds

Cultivation has significantly reduced the once extensive grasslands that border Nepal's lowland rivers, and formed the northern extension of the huge Gangetic plain. The remaining areas are now small, and lie in a fragmented matrix only within protected areas. A total of 14 grassland birds are nationally threatened (Baral *et al.* 1996), including, the Bengal Florican *Houbaropsis bengalensis* and Lesser Florican *Sypheotides indica*, two of the world's most endangered bustards (Collar *et al.* 1994). Intensive annual cutting and burning of grasslands are likely to alter their species composition yet further, effects which are still poorly understood. The numbers of Bengal Floricans have declined in Royal Chitwan National Park, possibly as a result of habitat loss, and it seems likely that other grassland species are also being adversely affected (Baral in prep.).

Royal Chitwan National Park and Sukila Phanta Wildlife Reserve still hold globally important grassland habitats (Peet 1997, Baral in prep.). Grasslands at Koshi Tappu, by contrast, are degraded by disturbance, livestock grazing and fodder collection. It is likely that pressure on Nepal's lowland tall grasslands will grow and threats will intensify in the future as the human population continues to increase.

Other Threats

Hunting is contributing to the decline of some species, including the globally threatened Greater Adjutant *Leptoptilos dubius*, Lesser Adjutant *L. javanicus*, Sarus Crane *Grus antigone*, Spot-billed Pelican *Pelecanus philippensis*, and Cheer Pheasant *Catreus wallichii*, as well as 12 species identified as nationally threatened. In some areas hunting is on the increase as traditional values wane. The slaughter of many larks and buntings for sale as snacks (locally known as *bagedi*) in village inns was recently observed in the terai. Illegal bird trading goes on near Koshi Barrage all the year round. Buyers from Bihar in India purchase birds for food, including species of ducks, jacanas, doves, moorhens, egrets, munias, larks and francolins. Once widespread throughout lowland Nepal, the Great Hornbill *Buceros bicornis* is now confined to Chitwan in central Nepal and Bardia in the west. The oil from the casque and the beak itself are much valued in the use of traditional medicine (Fleming *et al.* 1984). Hunters and villagers routinely shoot such large and conspicuous birds both for medicine and for food. Some globally threatened species, such as Lesser Adjutant and Sarus Crane, live close to human settlements making them easy targets. The establishment of reserves does not necessarily help their conservation. What is needed is improved conservation awareness amongst local people. The increased illegal bird trade in the Kathmandu Valley is a threat to some bird species (Mainali 1997), but the efforts of government officials to prevent it are wholly inadequate. These birds may not have a secure future even inside protected areas. Overfishing has been suggested as a threat to large fish-eating birds of prey at Chitwan, such as Grey-headed *Ichthyophaga ichthyaetus* and Lesser Fish Eagles *I. humilis* (Baral *et al.* 1996).

Introduced species of fauna and flora are a common threat to native birds and other wildlife worldwide. In Nepal many pools and small lakes have become overgrown by an exotic plant species, water hyacinth *Eichhornia crassipes*, making them less suitable for many wetland birds. To date no bird species have been introduced to Nepal, although the increasing bird trade carries some risks. Budgerigars *Melopsittacus undulatus* have been noted in city parks, but so far they have not been able to establish a wild population. We must take some preventative measures now rather than ignoring the problem and looking for solutions at a later stage when things are beyond our control.

Recently, there have been indications of bird poisoning by pesticides and other chemicals, although this is so far not proven in Nepal. The use of pesticides in agriculture including the use of the organochlorines DDT and aldrin has increased. Both are toxic to birds, the former largely by eggshell thinning, and the latter by direct toxicity. DDT is still sprayed in terai districts in spite of being banned in many countries due to problems associated with resistance in insect pests, persistence in the environment, and its harmful health effects. People selling pesticides do not have adequate knowledge and even date-expired chemicals are being sold. Out of 137 metric tons of date-expired pesticides about 70 metric tons were buried or spread in terai areas such as Amlekhgunj, Siddarthanagar (Bhairahawa), Nepalgunj and Biratnagar under the supervision of foreign consultants (Dahal 1994). Disposal of chemicals in such large quantities is hazardous for the total environment and we may face the effects in the near future. In Europe, pesticide use has been shown to cause widespread declines of numerous bird species, many of which were previously common, including birds of prey and finches (Tucker and Heath 1994). Nepal's dependence on pesticides is fairly recent and limited; it should, therefore, be easier to correct the mistakes if the necessary steps are taken now.

There are indications that the once common White-rumped Vulture *Gyps bengalensis* has recently sharply declined in the lowlands as a breeding bird, although the root cause of this apparent decline is still unknown.

Tourism is a major industry and source of foreign exchange in Nepal, and the number of tourists coming to Nepal is rising. There are indications that tourism-based industries may cause some damage to wildlife if not planned carefully (Peet 1997, pers. obs.). New lodges are built almost every year in several trekking areas. This involves clearing patches of dense forests and subsequently leads to forest thinning and degradation. As a consequence, bird species that are sensitive to even small changes in the ecosystem decline because of their specific habitat requirements (Baral *et al.* 1996). Adequate knowledge is necessary while running such industries to minimise the impact of tourism on birds and other wildlife.

Conservation Measures

The Forest Act of 1993 decentralised forest management and many village communities have now started to manage their own forest resources. Forests and wildlife outside protected areas are managed by the Department of Forest, but this is a large department and has a difficult task. Forests in their control are often species-poor as protection is not afforded adequately.

The Department of National Parks and Wildlife Conservation (DNPWC) is the authorised body for the maintenance and conservation of the protected areas in Nepal. Some areas are better protected than others because of their location and the nature of the local community. All protected areas except Annapurna, Makalu Barun and

Kanchenjunga, are guarded by the Royal Nepal Army. In the above areas local people and park staff take an active part in conservation. The Annapurna Conservation Area which is managed by the King Mahendra Trust for Nature Conservation with help from local people, is regarded as one of the most biologically diverse reserves in the world (UNEP 1995). The National Parks and Wildlife Conservation Act-1973 regulates wildlife laws in Nepal. It is implemented through the DNPWC.

While a number of threatened bird species occur in this country, so far only nine have been declared as protected by law. There is an urgent need to revise this list and include other species that really need protection. Inskipp (1989) identified some important omissions in the representation of vegetation types at lower altitudes in the protected area network. While there have been significant extensions since then and Nepal has good protected area coverage, middle-hill broadleaf forests, broadleaf Churia hill forests and tropical evergreen forests that are now restricted in small patches in the east are still not well represented. Nearly 49% (64 species) of the nationally threatened birds are lowland (75–1000 m) birds; 28% (36 species) are found in lowlands as well as in the middle hills (75–3000 m); 11% (14 species) are strictly found in the middle hills (1000–3000 m) and the remaining 12% (16 species) are birds that belong to higher altitudes (Baral *et al.* 1996). There is a varying degree of pressure on habitats in different regions and inadequate or poor representation of habitats at different elevations.

There is growing concern amongst the numerous young Nepalese working in the field of conservation resulting in many critical management issues now being addressed. Many national and international organisations are taking the lead in this respect and a database is being developed on the status, inventorying and conservation of biodiversity in Nepal (Bhandari *et al.* 1994, Bhandari 1998). The phenomenal growth in the number of people interested in avian conservation is encouraging. Several bird conservation and education organisations are now established throughout the country. Nepal may have lost a good deal of its native biota, and will doubtless lose more, but nonetheless, it has a good chance of saving much of what remains.

References

Baral, H.S. (1999) Decline of wetland dependent birds in Nepal with reference to Chitwan. *Danphe* 8(1): 4.

Baral, H.S. (*in prep.*) Community structure and habitat associations of lowland grassland birds in Nepal. PhD thesis. University of Amsterdam, Amsterdam.

Baral, H.S., Inskipp, C., Inskipp, T.P. and Regmi, U.R. (1996) *Threatened Birds of Nepal*. Bird Conservation Nepal and Department of National Parks and Wildlife Conservation, Kathmandu.

Basnet, K. (1992) Conservation practices in Nepal: past and present. *Ambio* 21(6): 390–393.

Bhandari, B. (1998) *An Inventory of Nepal's Terai Wetlands*. Final report. Wetland and Heritage Unit. IUCN-Nepal, Kathmandu.

Bhandari, B., Shrestha, T.B. and McEachern, J. (1994) *Safeguarding Wetlands in Nepal*. Proceedings of the National Workshop on Wetlands Management in Nepal, 3–5 March 1993. IUCN-Nepal, Kathmandu.

CBS (1998) *Statistical pocket book of Nepal*. Central Bureau of Statistics. His Majesty's Government of Nepal, Kathmandu.

Collar, N.J., Crosby, M. J. & Stattersfield, A.J. (1994) *Birds to Watch 2: The World List of Threatened Birds*. BirdLife International, Cambridge.

Dahal, L. (1994) A study on pesticide pollution in Nepal. *NCS Nepal.* 4(3/4): 1–3.

Dharmadhikary, S. (1998) Dam fundamentalism. *Himal* 11(3): 18–22.

Fleming, R.L. Sr, Fleming, R.L. Jr and Bangdel, L.S. (1984) *Birds of Nepal*. Third edition. Nature Himalayas, Kathmandu.

Giri, T. (1997) Habitat loss at Koshi. *Danphe* 6(2): 1.

Heinen, J.T. (1993) Park-people relations in Kosi Tappu Wildlife Reserve: a socio-economic analysis. *Environmental Conservation* 20(1): 25–34.

Inskipp, C. (1989) *Nepal's Forest Birds: Their Status and Conservation*. International Council for Bird Preservation, Monograph No. 4, Cambridge.

Inskipp, C. and Inskipp, T.P. (1991) *A Guide to the Birds of Nepal*. Second edition. Christopher Helm, London.

Karki, A.B. and Thapa, K.B. (1999) Khaste and other wetlands in Pokhara Valley. *Danphe* 8(1): 6.

Mainali, A. (1997) Illegal trade threatens birds. *Danphe* 6(2): 9-10.

Oli, K.P. (ed.) (1995) *Guidelines for Phewa Lake Conservation*. National Conservation Strategy Implementation Project. IUCN-Nepal, Kathmandu.

Peet, N.B. (1997) Biodiversity and management of tall grasslands in Nepal. PhD thesis. University of East Anglia, Norwich.

Tucker, G. and Heath, M. (1994) *Birds in Europe*. BirdLife International, Cambridge.

UNEP (1995) *Global Biodiversity Assessment*. United Nations Environment Programme, Nairobi.

NATIONAL ORGANISATIONS

Department of National Parks and Wildlife Conservation (DNPWC)
PO Box 860, Kathmandu. http://www.south-asia.com/dnpwc
The DNPWC is the government authority responsible for wildlife conservation. It manages eight National Parks, four Wildlife Reserves, one hunting Reserve and three Conservation Areas, as well as buffer zones.

Bird Conservation Nepal (BCN)
PO Box 12465, Kathmandu
BCN, previously known as the Nepal Bird Watching Club, is the biggest and oldest society dedicated to the interest of ornithology and birdwatching in Nepal. BCN was established in 1982 and has the following aims:

- to promote an interest in birds among the general public
- to encourage basic research on diverse aspects of bird biology and ecology
- to identify the major threats to birds' continued survival
- to help and suggest management measures to the related agencies to conserve birds and their habitats.

BCN provides the most up-to-date information on birds and their habitats all over Nepal. They are also committed to conservation education, educating the public about the value of birds, the relationship between birds and people, and the importance of community involvement and stewardship.

BCN publishes a quarterly newsletter *Danphe*, a journal *Ibisbill* and conservation booklets in local Nepali languages as well as materials to fit the curricula of schools and campuses in Nepal.

Regular Saturday birdwatching trips are organised to various bird habitats in the Kathmandu Valley.

Himalayan Nature *(Himali Prakriti)*
PO Box 7860, Lazimpat, Kathmandu. birdlife@mos.com.np. Fax: 00977 1439331
Himalayan Nature is a science-based research and conservation institute which takes an independent view of conservation issues in the Himalayan region. The institute offers advice over aspects of sound environmental research and management on various aspects of the natural environment. It is supported by several acknowledged and world-famous Himalayan scientists and conservationists. It publishes science-based reports and authentic publications on the wildlife and natural environment of the Himalayan region.

Bird Education Society (BES)
Bachhauli-2, Sauraha, Chitwan
BES is a non-profit-making non-governmental organisation that was established in 1994 in the vicinity of the Royal Chitwan National Park at Sauraha. The objectives are to:

- generate public awareness by organising seminars, workshops and conferences on birds of Nepal
- organise conservation education activities in schools
- discourage activities which threaten bird populations, such as hunting, trapping, poisoning and shooting
- emphasise and support various activities related to environmental protection and wildlife conservation.

Activities include a birdwatching programme every Saturday in and around the Royal Chitwan National Park.

A newsletter, *Panchhi*, written in the Nepali language is published three times a year.

The National Trust for Nature Conservation
PO Box 3712, Jawalakhel, Lalitpur, Kathmandu. http://www.kmtnc.org.np
The KMTNC is an autonomous, non-profit and non-governmental organisation working for nature conservation in Nepal. Holistic and integrated conservation and development programmes aimed at promoting local guardianship have been the focus of all KMTNC activities. Currently, the projects of the Trust are divided into three geographical areas – the Tarai Environment Program, the Mountain Environment Program and Kathmandu Valley. The Nepal Conservation, Research and Training Center (NCRTC) and the Bardia Conservation Project (BCP) are two major projects in the Tarai. Similarly, the Annapurna Conservation Area Project (ACAP) and the Manasalu Conservation Area Project (MCAP) are two projects in mountain environments. The Central Zoo is the only project in the Kathmandu Valley.

The mission statement of the KMTNC is to conserve, manage and promote nature in all its diversity, balancing human needs with the environment on a sustainable basis for posterity, ensuring maximum community participation with due cognisance of the linkages between economics, environment and ethics through a process in which people are both the principal actors and beneficiaries.

WWF Nepal Program
Baluwatar Avenue, Pavitra Pyara 124, Kathmandu. http://www.south-asia.com/wwfnepal/
A steadfast proponent of conservation of Nepal's wild and natural heritage is the WWF Nepal Program, known as the World Wildlife Fund in the United States and the World Wide Fund for Nature elsewhere. The WWF Nepal office, opened in 1993, is currently involved in conservation and development programmes such as the Bardia Integrated Conservation Project, the Northern Mountains Conservation Project, the Sagarmatha

Community Agroforestry Project and the Kanchenjunga Conservation Area Project. The focus of these projects is to strengthen park management as well as developing community-based natural resources management in the buffer zones. Applied research and monitoring of ecology and wildlife are emphasised in the projects.

In addition to implementing projects, the WWF Nepal Program acts as a facilitator between relevant Nepalese government and non-government organisations and donor agencies to forge relevant links. WWF also aims to assist other conservation programmes which are consistent with and reflect the Nepal Program's conservation priorities.

International Center for Integrated Mountain Development (ICIMOD)
4/80 Jawalakhel, PO Box 3226, Kathmandu. http://www.icimod.org.sg
The ICIMOD is the international centre devoted to integrated mountain development. The long-term objective of the centre is to contribute to attaining environmental stability and poverty eradication in the Hindu Kush and the Himalayas.

IUCN – The World Conservation Union
PO Box 3923, Kupondole, Lalitpur. http://www.iucn.org/places/nepal
IUCN – The World Conservation Union is an alliance of active conservation institutions, agencies and interest groups. IUCN has been active since 1973 in Nepal and it was one of the first states in Asia to obtain membership. IUCN developed a National Conservation Strategy (NCS) for Nepal in the 1980s.

INTERNATIONAL ORGANISATIONS

BirdLife International
Wellbrook Court, Girton Road, Cambridge CB3 0NA, UK
BirdLife International (formerly the International Council for Bird Preservation) is now the world's leading authority on the status of the world's birds, their habitats and the urgent problems facing them.

Wetlands International – Asia Pacific
3A39, Block A, Kelana Centre Point, Jalan SS7/19, Petaling Jaya, Malaysia
Wetlands International promotes the protection and sustainable utilisation of wetlands and wetland resources.

Bombay Natural History Society
Hornbill House, Dr Salim Ali Chowk, Shaheed Bhagat Singh Road, Mumbai 400 023, India
Carries out ornithological research in the region and creates conservation awareness.

Oriental Bird Club
PO Box 324, Beford, MK42 0WG, UK
Aims to encourage an interest in Oriental birds and their conservation.

World Pheasant Association
7/9 Shaftesbury Street, Fordingbridge, Hampshire, SP6 1JF, UK
Carries out survey work on pheasants. Runs the Pipar Reserve in the Annapurna Conservation Area.

REFERENCES

BirdLife International (in prep.) *Threatened Birds of Asia*. BirdLife International, Cambridge.

Dobremez, J.F. (1976) *Le Nepal Ecologie et Biogéographie*. Centre National de la Recherche, Paris, France.

Grant, P. and Mullarney, K. (1988–1989). The new approach to bird identification. *Birding World* 1:266–267, 350–354, 387–391, 422–425; 2:15–17, 65–68, 97–99, 132–134, 180–184, 204–206.

Gray, J.R. (1863) *Catalogue of the Specimens and Drawings of Mammals, Birds, Reptiles and Fishes of Nepal and Tibet presented by B. H. Hodgson Esq. to the British Museum*. 2nd Edition. British Museum, London.

Grimmett, R., Inskipp, C. and Inskipp, T. (1998) *Birds of the Indian Subcontinent*. Christopher Helm, London.

Inskipp, C. and Inskipp, T. (1991) *A Guide to the Birds of Nepal*. 2nd edition. Christopher Helm, London.

Inskipp, T., Lindsey, N. and Duckworth, W. (1996) *An Annotated Checklist of the Birds of the Oriental Region*. Oriental Bird Club, Sandy.

Martens, J. and Eck, S. (1991) *Pnoepyga immaculata* n. sp. eine neue bodenbewohnende Timalie aus dem Nepal – Himalaya. *Journal of Ornithology* 132:179–198.

Robson, C. (1999) Nepal Wren Babbler *Pnoepyga immaculata:* no more a Nepal endemic. *Danphe* 8(1):1.

Stattersfield, A.J., Crosby M.J., Long, A.J. and Wege, D.C. (1998) *Endemic Bird Areas of the World: Priorities for Biodiversity Conservation*. BirdLife International, Cambridge.

ACKNOWLEDGEMENTS

The authors are grateful to the artists whose work illustrates this book including John Cox who executed the cover and Craig Robson who prepared the line drawings in the introduction. Numerous people generously provided Richard Grimmett assistance in the preparation of the identification texts which are based on our book *Birds of the Indian Subcontinent*, published by Christopher Helm (1998), and these people are acknowledged in that work.

Carol Inskipp warmly thanks the following Nepalese ornithologists for their invaluable comments on draft texts of species distribution and status: Hem Sagar Baral, Suchit Basnet, Badri Choudhary, Hathan Choudhary, Shambhu Nath Ghimire, Tika Ram Giri and Ramesh Karki. Tim and Carol Inskipp are also grateful to the many observers who have sent them their bird records from Nepal. The authors are indebted to Hem Sagar Baral for his contribution to this book. In addition to writing the conservation section and providing useful comments on the text, he also kindly arranged for the assistance of the other Nepalese ornithologists.

Mike Crosby provided up-to-date information on the status of globally threatened species on behalf of BirdLife International.

Once again we thank Robert Kirk, who managed the project for the publisher, for his constant encouragement and understanding.

Richard Grimmett would like to thank Ani Kartikasari and Dwiati Novita Reni for their assistance in the preparation of the typescript.

GLOSSARY

See also figures on p.8, which cover bird topography.

Altitudinal migrant: a species which breeds at high altitudes (in mountains) and moves to lower levels and valleys in non-breeding season.

Arboreal: tree-dwelling.

Axillaries: the feathers in the armpit at the base of the underwing.

Cap: a well-defined patch of colour or bare skin on the top of the head.

Carpal: the bend of the wing, or carpal joint.

Carpal patch: a well-defined patch of colour on the underwing in the vicinity of the carpal joint.

Casque: an enlargement on the upper surface of the bill, in front of the head, as on hornbills.

Cere: a fleshy (often brightly coloured) structure at the base of the bill and containing the nostrils.

Collar: a well-defined band of colour that encircles or partly encircles the neck.

Culmen: the ridge of the upper mandible.

Eclipse plumage: a female-like plumage acquired by males of some species (e.g. ducks or some sunbirds) during or after breeding.

Edgings or edges: outer feather margins, which can frequently result in distinct paler or darker panels of colour on wings or tail.

Flight feathers: the primaries, secondaries and tail feathers (although not infrequently used to denote the primaries and secondaries alone).

Fringes: complete feather margins, which can frequently result in a scaly appearance to body feathers or wing coverts.

Gape: the mouth and fleshy corner of the bill, which can extend back below the eye.

Gonys: a bulge in the lower mandible, usually distinct on gulls and terns.

Graduated tail: a tail in which the longest feathers are the central pair and the shortest the outermost, with those in between intermediate in length.

Gregarious: living in flocks or communities.

Gular pouch: a loose and pronounced area of skin extending from the throat (e.g. hornbills).

Gular stripe: a usually very narrow (and often dark) stripe running down the centre of the throat.

Hackles: long and pointed neck feathers which can extend across mantle and wing-coverts (e.g. on junglefowls).

Hand: the outer part of the wing, from the carpal joint to the tip of the wing.

Hepatic: used with reference to the rufous-brown morph of some (female) cuckoos.

Iris (plural irides): the coloured membrane which surrounds the pupil of the eye and which can be brightly coloured.

Lappet: a wattle, particularly one at the gape.

Leading edge: the front edge of the forewing. *See also* Trailing edge.

Local: occurring or common within a small or restricted area.

Mandible: the lower or upper half of the bill.

Mask: a dark area of plumage surrounding the eye and often covering the ear-coverts.

Morph: a distinct plumage type which occurs alongside one or more other distinct plumage types exhibited by the same species.

Nomenclature: the scientific naming of species and subspecies, and of the genera, families, and other categories in which species may be classified.

Nominate: the first-named race of a species, that which has its scientific racial name the same as the specific name.

Nuchal: relating to the hindneck, used with reference to a patch or collar.

Ocelli: eye-like spots of iridescent colour; a distinctive feature in the plumage of peafowls.

Orbital ring: a narrow circular ring of feathering or bare skin surrounding the eye.

Plantation: a group of trees (usually exotic or non-native species) planted in close proximity to each other, used for timber or as a crop.

Primary projection: the extension of the primaries beyond the longest tertial on a closed wing; this can be of critical importance in identification (e.g. of larks or *Acrocephalus* warblers).

Race: subspecies, a geographical population whose members all show constant differences (e.g. in plumage or size) from those of other populations of the same species.

Rectrices (singular rectrix): the tail feathers.

Remiges (singular remex): the primaries and secondaries.

Rictal bristles: bristles, often prominent, at the base of the bill.

Shaft streak: a fine line of pale or dark colour in the plumage, produced by the feather shaft.

Speculum: the often glossy panel across the secondaries of, especially, dabbling ducks, often bordered by pale tips to these feathers and a greater-covert wing-bar.

Subspecies: *see* Race.

Subterminal band: a dark or pale band, usually broad, situated inside the outer part of a feather or feather tract (used particularly in reference to the tail).

Taxonomy: the science of classification of species, subspecies, genera, families and other categories in which species may be classified.

Terai: the undulating alluvial, often marshy strip of land 25–45-km wide lying north of the Gangetic plain, extending from Uttar Pradesh through Nepal and northern West Bengal to Assam; naturally supports tall Elephant Grass interspersed with dense forest, but large areas have been drained and converted to cultivation.

Terminal band: a dark or pale band, usually broad, at the tip of a feather or feather tract (especially the tail); cf. subterminal band.

Terrestrial: living or occurring mainly on the ground.

Trailing edge: the rear edge of the wing, often darker or paler than the rest of the wing; cf. leading edge.

Vent: the area around the cloaca (anal opening), just behind the legs (should not be confused with the undertail-coverts).

Vermiculated: marked with narrow wavy lines, usually visible only at close range.

Wattle: a lobe of bare, often brightly coloured skin attached to the head (frequently at the bill-base), as on the mynas or the wattled lapwings.

Wing-linings: the entire underwing-coverts.

Wing panel: a pale or dark band across the upperwing (often formed by pale edges to the remiges or coverts), broader and generally more diffuse than a wing-bar.

Wing-bar: generally a narrow and well-defined dark or pale bar across the upperwing, and often referring to a band formed by pale tips to the greater or median coverts (or both, as in 'double wing-bar').

FAMILY SUMMARIES

Some families are divided into subfamilies and some of these are further divided into tribes.

▪ ▫ ▪ Partridges, Francolins, Snowcocks, Quails and Pheasants Phasianidae ▪ ▫ ▪

Terrestrial, feeding and nesting on the ground, but many species roost in trees at night. They are good runners, often preferring to escape on foot rather than taking to the air. Their flight is powerful and fast, but, except in the case of the migratory quails, it cannot be sustained for long periods. Typically, they forage by scratching the ground with their strong feet to expose food hidden among dead leaves or in the soil. They mainly eat seeds, fruit, buds, roots and leaves, complemented by invertebrates. **pp.46–52**

▪ ▫ ▪ Whistling-ducks Dendrocygnidae and Geese and Ducks Anatidae ▪ ▫ ▪

Aquatic and highly gregarious, typically migrating, feeding, roosting and resting together, often in mixed flocks. Most species are chiefly vegetarian when adult, feeding on seed, algae, plants and roots, often supplemented by aquatic invertebrates. Their main foraging methods are diving, surface-feeding or dabbling, and grazing. They also upend, wade, filter and sieve water and debris for food, and probe with the bill. They have a direct flight with sustained fast wingbeats, and characteristically they fly in V-formation. **pp.54–60**

▪ ▫ ▪ Buttonquails Turnicidae ▪ ▫ ▪

Small, plump terrestrial birds. They are found in a wide variety of habitats having a dry, often sandy substrate and low ground cover under which they can readily run or walk. Buttonquails are very secretive and fly with great reluctance, with weak whirring beats low over the ground, dropping quickly into cover. They feed on grass and weed seeds, grain, greenery and small insects, picking food from the ground surface, or scratching with the feet. **p.48**

▪ ▫ ▪ Honeyguides Indicatoridae ▪ ▫ ▪

Small, inconspicuous birds that inhabit forest or forest edge. All species eat insects, but a peculiarity shared by the family is that they also eat wax, usually as bee combs. Spend long periods perched upright and motionless. Feeds by clinging to bee combs, often upside-down and by aerial sallies. **p.62**

▪ ▫ ▪ Wrynecks, Piculets and Woodpeckers Picidae ▪ ▫ ▪

Chiefly arboreal, and usually seen clinging to, and climbing up, vertical trunks and lateral branches. Typically, they work up trunks and along branches in jerky spurts, directly or in spirals. Some species feed regularly on the ground, searching mainly for termites and ants. The bill of many species is powerful, for boring into wood to extract insects and for excavating nest holes. Woodpeckers feed chiefly on ants, termites, and grubs and pupae of wood-boring beetles. Most woodpeckers also hammer rapidly against tree trunks with their bill, producing a loud rattle, known as 'drumming', which is used to advertise their territories. Their flight is strong and direct, with marked undulations. Many species can be located by their characteristic loud calls. **pp.62–66**

▪ ▫ ▪ Asian Barbets Megalaimidae ▪ ▫ ▪

Arboreal, and usually found in the treetops. Despite their bright coloration, they can be very difficult to see, especially when silent, their plumage blending remarkably well with tree foliage. They often sit motionless for long periods. Barbets call persistently and monotonously in the breeding season, sometimes throughout the day; in the non-breeding season they are usually silent. They are chiefly frugivorous, many species favouring figs *Ficus*. Their flight is strong and direct, with deep woodpecker-like undulations. **p.68**

▪ ▫ ▪ Hornbills Bucerotidae ▪ ▫ ▪

Medium-sized to large birds with massive bills with variable-sized casque. Mainly arboreal, feeding chiefly on wild figs *Ficus*, berries and drupes, supplemented by small animals and insects. Flight is powerful and slow, and for most species consists of a few wingbeats followed by a sailing glide with the wing-tips upturned. In all but the smaller species, the wingbeats make a distinctive loud puffing sound audible for some distance. Hornbills often fly one after another in follow-my-leader fashion. Usually found in pairs or small parties, sometimes in flocks of up to 30 or more where food is abundant. **p.70**

▪ ▪ ▪ Hoopoes Upupidae ▪ ▪ ▪

Have a distinctive appearance, with a long decurved bill, short legs, rounded wings. They are insectivorous and forage by pecking and probing the ground. Flight is undulating, slow and butterfly-like.   **p.72**

▪ ▪ ▪ Trogons Trogonidae ▪ ▪ ▪

Brightly coloured, short-necked, medium-sized birds with a long tail, short rounded wings and a rather short, broad bill. They usually keep singly or in widely separated pairs. Characteristically, they perch almost motionless in upright posture for long periods in the middle or lower storey of dense forests. Trogons are mainly insectivorous and also eat leaves and berries. They capture flying insects on the wing when moving from one vantage point to another, twisting with the agility of a flycatcher.   **p.72**

▪ ▪ ▪ Rollers Coraciidae ▪ ▪ ▪

Stoutly built, medium-sized birds with large head and short neck, which mainly eat large insects. Typically, they keep singly or in widely spaced pairs. Flight is buoyant, with rather rapid deliberate wingbeats.   **p.72**

▪ ▪ ▪ Small Kingfishers Alcedinidae, Large Kingfishers Halcyonidae and Pied Kingfishers Cerylidae ▪ ▪ ▪

Small to medium-sized birds, with large head, long strong beak and short legs. Most kingfishers spend long periods perched singly or in well-separated pairs, watching intently before plunging swiftly downwards to seize prey with bill; they usually return to the same perch. They eat mainly fish, tadpoles and invertebrates; larger species also eat frogs, snakes, crabs, lizards and rodents. Their flight is direct and strong, with rapid wingbeats and often close to the surface.   **p.74**

▪ ▪ ▪ Bee-eaters Meropidae ▪ ▪ ▪

Brightly coloured birds with long decurved beak, pointed wings and very short legs. They catch large flying insects on the wing, by making short, swift sallies like a flycatcher from an exposed perch such as a treetop, branch, post or telegraph wire; insects are pursued in a lively chase with a swift and agile flight. Some species also hawk insects in flight like swallows. Most species are sociable. Their flight is graceful and undulating, a few rapid wingbeats followed by a glide.   **p.72**

▪ ▪ ▪ Old World Cuckoos Cuculidae ▪ ▪ ▪

Have an elongated body with fairly long neck, tail varying from medium length to long and graduated, and quite long, decurved bill. Almost all Cuculidae are arboreal and eat hairy caterpillars. Apart from the Green-billed Malkoha, male cuckoos are very noisy in the breeding season, calling frequently during the day, especially if cloudy, and often into the night. When not breeding they are silent and unobtrusive, and as a result their status and distribution at this season are very poorly known. Cuckoos (apart from Green-billed Malkoha) are notorious for their nest parasitism.   **pp.76–78**

▪ ▪ ▪ Coucals Centropodidae ▪ ▪ ▪

Large, skulking birds with long graduated tail and weak flight. Coucals are terrestrial, frequenting dense undergrowth, bamboo, tall grassland or scrub jungle. They eat small animals and invertebrates.   **p.80**

▪ ▪ ▪ Parrots Psittacidae ▪ ▪ ▪

Have a short neck and short, stout hooked bill with the upper mandible strongly curved and overlapping the lower mandible. Most parrots are noisy and highly gregarious. They associate in family parties and small flocks and gather in large numbers at concentrations of food, such as paddy-fields. Their diet is almost entirely vegetarian: fruit, seeds, buds, nectar and pollen. The flight of *Psittacula* parrots is swift, powerful and direct.   **p.80**

Swifts Apodidae and Treeswifts Hemiprocnidae

Have long pointed wings, compact body, short bill with a wide gape and very short legs. Swifts spend most of the day swooping and wheeling in the sky with great agility and grace. Typical swift flight is a series of rapid shallow wingbeats interspersed with short glides. They feed entirely in the air, drink and bathe while swooping low over water, and regularly pass the night in the air. Swifts eat mainly tiny insects, caught by flying back and forth among aerial concentrations of these with their large mouth open; they also pursue individual insects. **p.82**

Barn Owls and Grass Owls Tytonidae and Typical Owls Strigidae

Have a large and rounded head, big forward-facing eyes surrounded by a broad facial disc, and a short tail. Most are nocturnal and cryptically coloured and patterned, making them inconspicuous when resting during the day. When hunting, owls either quarter the ground or scan and listen for prey from a perch. Their diet consists of small animals and invertebrates. Owls are usually located by their distinctive and often weird calls, which are diagnostic of the species and advertise their presence and territories. **pp.84–88**

Nightjars Caprimulgidae

Small to medium-sized birds with long, pointed wings, and gaping mouth with long bristles that help to catch insects in flight. Nightjars are crepuscular and nocturnal in habit, with soft, owl-like, cryptically patterned plumage. By day they perch on the ground or lengthwise on a branch, and are difficult to detect. They eat flying insects that are caught on the wing. Typically, they fly erratically to and fro over and among vegetation, occasionally wheeling, gliding and hovering to pick insects from foliage. Most easily located by the calls. **p.88**

Pigeons and Doves Columbidae

Have a stout compact body, rather short neck, and small head and bill. Their flight is swift and direct, with fast wingbeats. Most species are gregarious outside the breeding season. Seeds, fruits, buds and leaves form their main diet, but many species also eat small invertebrates. They have soft plaintive cooing or booming voices that are often monotonously repeated. **pp.90–94**

Bustards Otididae

Medium-sized to large terrestrial birds that inhabit grasslands in Nepal. They have fairly long legs, stout body, long neck, and crests and neck plumes, which are exhibited in display. The wings are broad and long, and in flight the neck is outstretched. Their flight is powerful and can be very fast. When feeding, bustards have a steady, deliberate gait. They are more or less omnivorous, and feed opportunistically on large insects, such as grasshoppers and locusts, young birds, shoots, leaves, seeds and fruits. Males perform elaborate and spectacular displays in the breeding season. **p.96**

Cranes Gruidae

Stately long-necked, long-legged birds with tapering body, and long inner secondaries which hang over the tail. The flight is powerful, with the head and neck extended forwards and legs and feet stretched out behind. Flocks of cranes often fly in V-formation; they sometimes soar at considerable heights. Most cranes are gregarious outside the breeding season, and flocks are often very noisy. Cranes have a characteristic resonant and far-reaching musical trumpet-like call. A wide variety of plant and animal food is taken. The bill is used to probe and dig for plant roots and to graze and glean vegetable material above the ground. Both sexes have a spectacular and beautiful dance that takes place throughout the year. **p.96**

Rails, Gallinules and Coots Rallidae

Small to medium-sized birds, with moderate-to-long legs for wading and short rounded wings. With the exception of the Common Moorhen and Common Coot, which spend much time swimming in the open, rails are mainly terrestrial. Many occur in marshes. They fly reluctantly and feebly, with legs dangling, for a short distance and then drop into cover again. The majority are heard more often than seen, and are most voluble at dusk and at night. Their calls consist of strident or raucous repeated notes. They eat insects, crustaceans, amphibians, fish and vegetable matter. **p.98**

■ Woodcocks, Snipes, Godwits, Sandpipers, Curlews and Phalaropes Scolopacidae ■

Woodcocks and Snipes Subfamily Scolopacinae

Woodcocks and snipes are small to medium-sized waders with a very long bill, fairly long legs and cryptically patterned plumage. They feed mainly by probing in soft ground and also by picking from the surface. Their diet consists mostly of small aquatic invertebrates. If approached, they usually first crouch on the ground and 'freeze', preferring to rely on their protective plumage pattern to escape detection. They inhabit marshy ground.   **p.100**

Godwits, Sandpipers, Curlews, Phalaropes Subfamily Tringinae

The Tringinae are wading birds with quite long to very long legs and a long bill. They feed on small aquatic invertebrates.   **pp.102–104, 268**

■ ■ ■ **Painted-snipes** Rostrarulidae ■ ■ ■

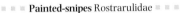

Frequent marshes and superficially resemble snipes, but have spectacular plumages. **p.100**

■ ■ ■ **Jacana** Jacanidae ■ ■ ■

Jacanas characteristically have very long toes, which enable them to walk over floating vegetation. They inhabit freshwater lakes, ponds and marshes.   **p.106**

■ ■ ■ **Thick-knees** Burhinidae ■ ■ ■

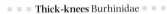

Medium-sized to large waders, mainly crepuscular or nocturnal, and with cryptically patterned plumages. They eat invertebrates and small animals.   **p.106**

■ ■ **Oystercatchers, Ibisbill, Avocets, Plovers and Lapwings** Charadriidae ■ ■

Oystercatchers, Ibisbill and Avocets Subfamily Recurvirostrinae

Oystercatchers are waders that usually inhabit the seashore and are only vagrants inland. They have all-black or black-and-white plumage. The bill is long, stout, orange-red and adapted for opening shells of bivalve molluscs. Stilts and avocets have a characteristic long bill, and longer legs in proportion to the body than any other birds except flamingos. They inhabit marshes, lakes and pools. The Ibisbill has a distinctive decurved bill and frequents rivers and streams. Both feed on aquatic invertebrates.   **pp.106, 268**

Plovers and Lapwings Subfamily Charadriinae

Plovers and lapwings are small to medium-sized waders with rounded head, short neck and short bill. Typically, they forage by running in short spurts, pausing and standing erect, then stooping to pick up invertebrate prey. Their flight is swift and direct.   **pp.108–110**

■ ■ ■ **Pratincoles and Coursers** Glareolidae *Subfamily Glareolinae* ■ ■ ■

Coursers and pratincoles have an arched and pointed bill, wide gape and long, pointed wings. Coursers are long-legged and resemble plovers; they feed on the ground. Most pratincoles are short-legged; they catch most of their prey in the air, although they also feed on the ground. All pratincoles live near water, whereas coursers frequent dry grassland and dry stony areas.   **pp.106, 110**

■ ■ ■ **Skimmers, Gulls and Terns** Laridae ■ ■ ■

This family comprises the subfamilies Larinae and Alcinae. Only the former occurs in Nepal and this is subdivided into three tribes.

Skimmers Tribe Rynchopini

Have very long wings, a short forked tail, a long bill and short red legs and toes, and are black above and white below. They frequent rivers and lakes.   **p.114**

Gulls Tribe Larini

Medium-sized to large birds with relatively long, narrow wings, usually a stout bill, moderately long legs and webbed feet. Immatures are brownish and cryptically patterned. In flight, gulls are graceful and soar easily in updraughts. All species swim buoyantly and well. They are highly adaptable, and most species are opportunistic feeders with a varied diet including invertebrates. Most species are gregarious.   **p.112**

Terns Tribe Sternini

Small to medium-sized aerial birds with a gull-like body but, with the exception of the largest species, more delicately built. The wings are long and pointed, typically narrower than those of the gulls, and the flight is buoyant and graceful. Terns are highly vocal and most species are gregarious. Two groups of terns occur in Nepal: the *Sterna* terns and the *Chlidonias* or marsh terns. The *Sterna* terns have a deeply forked tail, and inhabit large rivers and other inland fresh waters. *Sterna* terns mainly eat small fish, tadpoles and crabs caught by hovering and then plunge-diving from the air, often submerging completely; also by picking prey from the surface. Marsh terns lack a prominent tail-fork and, compared with *Sterna* terns, are smaller, more compact and short-tailed, and have a more erratic and rather stiff-winged flight. They frequent marshes, lakes and rivers. Typically, marsh terns hawk insects or swoop down to pick small prey from the water surface.   **p.114**

▪ ▪ ▪ Osprey, Hawks, Eagles, Harriers and Vultures etc. Accipitridae ▪ ▪ ▪

A large and varied family of raptors, ranging from the Besra to the huge Himalayan Griffon. In most species, the vultures being an exception, the female is larger than the male and is often duller and brownish. The Accipitridae feed on mammals, birds, reptiles, amphibians, fish, crabs, molluscs and insects – dead or alive. All have a hooked, pointed bill and very acute sight, and all except the vultures have powerful feet with long curved claws. They frequent all habitat types, ranging from dense forest, deserts and mountains to fresh waters.   **pp.116–136**

▪ ▪ ▪ Falcons Falconidae ▪ ▪ ▪

Small to medium-sized birds of prey, which resemble the Accipitridae in having a hooked beak, sharp curved talons, and remarkable powers of sight and flight. Like other raptors they are mainly diurnal, although a few are crepuscular. Two genera occur in Nepal: the falconets *Microhierax* and the falcons *Falco*. The falconets prey mainly on insects. Some falcons kill flying birds in a surprise attack, often by stooping at great speed (e.g. Peregrine); others hover and then swoop on prey on the ground (e.g. Common Kestrel), and several species hawk insects in flight (e.g. Eurasian Hobby).   **pp.138–140**

▪ ▪ ▪ Grebes Podicipedidae ▪ ▪ ▪

Aquatic birds adapted for diving from the surface and swimming under the water to catch fish and aquatic invertebrates. Their strong legs are placed near the rear of their almost tailless body, and the feet are lobed. In flight, grebes have an elongated appearance, with the neck extended, and feet hanging lower than the humped back. They usually feed singly, but may form loose congregations in the non-breeding season.   **p.142**

▪ ▪ ▪ Anhingas Anhingidae ▪ ▪ ▪

Large aquatic birds adapted for hunting fish underwater. Anhingas have a long, slender neck and head, long wings and a very long tail.   **p.142**

▪ ▪ ▪ Cormorants Phalacrocoracidae ▪ ▪ ▪

Medium-sized to large aquatic birds. They are long-necked, with a hooked bill of moderate length and a long, stiff tail. Cormorants swim with the body low in the water, with the neck straight and the head and bill pointing a little upwards. They eat mainly fish, which are caught by underwater pursuit. In flight, the neck is extended and the head is held slightly above the horizontal. Typically they often perch for long periods in upright posture, with spread wings and tail, on trees, posts or rocks.   **p.142**

▪ ▪ ▪ Herons & Bitterns Ardeidae ▪ ▪ ▪

Medium-sized to large birds with long legs for wading. The diurnal herons have a slender body and long head and neck; the night herons are more squat, with shorter neck and legs. They fly with leisurely flaps, with the legs outstretched and projecting beyond the tail, and nearly always with head and neck drawn back. They frequent marshes and the shores of lakes and rivers. Typically, herons feed by standing motionless at the water's edge, waiting for prey to swim within reach, or by slow stalking in shallow water or on land. Bitterns usually skulk in reedbeds, although occasionally one may forage in the open, and they can clamber about reed stems with agility. Normally they are solitary and crepuscular and most often seen flying low over reedbeds with slow wingbeats, soon dropping into cover again. Herons and bitterns feed on a wide variety of aquatic prey.   **pp.144–146**

▪ ▪ ▪ Flamingos Phoenicopteridae ▪ ▪ ▪

Large wading birds with long neck, very long legs, webbed feet and pink plumage. The bill is highly specialised for filter-feeding. Flamingos often occur in huge numbers and are found mainly on salt lakes and lagoons.   **p.268**

▪ ▪ ▪ Ibises and Spoonbills Threskiornithidae ▪ ▪ ▪

Large birds with long neck and legs, partly webbed feet and long, broad wings. Ibises have a long decurved bill, and forage by probing in shallow water, mud and grass. Spoonbills have a long spatulate bill, and catch floating prey in shallow water.   **p.148**

▪ ▪ ▪ Pelicans Pelecanidae ▪ ▪ ▪

Large, aquatic, gregarious fish-eating birds. The wings are long and broad, and the tail is short and rounded. They have a characteristic long, straight, flattened bill, hooked at the tip, and with a large expandable pouch suspended beneath the lower mandible. Many pelicans often fish cooperatively by swimming forward in a semicircular formation, driving the fish into shallow waters; each bird then scoops up fish from the water into its pouch, before swallowing the food. Pelicans fly either in V-formation or in lines, and often soar for considerable periods in thermals. They are powerful fliers, proceeding by steady flaps and with the head drawn back between the shoulders. When swimming, the closed wings are typically held above the back.   **p.148**

▪ ▪ ▪ Storks Ciconiidae ▪ ▪ ▪

Large or very large birds with long bill, neck and legs, long and broad wings and a short tail. In flight, the legs are extended behind and the neck is outstretched. They have a powerful slow-flapping flight and frequently soar for long periods, often at great heights. They capture fish, frogs, snakes, lizards, large insects, crustaceans and molluscs while walking slowly in marshes, at edges of lakes and rivers and in grassland.   **pp.150–152**

▪ ▪ ▪ Pittas Pittidae ▪ ▪ ▪

Brilliantly coloured, terrestrial forest passerines. They are of medium size, stocky and long-legged, with short square tail, stout bill and an erect carriage. Most of their time is spent foraging for invertebrates on the forest floor, flicking leaves and other vegetation, and probing with their strong bill into leaf litter and damp earth. Pittas usually progress on the ground by long hopping bounds. Typically, they are skulking and are often most easily located by their high-pitched whistling calls or songs. They sing in trees or bushes.   **p.154**

▪ ▪ ▪ Broadbills Eurylaimidae ▪ ▪ ▪

Small to medium-sized plump birds with rounded wings and short legs, most species having a distinctively broad bill. Typically, they inhabit the middle storey of forest and feed mainly on invertebrates gleaned from leaves and branches. Broadbills are active when foraging, but are often unobtrusive and lethargic at other times.   **p.154**

▪ ▪ ▪ Fairy Bluebirds and Leafbirds Irenidae ▪ ▪ ▪

Small to medium-sized passerines having a fairly long, slender bill with the upper mandible decurved at the tip. All are arboreal, typically frequenting thick foliage in the canopy. They search leaves for insects and also feed on berries and nectar. Their flight is swift, usually over a short distance.   **p.154**

▪ ▪ ▪ Shrikes Laniidae ▪ ▪ ▪

Medium-sized, predatory passerines with a strong stout bill, hooked at the tip of the upper mandible, strong legs and feet, a large head, and a long tail with graduated tip. Shrikes search for prey from a vantage point, such as the top of a bush or small tree or post. They swoop down to catch invertebrates or small animals from the ground or in flight. Over long distances their flight is typically undulating. Their calls are harsh, but most have quite musical songs and are good mimics. Shrikes typically inhabit open country with scattered bushes or light scrub.   **p.156**

▪ ▪ ▪ **Corvids** Corvidae ▪ ▪ ▪

This is very large family, represented in Bhutan by four subfamilies (in some cases further subdivided into tribes).

Subfamily Corvinae

Jays, Magpies, Treepies, Choughs, Nutcrackers, Crows, Ravens Tribe Corvini
These are all robust perching birds which differ considerably from each other in appearance, but which have a number of features in common: a fairly long straight bill, very strong feet and legs, and a tuft of nasal bristles extending over the base of the upper mandible. The sexes are alike or almost alike in plumage. They are strong fliers. Most are gregarious, especially when feeding and roosting. Typically, they are noisy birds, uttering loud and discordant squawks, croaks or screeches. The Corvini are highly inquisitive and adaptable.

pp.158–160

Woodswallows Tribe Artamini
Plump birds with long, pointed wings, short tail and legs, and a wide gape. They feed on insects, usually captured in flight and spend prolonged periods on the wing. They perch close together on a bare branch or wire, and often waggle the tail from side to side. **p.162**

Orioles, Cuckooshrikes, Minivets, Flycatcher-shrikes Tribe Oriolini
Orioles Genus *Oriolus* Medium-sized arboreal passerines that usually keep hidden in the leafy canopy. Orioles have beautiful, fluty, whistling songs and harsh grating calls. They are usually seen singly, in pairs or in family parties. Their flight is powerful and undulating, with fast wingbeats. They feed mainly on insects and fruit. **pp.162–164**

Cuckooshrikes Genus *Coracina* Arboreal, insectivorous birds that usually keep high in the trees. They are of medium size, with long pointed wings, a moderately long rounded tail, and an upright carriage when perched. **p.162**

Minivets Genus *Pericrocotus* Small to medium-sized, brightly coloured passerines with a moderately long tail and an upright stance when perched. They are arboreal, and feed on insects by flitting about in the foliage to glean prey from leaves, buds and bark, sometimes hovering in front of a sprig or making short aerial sallies. They usually keep in pairs in the breeding season, and in small parties when not breeding. When feeding and in flight, they continually utter contact calls. **p.164**

Subfamily Dicrurinae

Fantails Tribe Rhipidurini
Small, confiding, arboreal birds, perpetually on the move in search of insects. Characteristically, they erect and spread the tail like a fan, and droop the wings, while pirouetting and turning from side to side with jerky, restless movements. When foraging, they flit from branch to branch, making frequent aerial sallies after winged insects. They call continually. Fantails are usually found singly or in pairs, and often join mixed hunting parties with other insectivorous birds. **p.164**

Drongos Tribe Dicrurini
Medium-sized passerines with characteristic black and often glossy plumage, long, often deeply forked tail, and a very upright stance when perched. They are mainly arboreal and insectivorous, catching larger winged insects by aerial sallies from a perch. Usually found singly or in pairs. Their direct flight is swift, strong and undulating. Drongos are rather noisy, and have a varied repertoire of harsh calls and pleasant whistles; some species are good mimics. **p.166**

Monarchs Tribe Monarchini
Most species are small to medium-sized, with long, pointed wings and a medium-length to long tail. They feed mainly on insects. **p.168**

Ioras Subfamily Aegithininae

Small, fairly lively passerines that feed in trees, mainly on insects and especially caterpillars.
p.168

Woodshrikes Subfamily Malaconotinae

Medium-sized, arboreal, insectivorous passerines. The bill is stout and hooked, the wings are rounded, and the tail is short.
p.168

▪ ▪ ▪ Waxwings Bombycillidae ▪ ▪ ▪

Have soft plumage, crested head, short broad-based bill, and short, strong legs and feet. Outside the breeding season, they are found wherever fruits are available.
p.269

▪ ▪ ▪ Dippers Cinclidae ▪ ▪ ▪

Have short wings and tail, and are adapted for feeding on invertebrates in or under running water. They fly low over the water surface on rapidly whirring wings.
p.168

▪ ▪ ▪ Thrushes, Shortwings, Old World Flycatchers and Chats Muscicapidae ▪ ▪ ▪

A large and varied family represented in Nepal by two subfamilies, the second of which is subdivided into two tribes.

Subfamily Turdinae

Thrushes Genera *Monticola, Myophonus, Zoothera* and *Turdus* Medium-sized passerines with rather long, strong legs, a slender bill and fairly long wings. On the ground they progress by hopping. All are insectivorous, and many eat fruit as well. Some species are chiefly terrestrial and others arboreal. Most thrushes have loud and varied songs, which are used to proclaim and defend their territories when breeding. Many species gather in flocks outside the breeding season.
pp.170–174

Shortwings Genus *Brachypteryx* Small, chat-like thrushes with short rounded wings, almost square tail, and strong legs. They are mainly terrestrial, and inhabit low bushes, undergrowth or thickets. Shortwings are chiefly insectivorous and found singly or in pairs.
p.182

Subfamily Muscicapinae

Old World Flycatchers Tribe Muscicapini

Small insectivorous birds with a small, flattened bill, and bristles at the gape that help in the capture of flying insects. They normally have a very upright stance when perched. Many species frequently flick the tail and hold the wings slightly drooped. Generally, flycatchers frequent trees and bushes. Some species regularly perch on a vantage point, from which they catch insects in mid-air in short aerial sallies or by dropping to the ground, often returning to the same perch. Other species capture insects while flitting among branches or by picking them from foliage. Flycatchers are usually found singly or in pairs; a few join mixed hunting parties of other insectivorous birds.
pp.176–180

Chats Tribe Saxicolini

A diverse group of small/medium-sized passerines that includes the chats, bush robins, magpie robins, redstarts, forktails, cochoas and wheatears. Most are terrestrial or partly terrestrial, some are arboreal, and some are closely associated with water. Their main diet is insects, and they also consume fruits, especially berries. They forage mainly by hopping about on the ground in search of prey, or by perching on a low vantage point and then dropping to the ground on to insects or making short sallies to catch them in the air. Found singly or in pairs.
pp.182–192

Starlings and Mynas Sturnidae

Robust, medium-sized passerines with strong legs and bill, moderately long wings and a square tail. The flight is direct; strong and fast in the more pointed-winged species (*Sturnus*), and rather slower with more deliberate flapping in the more rounded-winged ones. Most species walk with an upright stance in a characteristic, purposeful jaunty fashion, broken by occasional short runs and hops. Their calls are often loud, harsh and grating, and the song of many species is a variety of whistles; mimicry is common. Most are highly gregarious at times. Some starlings in Nepal are mainly arboreal and feed on fruits and insects; others are chiefly ground-feeders, and are omnivorous. Many are closely associated with human cultivation and habitation. **p.194**

Nuthatches and Wallcreeper Sittidae

Nuthatches and the Wallcreeper are small, energetic passerines with a compact body, short tail, large strong feet and a long bill. The Wallcreeper is adept at clambering over rock faces. Nuthatches are also agile tree climbers. They can move with ease upwards, downwards, sideways and upside-down over trunks or branches progressing by a series of jerky hops. Unlike woodpeckers and treecreepers, they usually begin near the top of a tree and work down the main trunk or larger branches, often head-first, and do not use the tail as a prop. Their flight is direct over short distances, and undulating over longer ones. Nuthatches capture insects, spiders, seeds and nuts. They are often found singly or in pairs; outside the breeding season, they often join foraging flocks of other insectivorous birds. **p.196**

Treecreepers and Wrens Certhiidae

A family of mainly small, rather similar-looking species with two subfamilies.

Treecreepers Subfamily Certhiinae

Small, quiet, arboreal passerines with a slender, decurved bill and a stiff tail that is used as a prop when climbing, like that of the woodpeckers. Treecreepers forage by creeping up vertical trunks and along the underside of branches, spiralling upwards in a series of jerks in search of insects and spiders; on reaching the top of a tree, they fly to the base of the next one. Their flight is undulating and weak, and is usually only over short distances. Treecreepers are non-gregarious, but outside the nesting season they usually join mixed hunting parties of other insectivorous birds. They inhabit broadleaved and coniferous forest, woodland, groves, and gardens with trees. Thin high-pitched contact calls are used continually. **p.196**

Wrens Subfamily Troglodytinae

Small, plump, insectivorous passerines with rather short, blunt wings, strong legs and the tail characteristically held erect. **p.200**

Tits Paridae and Long-tailed Tits Aegithalidae

Small, active (except for Sultan Tit), highly acrobatic passerines with a short bill and strong feet. Their flight over long distances is undulating. They are mainly insectivorous, although many species also depend on seeds, particularly from trees in winter, and some also eat fruit. They probe bark crevices, search branches and leaves, and frequently hang upside-down from twigs. Tits are chiefly arboreal, but also descend to the ground to feed, hopping about and flicking aside leaves and other debris. They are very gregarious; in the non-breeding season most species join roving flocks of other other insectivorous birds. **pp.198–200**

Swallows and Martins Hirundinidae

Gregarious, rather small passerines with a distinctive slender, streamlined body, long, pointed wings and a small bill. The long-tailed species are often called swallows, and the shorter-tailed species termed martins. All hawk day-flying insects in swift, agile, sustained flight, sometimes high in the air. Many species have a deeply forked tail, which affords better manoeuvrability. Hirundines catch most of their food while flying in the open. They perch readily on exposed branches and wires. **p.202**

▪ ▪ ▪ Bulbuls Pycnonotidae ▪ ▪ ▪

Medium-sized passerines with soft, fluffy plumage, rather short and rounded wings, a medium-long to long tail, slender bill and short, weak legs. Bulbuls in Nepal feed on berries and other fruits, often supplemented by insects, and sometimes also nectar and buds of trees and shrubs. Many species are noisy, especially when feeding. Typically, bulbuls have a variety of cheerful, loud, chattering, babbling and whistling calls. Most species are gregarious in the non-breeding season.   **p.204**

▪ ▪ ▪ Prinias and Cisticolas Cisticolidae ▪ ▪ ▪

Prinias *Prinia* Have a long, graduated tail that is longer in winter than in summer. Most inhabit grassland, marsh vegetation or scrub. They forage by gleaning insects and spiders from vegetation, and some species also feed on the ground. When perched, the tail is often held cocked and slightly fanned. Flight is weak and jerky.   **p.206**

Cisticolas *Cisticola* Tiny, short-tailed, insectivorous passerines. The tail is longer in winter than in summer. They are often found in grassy habitats, and many have aerial displays.
                                                                                      p.208

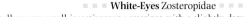

▪ ▪ ▪ White-Eyes Zosteropidae ▪ ▪ ▪

Small or very small insectivorous passerines with a slightly decurved and pointed bill, a brush-tipped tongue, and a white ring around each eye. White-eyes frequent forest, forest edge, and bushes in gardens.   **p.208**

▪ ▪ ▪ Warblers, Grassbirds, Laughingthrushes and Babblers Sylviidae ▪ ▪ ▪

A huge and varied family of mostly small species, represented in Nepal by four subfamilies.

Warblers Subfamily Acrocephalinae

A large group of small, active perching birds with a fine pointed bill. Insects and spiders form their main diet; some species also consume berries, seeds and nectar. They usually capture their prey by gleaning from foliage, but sometimes also from the ground. Warblers inhabit all types of vegetation, often in dense habitats.

Tesias Tiny, active, almost tailless warblers inhabiting forest. Mainly terrestrial. **p.208**

Bush Warblers Medium-sized warblers with rounded wings and tail that inhabit marshes, grassland and forest undergrowth. They are usually found singly. Bush warblers call frequently, and are usually heard more often than seen. *Cettia* species have surprisingly loud voices, and some can be identified by their distinctive melodious songs. Bush warblers seek insects and spiders by actively flitting and hopping about in vegetation close to the ground. They are reluctant to fly, and usually cover only short distances at low level before dropping into dense cover again. When excited, they flick their wings and tail.   **p.210**

Warblers Genus *Locustella* Very skulking, medium-sized warblers with a rounded tail, usually found singly. Characteristically, they keep low down or on the ground among dense vegetation, walking furtively and scurrying off when startled. Their plumage is dull brownish, and they differ from Spotted, Chinese and Brown Bush Warblers, which are similar in behaviour and winter in the same habitat, in having noticeable streaking on the upperparts. They fly at low level, flitting between plants, or rather jerkily over longer distances, ending in a sudden dive into cover.   **p.270**

Warblers Genus *Acrocephalus* Medium-sized to large warblers with prominent bill and rounded tail. They usually occur singly. Many species are skulking, typically keeping low down in dense vegetation. Most frequent marshy habitats, and are able to clamber about readily in reeds and other vertical stems of marsh plants. Their songs are harsh and often monotonous.   **pp.210–212**

Warblers Genus *Hippolais* Medium-sized warblers with a large bill, square-ended tail, and rather sloping forehead and peaked crown giving a distinctive domed head shape. Their songs are harsh and varied. They clamber about vegetation with a rather clumsy action.
                                                                                      p.212

Tailorbirds Have a long, decurved bill, short wings and a graduated tail, the latter held characteristically cocked.   **p.208**

Tit Warblers Small warblers with soft, copious plumage. Inhabit scrub or coniferous forest.   **p.208**

Warblers Genus *Phylloscopus* Rather small, slim and short-billed warblers. Useful identification features are voice, strength of supercilium, colour of underparts, rump, bill and legs, and presence or absence of wing-bars, of coronal bands or of white on the tail. The coloration of upperparts and underparts and the presence or prominence of wing-bars are affected by wear. Leaf warblers are fast moving and restless, hopping and creeping about actively and often flicking the wings. They mostly glean small insects and spiders from foliage, twigs and branches, often first disturbing prey by hovering and fluttering; they also make short fly-catching sallies.   **pp.214–216**

Warblers Genera *Seicercus* and *Abroscopus* Small and active warblers. They feed in a similar manner to *Phylloscopus* warblers, by gleaning from foliage and twigs and making frequent aerial sallies, but have a broader bill and brighter plumage than those species.   **p.218**

Grassbirds Subfamily Megalurinae

Brownish warblers with a longish tail which inhabit damp tall grassland. The males perform song flights in the breeding season.   **p.212**

Laughingthrushes Subfamily Garrulacinae

Medium-sized, long-tailed passerines that are gregarious even in the breeding season. At the first sign of danger, they characteristically break into a concert of loud hissing, chattering and squealing. They often feed on the ground, moving along with long springy hops, rummaging among leaf litter, flicking leaves aside and into the air, and digging for food with their strong bill. Their flight is short and clumsy, the birds flying from tree to tree in follow-my-leader fashion   **pp.220–222**

Babblers Subfamily Sylviinae, Tribe Timaliini

A large and diverse group of small to medium-sized passerines. They have soft, loose plumage, short or fairly short wings, and strong feet and legs. The sexes are alike in most species. With the exception of most wren babblers, the members of this tribe associate in flocks outside the breeding season, and some species do so throughout the year. Babbler flocks are frequently a component of mixed-species feeding parties. Most babblers have a wide range of chatters, rattles and whistles; some have a melodious song. Many are terrestrial or inhabit bushes or grass close to the ground, while other species are arboreal. Babblers are chiefly insectivorous, and augment their diet with fruits, seeds and nectar. Arboreal species collect food from leaves, moss, lichen and bark; terrestrial species forage by probing, digging, and tossing aside dead foliage.   **pp.224–236**

Subfamily Sylviinae, Tribe Sylviini

Small to medium-sized passerines with a fine bill, closely resembling the true warblers. Typically, they inhabit bushes and scrub and feed chiefly by gleaning insects from foliage and twigs; they sometimes also consume berries in autumn and winter.   **p.212**

▪ ▪ ▪ Larks Alaudidae ▪ ▪ ▪

Terrestrial cryptically coloured passerines, generally small-sized, which usually walk and run on the ground and often have a very elongated hindclaw. Their flight is strong and undulating. Larks take a wide variety of food, including insects, molluscs, arthropods, seeds, flowers, buds and leaves. Many species have a melodious song, which is often delivered in a distinctive, steeply climbing or circling aerial display, but also from a conspicuous low perch. They live in a wide range of open habitats, including grassland and cultivation.   **p.238**

▪ ▪ ▪ Flowerpeckers, Sunbirds and Spiderhunters
Nectariniidae, *Subfamily Nectariniinae* ▪ ▪ ▪

These birds are represented in Nepal by two discrete tribes.

Flowerpeckers Tribe Dicaeini

Very small passerines with short beak and tail, with a tongue adapted for nectar-feeding. They usually frequent the tree canopy and feed mainly on soft fruits, berries and nectar; also on small insects and spiders. Many species are especially fond of mistletoe *Loranthus* berries. Flowerpeckers are very active, continually flying about restlessly, and twisting and turning in different attitudes when perched, while calling frequently with high-pitched notes. Normally they live singly or in pairs; some species form small parties in the non-breeding season. **p.240**

Sunbirds and Spiderhunters Tribe Nectariniini

Sunbirds and spiderhunters have a bill and tongue adapted to feed on nectar; they also eat small insects and spiders. The bill is long, thin and curved for probing the corollas of flowers. The tongue is very long, tubular and extensible far beyond the bill, and is used to draw out nectar.

Sunbirds   Small to very small passerines. Sunbirds feed mainly at the blossoms of flowering trees and shrubs. They flit and dart actively from flower to flower, clambering over the blossoms, often hovering momentarily in front of them, and clinging acrobatically to twigs. Sunbirds usually keep singly or in pairs, although several may congregate in flowering trees, and some species join mixed foraging flocks. They have sharp, metallic calls and high-pitched trilling and twittering songs. **pp.240–242**

Spiderhunters   Have similar foraging behaviour to the sunbirds, but are larger and bulkier, have a longer bill and utter explosive chattering calls. The sexes are alike. They are usually found singly or in pairs. **p.242**

▪ ▪ ▪ Passeridae ▪ ▪ ▪

Represented in Nepal by five subfamilies: sparrows, wagtails and pipits, accentors, weavers and estrildine finches.

Sparrows and Snowfinches Subfamily Passerinae

Small passerines with a thick conical bill. There are four genera: *Passer*, the true sparrows, some of which are closely associated with human habitation; *Petronia*, the rock sparrows, which inhabit dry rocky country or light scrub; and *Montifringilla* and *Pyrgilauda*, the snowfinches, which occur in mountains. They are mainly brown and grey in coloration, sometimes with black, except for the snowfinches, which have some conspicuous white in the plumage. Most species feed on seeds, taken on or near the ground; snowfinches also consume a high proportion of insects when available. The *Passer* sparrows are rather noisy, using a variety of harsh, chirping notes; the others have more varied songs and rather harsh calls. **p.244**

Wagtails And Pipits Subfamily Motacillinae

Small, slender, terrestrial birds with long legs, relatively long toes and a thin, pointed bill. Some wagtails exhibit wide geographical plumage variation. All walk with a deliberate gait and run rapidly. The flight is undulating and strong. Most wagtails wag the tail up and down, and so do some pipits. They feed mainly by picking insects from the ground as they walk along, or by making short rapid runs to capture insects they have flushed; they also catch prey in mid-air. Song flights are characteristic of many pipits. Both wagtails and pipits call in flight, and this is often a useful identification feature. They are usually found singly or in pairs in the breeding season and in scattered flocks in autumn and winter. **pp.246–250**

Accentors Subfamily Prunellinae

Small, compact birds resembling *Passer* sparrows in appearance, but with a more slender and pointed bill. Accentors forage quietly and unobtrusively on the ground, moving by hopping or in shuffling walk; some species also run. In summer accentors are chiefly insectivorous, and in winter they feed mainly on seeds. Their flight is usually low over the ground and sustained only over short distances. **p.252**

Weavers Subfamily Ploceinae

Small, rather plump, finch-like passerines with a large, conical bill. Adults feed chiefly on seeds and grain, supplemented by invertebrates; the young are often fed on invertebrates. Weavers inhabit grassland, marshes, cultivation and very open woodland. They are highly gregarious, roosting and nesting communally, and are noted for their elaborate roofed nests. **p.254**

Estrildine Finches Subfamily Estrildinae

Small, slim passerines with a short, stout, conical beak. They feed chiefly on small seeds, which they pick up from the ground or gather by clinging to stems and pulling the seeds directly from seed heads. Their gait is a hop or occasionally a walk. Outside the breeding season all species are gregarious. Flight is fast and undulating. **p.254**

▪ ▪ ▪ Finches and Buntings Fringillidae ▪ ▪ ▪

Finches Subfamily Fringillinae

Small to medium-sized passerines with a strong conical bill used for eating seeds. Forage on the ground; some species also feed on seedheads of tall herbs, and blossoms or berries of bushes and trees. Finches are highly gregarious outside the breeding season. Their flight is fast and undulating. **pp.256–262**

Buntings Subfamily Emberizinae

Small to medium-sized, terrestrial passerines with a strong, conical bill designed for shelling seeds, usually of grasses; adults also eat insects in summer. They forage by hopping or creeping on the ground. Their flight is undulating. Buntings are usually gregarious outside the breeding season, feeding and roosting in flocks. Buntings occur in a wide variety of open habitats. **p.264**

Snow Partridge *Lerwa lerwa* 38 cm

ADULT Fairly common resident; summers mainly 4000–5000 m, winters down to 3050 m. Vermiculated dark brown and white upperparts, chestnut streaking on underparts, and red bill and legs. Often occurs in large parties, and can be very tame. High-altitude rocky and grassy slopes with scrub.

Tibetan Snowcock *Tetraogallus tibetanus* 51 cm

ADULT Locally fairly common resident; summers mainly 4500–5500 m, winters down to 3650 m. Large size, white ear-covert patch, grey bands across breast, and white underparts with black flank stripes. In flight, shows only a small amount of white in primaries, extensive white patch in secondaries, and chestnut rump. Call is a far-carrying *keep-kweep-kweep*. High-altitude rocky slopes and alpine meadows.

Himalayan Snowcock *Tetraogallus himalayensis* 72 cm

ADULT Fairly common resident, mainly in the west, also in upper Langtang; 4250–5500 m (–5900 m). Very large, with chestnut neck stripes, whitish breast contrasting with dark grey underparts, and chestnut flank stripes. In flight, shows extensive white in primaries, little or no white in secondaries, and greyish rump. Call is not markedly different from Tibetan Snowcock, a far-carrying *cour-lee-whi-whi*. High-altitude rocky slopes and alpine meadows.

Chukar *Alectoris chukar* 38 cm

ADULT Resident, fairly common in the west, rare in the east; mainly 2100–3960 m. Black gorget encircling throat, barring on flanks, and red bill and legs. Call is a rapidly repeated *chuck, chuck-aa*. Open rocky or grassy hills; dry terraced cultivation.

Black Francolin *Francolinus francolinus* 34 cm

a MALE and **b** FEMALE Common and widespread resident up to 2050 m. Male has black face with white ear-covert patch, rufous neck band, and black underparts with white spotting. Female has rufous hindneck, buffish supercilium and dark eye-stripe, streaked appearance to upperparts, and heavily barred or spotted underparts. Male usually calls from vantage point; a loud, harsh *kar-kar, kee, ke-kee*. Cultivation, tall grass and scrub in plains and hills.

Grey Francolin *Francolinus pondicerianus* 33 cm

ADULT Resident, mainly in the west; uncommon below 200 m. Buffish throat with fine dark necklace. Finely barred upperparts with shaft streaking, and finely barred underparts. Sexes similar, but female lacks spurs. Male usually calls from vantage point; a rapidly repeated *khateeja-khateeja-khateeja*. Dry grass and thorn scrub.

Swamp Francolin *Francolinus gularis* 37 cm

ADULT Local resident, common at Koshi Tappu and Sukila Phanta, rare elsewhere; below 200 m. Rufous-orange throat, finely barred upperparts, and bold white streaking on underparts. Sexes similar, but female lacks spurs. Call is a long series of sharp notes, *chuill-chuill-chuill*. Often wades in water, or climbs onto reeds in deep water. Tall wet grassland and marshes. Globally threatened.

Tibetan Partridge *Perdix hodgsoniae* 31 cm

ADULT Uncommon resident in the trans-Himalayas in the north-west, also in upper Langtang; winters 3700–4100 m, summers up to 5000 m. Black patch on white face, rufous collar, and black and rufous barring on underparts. Occurs in large coveys outside breeding season. Call is a rattling and repeated *scherrrrreck-scherrrrreck*. High-altitude semi-desert, rock and scrub slopes.

Common Quail *Coturnix coturnix* 20 cm
a MALE and **b** FEMALE Scarce winter visitor and passage migrant; possibly resident; below 915 m (–2900 m). Male has black 'anchor' mark on throat (which may be lacking), and buff or rufous breast with pale streaking. Female lacks 'anchor' mark and has blackish spotting on buffish breast. Song is a far-carrying *whit, whit-tit*, repeated in quick succession. Crops and grassland.

Blue-breasted Quail *Coturnix chinensis* 14 cm
a MALE and **b** FEMALE Rare resident up to 1280 m. Small size. Male has black-and-white head pattern, slaty-blue flanks, and chestnut belly. Female has rufous forehead and supercilium, and barred breast and flanks. Song is a high-pitched, descending *ti-yu* or *quee-kee-kew*. (*see* Appendix 1 for comparison with Rain Quail). Wet grassland, field edges and scrub.

Small Buttonquail *Turnix sylvatica* 13 cm
MALE Scarce and very local, presumably resident; 250 m. Very small size and pointed tail. Buff edges to scapulars form prominent lines, and rufous mantle and coverts are boldly fringed buff, creating scaly appearance. Underparts are similar to many Yellow-legged, but very different to those of Barred Buttonquail. Has repetitive booming call. Bill grey and legs are pinkish. Tall grassland.

Yellow-legged Buttonquail *Turnix tanki* 15–16 cm
a MALE and **b** FEMALE Resident, fairly common at Chitwan, scarce elsewhere; below 915 m (–1500 m). Widespread, chiefly in lowlands. Yellow legs and bill. Comparatively uniform upperparts (lacking scaly or striped appearance), and buff coverts with bold black spotting. Pattern and coloration of underparts very different from Barred Buttonquail. Utters a low-pitched hoot, repeated with increasing strength to become human-like moan. Scrub and grassland, and crops.

Barred Buttonquail *Turnix suscitator* 15 cm
a MALE and **b** FEMALE Fairly common and widespread resident; below 300 m (–2050 m). Grey bill and legs, and bold black barring on sides of neck, breast and wing coverts. Orange-rufous flanks and belly clearly demarcated from barred breast. Female has black throat and centre of breast. Utters a motorcycle-like *drr-r-r-r-r-r*, and a far-carrying *hoon-hoon-hoon-hoon*. Scrub, grassland, and field edges.

Hill Partridge *Arborophila torqueola* 28 cm
a MALE and **b** FEMALE Fairly common and quite widespread resident; mainly 1830–3200 m (–3550 m). Male has rufous crown and ear-coverts, black eye-patch and eye-stripe, white neck sides streaked with black, and white collar. Female has black barring on mantle, and rufous-orange foreneck lacks black lower border (which is present in Rufous-throated Partridge). Grey or brown legs and feet. Call is a single mournful, drawn-out whistle, repeated two or three times, followed by a series of three to six double whistles; call often preceded by a shrill, continuous *kwik kwik kwik kwik kwik* thought to be female's call. Broadleaved evergreen forest.

Rufous-throated Partridge *Arborophila rufogularis* 27 cm
a MALE and **b** FEMALE Rare resident; mainly 1450–1830 m (250–2050 m). Greyish-white supercilium, diffuse whitish moustachial stripe, unbarred mantle, and black border between rufous-orange foreneck and grey breast. Pinkish or red legs and feet. Sexes similar. Call is a mournful double whistle *wheea-whu* repeated constantly and on slightly ascending scale; the first note prolonged and the second short and sharp. Broadleaved evergreen forest.

Size of illustrations:
1–5, 27% of actual size;
6 & 7, 17% of actual size.

Blood Pheasant *Ithaginis cruentus* 38 cm

a MALE and **b** FEMALE Locally fairly common resident; mainly in centre and east, where widespread; 3200–4400 m. Crested head, and red orbital skin and legs/feet. Male has grey upperparts streaked with white, and greenish underparts, and plumage is splashed with red. Female has grey crest and nape, rufous-orange face, dark-brown upperparts, and rufous-brown underparts. Bamboo clumps, forests or scrub of rhododendron, birch and juniper.

Satyr Tragopan *Tragopan satyra* M 67–72 cm, F 57.5 cm

a MALE and **b** FEMALE Scarce resident; mainly summers 2500–3800 m, winters down to 2100 m. Male has red underparts with black-bordered white spots, and olive-brown coloration to upperparts. Female is rufous-brown with white streaking and spotting. Call a deep, wailing, drawn-out *wah, waah! oo-ah! oo-aaaaa!* uttered 12–14 times mainly at dawn, the series rising in volume and becoming more protracted; also a *wah wah* at any time. Moist evergreen forest with dense undergrowth.

Koklass Pheasant *Pucrasia macrolopha* M 58–64 cm, F 52.5–56 cm

a MALE and **b** FEMALE *P. m. macrolopha*; **c** MALE *P. m. nipalensis* Locally fairly common resident in the west; mainly summers 2680–3200 m (–3500 m), winters down to 2135 m. Race in Nepal is mainly *nipalensis*; birds in the far west may be *macrolopha*. Male has bottle-green head and ear-tufts, chestnut on underparts, and streaked appearance to upperparts. Female has white throat, short buff ear-tufts, and heavily streaked body. Both sexes have wedge-shaped tail. Call of male is a far-carrying, raucous *kok, kark, kuku...kukuk*. Conifer, oak and rhododendron forests.

Himalayan Monal *Lophophorus impejanus* M 70 cm, F 63.5 cm

a MALE and **b** FEMALE Fairly common and widespread resident; chiefly summers 3300–4570m (–2500 m), winters down to 2500 m. Male is iridescent green, copper and purple, with white patch on back and cinnamon-brown tail. Female has white throat, short crest, boldly streaked underparts, white crescent on uppertail-coverts, and narrow white tip to tail. Both sexes utter a series of upward-inflected whistles, *kur-leiu* or *kleeh-vick* which are often strung together, alternated with higher-pitched *kleeh* calls. Summers on rocky and grass-covered slopes; winters in forest.

Red Junglefowl *Gallus gallus* M 65–75 cm, F 42–46 cm

a MALE and **b** FEMALE Locally fairly common and quite widespread resident, usually below 300 m (–1280 m). Male has red comb and wattles, orange and golden-yellow neck hackles, blackish-brown underparts, and long greenish-black sickle-shaped tail. In eclipse plumage, male lacks neck hackles and elongated central tail feathers. Female has naked, reddish face, black-streaked golden 'shawl', and rufous-brown underparts streaked with buff. Male's call at dawn and dusk, a loud *cock-a-doodle-doo*, very similar to the crowing of a domestic cockerel. Forest undergrowth and scrub.

Kalij Pheasant *Lophura leucomelanos* M 65–73 cm, F 50–60 cm

a MALE and **b** FEMALE *L. l. hamiltonii*; **c** MALE *L. l. leucomelanos*; **d** MALE *L. l. melanota* Fairly common and widespread resident; 245–3050 m (–3700 m). Both sexes have red facial skin and down-curved tail. Three intergrading races occur: *L. l. leucomelanos* which is endemic to Nepal (male has blue-black crest and white barring on rump); *L. l. hamiltonii* of W Nepal (male has white or grey-brown crest, broad white barring on rump, and heavily-scaled upperparts) and *L. l. melanota* of E Nepal (male has blue-black crest, and blue-black rump that lacks pale scaling). Female is reddish-brown, with greyish-buff fringes producing scaly appearance. All types of forest with dense undergrowth.

Cheer Pheasant *Catreus wallichii* M 90–118 cm, F 61–76 cm

a **c** MALE and **b** FEMALE Resident in the west, current status uncertain, recent records from only a few localities; 1800–3050 m. Long, broadly barred tail, pronounced crest, and red facial skin. Male is more cleanly and strongly marked than female, with pronounced barring on mantle, unmarked neck, and broader barring across tail. Utters distinctive pre-dawn and dusk contact calls, including high piercing whistles, *chewewoo*. Steep, craggy hillsides with scrub, secondary growth. Globally threatened.

Indian Peafowl *Pavo cristatus* M 180–230 cm, F 90–100 cm

a MALE and **b** FEMALE Locally common and quite widespread resident; mainly below 300 m. Male has blue neck and breast, and spectacular glossy green train of elongated uppertail-covert feathers with numerous ocelli. Female has whitish face and throat and white belly, and lacks elongated uppertail-coverts. Call is a trumpeting, far-carrying and mournful *kee-ow, kee-ow, kee-ow*. Dense riverine vegetation and open sal forest.

Greylag Goose *Anser anser* 75–90 cm

a **b** ADULT Uncommon winter visitor and passage migrant; mainly below 275 m (–3050 m on passage). Large grey goose with pink bill and legs. Shows pale grey forewing in flight. (*See* Appendix 1 for comparison with Bean Goose.) Crops, lakes and large rivers.

Bar-headed Goose *Anser indicus* 71–76 cm

a **b** ADULT and **c** JUVENILE Fairly common and quite widespread passage migrant; recorded up to 9375 m, sometimes winters below 275 m. Adult has white head with black banding, and white line down grey neck. Has black-tipped yellowish bill, and yellowish legs. Juvenile has white face and dark-grey crown and hindneck. Plumage paler steel-grey, with paler grey forewing, compared with Greylag Goose. Large rivers and lakes.

Lesser Whistling-duck *Dendrocygna javanica* 42 cm

a **b** ADULT Locally common resident, winter visitor and passage migrant; mainly below 305 m (–1350 m). Smaller than Fulvous Whistling-duck (*see* Appendix 1), and from that species by greyish-buff head and neck, dark-brown crown, lack of well-defined dark line down hind neck, bright chestnut patch on forewing, and chestnut uppertail-coverts. Both species of Whistling-duck have rather weak, deep-flapping flight, when they show dark upperwing and underwing, and are very noisy with much whistling. Wetlands.

Ruddy Shelduck *Tadorna ferruginea* 61–67 cm

a **b** MALE and **c** FEMALE Common and quite widespread winter visitor below 305 m, regular on passage up to 4800 m; also a rare breeder at 4300 m. Rusty-orange, with buffish head; white upperwing- and underwing-coverts contrast with black remiges in flight. Breeding male has black neck-band. Wetlands.

Common Shelduck *Tadorna tadorna* 58–67 cm

a **b** MALE and **c** JUVENILE Rare winter visitor and spring passage migrant; below 275 m. Adult has.greenish-black head and neck, and largely white body with chestnut breast-band and black scapular stripe. Female is very similar to male, but slightly duller, and lacks knob on bill. Juvenile lacks breast-band and has sooty-brown upperparts. White upperwing- and underwing-coverts contrast with black remiges in flight in all plumages. Wetlands.

Comb Duck *Sarkidiornis melanotos* 56–76 cm

a **b** MALE and **c** FEMALE Local and uncommon resident; below 150 m. Whitish head, speckled with black, and whitish underparts with incomplete narrow black breast-band. Upperwing and underwing blackish. Male has fleshy comb. Comb lacking in female and she is much smaller with duller upperparts. Pools in well-wooded country.

Gadwall *Anas strepera* 39–43 cm

a b MALE and **c d** FEMALE Locally common winter visitor and passage migrant; mainly below 915 m (–4750 m). White patch on inner secondaries in all plumages. Male is mainly grey with white belly and dark patch at rear; bill is dark grey. Female similar to female Mallard, but has orange sides to dark bill and clear-cut white belly. Wetlands.

Falcated Duck *Anas falcata* 48–54 cm

a b MALE and **c d** FEMALE Local and uncommon, but regular winter visitor below 915 m (–1310 m). Male has bottle-green head with maned hindneck, and elongated black-and-grey tertials; shows pale grey forewing in flight. Female has rather plain greyish head, a dark bill, dark spotting and scalloping on brown underparts, and greyish-white fringes to exposed tertials; shows greyish forewing and white greater covert-bar in flight, but does not show striking white belly (compare with female Eurasian Wigeon). Lakes and large rivers.

Eurasian Wigeon *Anas penelope* 45–51 cm

a b MALE and **c d** FEMALE Locally common winter visitor and passage migrant; mainly below 250 m (–4570 m on passage). Male has yellow forehead and forecrown, chestnut head, and pinkish breast; shows white forewing in flight. Female has rather uniform head, breast and flanks. In all plumages, shows white belly and rather pointed tail in flight. Male has distinctive whistled *wheeooo* call. Wetlands.

Mallard *Anas platyrhynchos* 50–65 cm

a b MALE and **c d** FEMALE Locally fairly common winter visitor and passage migrant below 3050 m; also resident and breeds at 2620 m. In all plumages, has white-bordered purplish speculum. Male has yellow bill, dark-green head and purplish-chestnut breast. Female is pale brown and boldly patterned with dark brown; bill variable, patterned mainly in dull orange and dark brown. Wetlands.

Spot-billed Duck *Anas poecilorhyncha* 58–63 cm

a b MALE and **c** FEMALE Frequent resident and winter visitor; mainly below 915 m (–3290 m on passage). Yellow tip to bill, dark crown and eye-stripe, spotted breast and boldly scalloped flanks, and white tertials. Sexes similar, but male has red loral spot and is more strongly marked than female. Wetlands.

Cotton Pygmy-goose *Nettapus coromandelianus* 30–37 cm

a **b** MALE, **c** ECLIPSE MALE and **d** **e** FEMALE Frequent and quite widespread resident and summer visitor; mainly below 250 m (–1280 m). Small size. Male has broad white band across wing, and female has white trailing edge to wing. Male has white head and neck, black cap, and black breast band. Eclipse male and female dark stripe through eye. Vegetation-covered wetlands.

Common Teal *Anas crecca* 34–38 cm

a **b** MALE and **c** **d** FEMALE Common and quite widespread winter visitor and passage migrant; mainly below 915 m (–4300 m on passage). Male has chestnut head with green band behind eye, white stripe along scapulars, and yellowish patch on undertail-coverts. Female has rather uniform head, lacking pale loral spot of female Garganey. In flight, both sexes have broad white band along greater coverts, and green speculum with narrow white trailing edge; forewing of female is brown. *See* Appendix 1 for comparison with Baikal Teal. Wetlands.

Garganey *Anas querquedula* 37–41 cm

a **b** MALE and **c** **d** FEMALE Mainly a passage migrant, a few wintering; locally common; chiefly below 915 m (–4570 m). Male has white stripe behind eye, and brown breast contrasting with grey flanks; shows blue-grey forewing in flight. Female has more patterned head than female Common Teal, with more prominent supercilium, whitish loral spot, pale line below dark eye-stripe, and dark cheek-bar; shows pale grey forewing and broad white trailing edge to wing in flight. Wetlands.

Northern Pintail *Anas acuta* 51–56 cm

a **b** MALE and **c** **d** FEMALE Locally common winter visitor and passage migrant; mainly below 915 m (–4650 m on passage). Long neck and pointed tail. Male has chocolate-brown head, with white stripe down sides of neck. Female has comparatively uniform buffish head and slender grey bill; in flight she shows combination of indistinct brownish speculum, prominent white trailing edge to secondaries, and greyish underwing. Wetlands.

Northern Shoveler *Anas clypeata* 44–52 cm

a **b** MALE and **c** **d** FEMALE Locally common passage migrant, also a rare winter visitor; mainly below 1350 m (–4570 m on passage). Long, spatulate bill. Male has dark-green head, white breast, chestnut flanks, and blue forewing. Female recalls female Mallard in plumage but has blue-grey forewing. Wetlands.

Red-crested Pochard *Rhodonessa rufina* 53–57 cm

a **b** MALE and **c** **d** FEMALE Frequent winter visitor and passage migrant; mainly below 915 m (–3050 m). Large, with square-shaped head. Shape at rest and in flight more like dabbling duck. Male has rusty-orange head, black neck and breast and white flanks. Female has pale cheeks contrasting with brown cap. Both sexes have largely white flight feathers on upperwing, and whitish underwing. Lakes and large rivers.

Common Pochard *Aythya ferina* 42–49 cm

a **b** MALE, **c** **d** FEMALE and **e** IMMATURE MALE Locally fairly common winter visitor and passage migrant; mainly below 915 m (–4570 m on passage). Large with domed head. Pale-grey flight feathers and grey forewing result in different upperwing pattern from other *Aythya*. Male has chestnut head, black breast and grey upperparts and flanks. Female has brownish head and breast contrasting with paler brownish-grey upperparts and flanks; lacks white undertail-coverts; eye is dark, and bill has grey central band. Lakes and large rivers.

Ferruginous Pochard *Aythya nyroca* 38–42 cm

a **b** MALE and **c** FEMALE Common and widespread winter visitor, also a passage migrant; below 915 m (–4575 m on passage). Smallest *Aythya* duck with dome-shaped head. Chestnut head, breast and flanks and white undertail-coverts. Female is duller than male with dark iris. In flight, shows extensive white wing-bar and white belly. Lakes and large rivers.

Baer's Pochard *Aythya baeri* 41–46 cm

a **b** MALE and **c** FEMALE Scarce and local, but regular passage migrant, mainly to Koshi; below 915 m. Greenish cast to dark head and neck, which contrast with chestnut-brown breast. White patch on fore-flanks visible above water. Female and immature male have duller head and breast than adult male. Female has dark iris and pale and diffuse chestnut-brown loral spot. Lakes and large rivers. Globally threatened.

Tufted Duck *Aythya fuligula* 40–47 cm

a **b** MALE, **c** IMMATURE MALE, **d** **e** FEMALE and **f** FEMALE WITH SCAUP-LIKE HEAD Fairly common winter visitor and passage migrant, some present all year; mainly below 915 m (–4900 m on passage). Breeding male is glossy black, with prominent crest and white flanks. Eclipse/immature males are duller, with greyish flanks. Female is dusky brown, with paler flanks; some females may show white face patch, recalling Greater Scaup (*see* Appendix 1) but they usually also show tufted nape and squarer head shape. Female has yellow iris. Lakes and large rivers.

Common Goldeneye *Bucephala clangula* 42–50 cm

a **b** MALE and **c** **d** FEMALE Uncommon winter visitor and passage migrant; below 915 m (–3050 m). Stocky, with bulbous head. Male has dark-green head, with large white patch on lores. Female and immature male have brown head, indistinct whitish collar, and grey body, with white wing patch usually visible at rest. Swims with body flattened, and partially spreads wings when diving. Lakes and large rivers.

Common Merganser *Mergus merganser* 58–72 cm

a **b** MALE and **c** **d** FEMALE Fairly common and widespread winter visitor; below 3000 m. Male has dark-green head, and whitish breast and flanks (with variable pink wash). Female and immature male have chestnut head and greyish body. *See* Appendix 1 for comparison with Red-breasted Merganser. Lakes, rivers and streams.

1 Yellow-rumped Honeyguide *Indicator xanthonotus* 15 cm

a MALE and **b** FEMALE Local and uncommon resident; mainly 1800–3300 m (–610 m in winter). Golden-yellow forehead, back and rump, streaked underparts, and square, blackish tail. Inner edges of tertials are white, and form parallel lines down back. Male has pronounced, yellow malar stripes. Near Giant Rock Bee nests on cliffs, and adjacent forest.

2 Eurasian Wryneck *Jynx torquilla* 16–17 cm

ADULT Frequent on passage and in winter; mainly below 915 m (–3445 m). Cryptically patterned with grey, buff and brown. Has dark stripe down nape and mantle, and long, barred tail. Scrub, secondary growth and cultivation edges.

3 Speckled Piculet *Picumnus innominatus* 10 cm

a MALE and **b** FEMALE Locally fairly common and quite widespread resident; mainly 915–1830 m. Tiny size. Whitish underparts with black spotting, black ear-covert patch and malar stripe, and white in black tail. Male has orange on forehead, which is lacking in female. Bushes and bamboo in broadleaved forest and secondary growth.

4 White-browed Piculet *Sasia ochracea* 9–10 cm

a MALE and **b** FEMALE Uncommon resident from west-central areas eastwards; 250–2135 m. Tiny size. Rufous underparts, and white supercilium behind eye. Male has golden-yellow on forehead, which is lacking in female. Bushes and bamboo in broadleaved forest and secondary growth.

5 Rufous Woodpecker *Celeus brachyurus* 25 cm

a MALE and **b** FEMALE Uncommon and quite widespread resident; below 305 m (–1525 m). Short black bill and shaggy crest. Rufous-brown, with prominent black barring. Male has scarlet patch on ear-coverts. Broadleaved forest and secondary growth.

6 Pale-headed Woodpecker *Gecinulus grantia* 25 cm

a MALE and **b** FEMALE Very rare and local resident in south-east; 275 m. Pale bill, golden-olive head, maroon upperparts, and pinkish barring to primaries. Male has crimson-pink on crown. Bamboo jungle.

7 Bay Woodpecker *Blythipicus pyrrhotis* 27 cm

a MALE and **b** FEMALE Local and uncommon resident; mainly 1525–2500 m (–75 m). Long, pale bill. Plumage rufous with dark-brown barring. Male has red on sides of neck. Dense broadleaved forest and secondary growth.

8 Great Slaty Woodpecker *Mulleripicus pulverulentus* 51 cm

a MALE and **b** FEMALE Local resident, frequent in the west, rare in central areas; below 245 m. Huge, slate-grey woodpecker with long bill and long neck and tail. Male has pinkish-red moustachial patch. Mature trees in sal forest and forest clearings.

Brown-capped Pygmy Woodpecker *Dendrocopos nanus* 13 cm

a MALE and **b** FEMALE Quite widespread resident, locally fairly common in the west, rare from central areas eastwards; below 250 m. Very small. Has fawn-brown crown and eye-stripe, brown coloration to upperparts, greyish- to brownish-white underparts (streaked with brown), and white spotting on central tail feathers. Light forest and trees in cultivation.

Grey-capped Pygmy Woodpecker *Dendrocopos canicapillus* 14 cm

a MALE and **b** FEMALE Quite widespread resident, fairly common from west-central areas eastwards, rare farther west; below 1370 m. Very small. Has grey crown, blackish eye-stripe, blackish coloration to upperparts, diffuse blackish malar stripe, dirty fulvous underparts streaked with black, and lacks white spotting on central tail feathers. Open broadleaved forest.

Brown-fronted Woodpecker *Dendrocopos auriceps* 19–20 cm

a MALE and **b** FEMALE Fairly common and widespread resident; 1065–2440 m. Brownish forehead and forecrown, yellowish central crown, white-barred upperparts, prominent black moustachial stripe, well-defined streaking on underparts, pink undertail-coverts, and unbarred central tail feathers. Coniferous and dry broadleaved forest.

Fulvous-breasted Woodpecker *Dendrocopos macei* 18–19 cm

a MALE and **b** FEMALE Widespread resident, common from west-central areas eastwards, uncommon farther west; mainly below 1830 m (–2745 m). White barring on mantle and wing-coverts, and diffusely-streaked buffish underparts. Male has red crown, which is black on female (compare with Brown-fronted Woodpecker). Forest edges and open forest.

Yellow-crowned Woodpecker *Dendrocopos mahrattensis* 17–18 cm

a MALE and **b** FEMALE Uncommon resident; mainly below 275 m (–1700 m). Yellowish forehead and forecrown, white-spotted upperparts, poorly defined moustachial stripe, dirty underparts with heavy but diffuse streaking, red patch on lower belly, and bold white barring on central tail feathers. Open woodland, open country with scattered trees.

Rufous-bellied Woodpecker *Dendrocopos hyperythrus* 20 cm

a MALE and **b** FEMALE Locally fairly common and widespread resident; 2135–2400 m. Whitish face and rufous underparts. Lacks white wing patch. Male has red crown. Female has black crown with white spots. Juvenile has barred underparts. Oak/rhododendron and coniferous forest.

Crimson-breasted Woodpecker *Dendrocopos cathpharius* 18 cm

a MALE and **b** FEMALE Frequent resident from west-central areas eastwards; 1500–2750 m. Small white wing patch, streaked underparts, and variable crimson patch on breast. Male has extensive red on nape and hindneck. Female has a diffuse, but fairly distinct, rufous patch at rear of ear-coverts. Undertail-coverts of both sexes are indistinctly streaked with pale scarlet (wholly pale scarlet in Darjeeling Woodpecker). Broadleaved forest.

Darjeeling Woodpecker *Dendrocopos darjellensis* 25 cm

a MALE and **b** FEMALE Fairly common and widespread resident from west-central areas eastwards; 1830–3500 m. Small white wing patch, black streaking on yellowish-buff underparts, and yellow patch on side of neck. Male has scarlet nape patch. Coniferous and broadleaved forest.

Himalayan Woodpecker *Dendrocopos himalayensis* 23–25 cm

a MALE and **b** FEMALE Fairly common resident in the west; 1980–3050 m. White wing patch, unstreaked underparts, and black rear border to ear-coverts. Coniferous and broadleaved forest.

Lesser Yellownape *Picus chlorolophus*   27 cm
a MALE and **b** FEMALE Fairly common resident; below 1750 m (–2135 m). Tufted yellow nape, scarlet and white markings on head, and barring on underparts. Smaller than Greater Yellownape, with less prominent crest and smaller bill. Broadleaved forest and secondary growth.

Greater Yellownape *Picus flavinucha*   33 cm
a MALE and **b** FEMALE Fairly common resident; 305–1450 m (–2135 m). Tufted yellow nape, yellow (male) or rufous-brown (female) throat, dark-spotted white foreneck, unbarred underparts, and rufous barring on secondaries. Broadleaved forest and forest edges.

Streak-throated Woodpecker *Picus xanthopygaeus*   30 cm
a MALE and **b** FEMALE Frequent resident; below 465 m (–915 m). Scaling on underparts. Smaller than Scaly-bellied Woodpecker, with dark bill and pale eye, streaked throat and upper breast, and indistinct barring on tail. Broadleaved forest and secondary growth.

Scaly-bellied Woodpecker *Picus squamatus*   35 cm
a MALE and **b** FEMALE Locally fairly common resident from eastcentral areas westwards; 1850–3700 m, mainly below 3300 m. Scaling on underparts. Larger than Streak-throated Woodpecker, with pale bill and reddish eye, prominent black eye-stripe and moustachial stripe, unstreaked throat and upper breast (although these parts are streaked in juvenile), and barred tail. Coniferous and oak/coniferous forest.

Grey-headed Woodpecker *Picus canus*   32 cm
a MALE and **b** FEMALE Common and widespread resident; below 2000 m. Plain grey face, black nape and moustachial stripe, and uniform greyish-green underparts. Male has scarlet forecrown. Broadleaved forest.

Himalayan Flameback *Dinopium shorii*   30–32 cm
a MALE and **b** FEMALE Local resident; common at Chitwan, frequent at Sukila Phanta and Bardia, uncommon elsewhere; below 275 m. Smaller bill than Greater Flameback, with unspotted black hindneck, and brownish-buff centre of throat (and breast on some) with black spotting forming irregular border. Centre of divided moustachial stripe is brownish-buff (with touch of red on some males). Breast less heavily marked with black than on Greater Flameback. Has reddish or brownish eyes, and three toes. Female has white streaking to black crest. Mature broadleaved forest.

Black-rumped Flameback *Dinopium benghalense*   26–29 cm
a MALE and **b** FEMALE Frequent and quite widespread resident; below 365 m. Black eye-stripe and throat (lacking dark moustachial stripe), spotting on wing coverts, and black rump. Light forest, groves and trees in open country.

Greater Flameback *Chrysocolaptes lucidus*   33 cm
a MALE and **b** FEMALE Frequent resident; below 915 m (–1700 m). Large size and long bill. White or black-and-white spotted hindneck and upper mantle, clean black line down centre of throat and neck, and white spotting on black breast. Moustachial stripe is clearly divided (with obvious white oval centre). Has pale eyes and four toes. Female has white spotting to black crest. Forest and groves.

White-naped Woodpecker *Chrysocolaptes festivus*   29 cm
a MALE and **b** FEMALE Uncommon resident in the far west; below 245 m. White hindneck and mantle, and black scapulars and back forming V-shape. Moustachial stripe is clearly divided. Rump is black. Female has yellow crown. Light broadleaved forest and scattered trees.

Great Barbet *Megalaima virens* 33 cm

ADULT Common and widespread resident; mainly 900–2200 m (305–2600 m). Large yellow bill, bluish head, brown breast and mantle, olive-streaked yellowish underparts, and red under-tail-coverts. Has a monotonous, incessant and far-reaching *piho, piho* uttered throughout the day; a repetitive *tuk tuk tuk* is often uttered in a duet, presumably by female. Subtropical and temperate forest.

Brown-headed Barbet *Megalaima zeylanica* 27 cm

ADULT Resident, locally fairly common in the far west, status elsewhere uncertain; below 300 m. Fine streaking on brown head and breast, brown throat, orange circumorbital skin and bill (when breeding), and white-spotted wing coverts. Streaking almost absent on belly and flanks. Call is a monotonous *kotroo, kotroo, kotroo*, or *kutruk, kutruk, kutruk*. Forest, wooded areas and trees near habitation.

Lineated Barbet *Megalaima lineata* 28 cm

ADULT Common and widespread resident; below 915 m. Bold white streaking on head and breast, whitish throat, and uniform unspotted wing coverts. Less extensive circumorbital skin (usually separated from bill) than Brown-headed Barbet. Call is a monotonous *kotur kotur kotur* (slightly mellower and softer than Brown-headed's) uttered throughout the day. Open sal forest and well-wooded areas.

Golden-throated Barbet *Megalaima franklinii* 23 cm

ADULT Frequent and local resident from west-central areas eastwards; 1500–2400 m. Yellow centre of crown and throat, greyish-white cheeks and lower throat, and broad black mask. Voice is a wailing, repetitive *peeyu, peeyu* recalling Great Barbet but higher pitched; also a monotonous *pukwowk, pukwowk, pukwowk*. Moist broadleaved forest.

Blue-throated Barbet *Megalaima asiatica* 23 cm

ADULT Widespread resident; common below 1500 m; frequent up to 2100 m. Blue 'face' and throat, red forehead and hind crown, and black band across crown. Juvenile has duller head pattern. Voice is a harsh and loud *took-a-rook, took-a-rook* uttered very rapidly. Open forest, groves and gardens.

Blue-eared Barbet *Megalaima australis* 17 cm

a ADULT and **b** JUVENILE Scarce and very local resident in the far east; 120–305 m. Small barbet with blue throat and ear-coverts, black forehead and malar stripe, and red patches on side of head. Juvenile lacks head patterning, but shows traces of blue on side of head and throat. Voice is a disyllabic *tk-trrt*, repeated very rapidly, and a throaty whistle. Dense, moist broadleaved forest.

Coppersmith Barbet *Megalaima haemacephala* 17 cm

a ADULT and **b** JUVENILE Widespread resident, common below 915 m; frequent up to 1830 m. Small barbet with crimson forehead and breast patch, yellow patches above and below eye, yellow throat, and streaked underparts. Juvenile lacks red on head and breast. Voice is a loud, metallic, repetitive and monotonous *tuk, tuk, tuk*. Open wooded country, groves and trees in cultivation and gardens.

Indian Grey Hornbill *Ocyceros birostris*   50 cm

a   **b**   MALE and   **c**   IMMATURE   Local and frequent resident, recorded from west to east; below 305 m (–760 m). Small hornbill with sandy brownish-grey upperparts, long tail that has dark subterminal band and elongated central feathers, and white trailing edge to wing. Prominent black casque and extensive black at base of bill. Female similar to male, but with smaller bill and casque. Territorial call is a loud cackling and squealing *k-k-k-ka-e* or rapid piping *pi-pi-pi-pi-pipipieu* etc.; normal contact call is a kite-like *chee-ooww*. Open broadleaved forest, groves and gardens with fruiting trees.

Oriental Pied Hornbill *Anthracoceros albirostris*   55–60 cm

a   **b**   MALE and   **c**   FEMALE   Local and frequent resident, recorded from west to east; below 250 m. Much smaller than Great Hornbill. Head and neck black. Tail mainly black with white tips to outer feathers. Both sexes have cylindrical casque, blue orbital skin and throat patch. Female has smaller casque than male, and has black at tip of bill. Calls include a variety of loud, shrill, nasal squeals, and raucous chucks. Mature broadleaved forest with fruiting trees.

Great Hornbill *Buceros bicornis*   95–105 cm

a   **b**   MALE   Local resident, uncommon at Chitwan, rare elsewhere; below 250 m. Huge size, with massive yellow casque and bill, and white tail with black subterminal band. Has white neck, wing-bars and trailing edge to wing which are variably stained with yellow (by preen-gland oils). Sexes alike, although female has white iris (red in male) and lacks black at ends of casque. Calls are loud and raucous, frequently given as a duet, *grongk-gonk, grongk-gongk*, and often becoming louder and more agitated prior to flight; flight call is a loud *ger-onk*. *See* Appendix 1 for comparison with Rufous-necked Hornbill. Mature broadleaved forest with fruiting trees.

Size of illustrations:
1 & 2, 20% of actual size;
3, 15% of actual size.

Common Hoopoe *Upupa epops* 31 cm

a **b** ADULT Fairly common and widespread; resident up to 1500 m; summers to 4400 m (–5900 m on passage). Orange-buff, with black-and-white wings and tail, and black-tipped fan-like crest. Voice is a repetitive and mellow *poop, poop, poop* similar to that of Oriental Cuckoo. Open country, cultivation and villages.

Red-headed Trogon *Harpactes erythrocephalus* 35 cm

a MALE and **b** FEMALE Local and uncommon resident; mainly 250–1000 m (–1830 m). Male has crimson head and breast, pink underparts, and black-and-grey vermiculated wing coverts. Female has dark-cinnamon head and breast, and brown-and-buff vermiculated coverts. Immature resembles female but has whitish underparts. Call is a descending series of notes, *tyaup, tyaup, tyaup, tyaup, tyaup*. Dense broadleaved forest.

Indian Roller *Coracias benghalensis* 33 cm

a **b** ADULT *C. b. benghalensis* and **c** ADULT *C. b. affinis* Common and widespread resident below 1050 m (–3655 m). Two races occur with intermediates. The nominate is rufous-brown on nape and underparts, has white streaking on ear-coverts and throat, and greenish mantle. In flight, shows turquoise band across primaries and dark-blue terminal band to tail. The eastern race *C. b. affinis* has purplish-brown underparts, blue streaking on throat, and dark corners to tail instead of dark terminal band. Cultivation, open woodland, groves and gardens.

Dollarbird *Eurystomus orientalis* 28 cm

a **b** ADULT Local summer visitor, common at Chitwan, uncommon elsewhere; mainly below 365 m (–1300 m). Dark greenish, appearing black at distance, with red bill and eye-ring. In flight, shows turquoise patch on primaries. Tropical forest and forest clearings.

Blue-bearded Bee-eater *Nyctyornis athertoni* 31–34 cm

ADULT Uncommon resident; mainly below 365 m (–2440 m). Large bee-eater with square-ended tail, and blue 'beard'. Has yellowish-buff belly and flanks with greenish streaking. Edges of broadleaved forest and open forest.

Green Bee-eater *Merops orientalis* 16–18 cm

ADULT Common resident and summer visitor to the terai; fairly common in lower hills; below 620 m (–2800 m). Small bee-eater, with blue cheeks, black gorget, and golden coloration to crown. Green tail with elongated central feathers. Juvenile has green crown and nape, lacks black gorget, and has square-ended tail. Open country with scattered trees.

Blue-tailed Bee-eater *Merops philippinus* 23–26 cm

ADULT Locally fairly common summer visitor, very rarely overwinters; below 300 m (–1525 m). Larger than Green Bee-eater with chestnut throat, green crown and nape, and blue tail. Green upperparts and underparts are washed with brown and blue. Juvenile is like washed-out version of adult; lacks elongated central tail feathers. Near water in open wooded country.

Chestnut-headed Bee-eater *Merops leschenaulti* 18–20 cm

ADULT Chiefly a summer visitor, some birds resident at lower altitudes; fairly common below 680 m, locally up to 1525 m (–2135 m). Chestnut crown, nape and mantle, and yellow throat with diffuse black gorget. Tail has slight fork; lacks elongated central tail feathers. Juvenile is like washed-out version of adult, but crown and nape dark green on some. Open broadleaved forest, often near water.

Size of illustrations:
1–4, 25% of actual size;
5–8, 35% of actual size.

1 Blyth's Kingfisher *Alcedo hercules* 22 cm

ADULT Very rare and local resident in the east; 250 m. Much larger than Common Kingfisher with huge bill. Ear-coverts are dark greenish-blue (orange in Common Kingfisher). Upperparts are a much darker greenish-blue than in Common Kingfisher. Streams in dense forest.

2 Common Kingfisher *Alcedo atthis* 16 cm

ADULT Fairly common and widespread resident below 1000 m; frequent up to 1800 m (–3050 m). Orange ear-coverts. Greenish-blue on head, scapulars and wings, and turquoise line down back. Freshwaters in open country.

3 Blue-eared Kingfisher *Alcedo meninting* 16 cm

a ADULT and **b** JUVENILE Local resident, fairly common at Chitwan, rare elsewhere; below 250 m. Blue ear-coverts. Lacks green tones to blue of head, scapulars and wings compared with Common. Confusingly, juvenile has orange ear-coverts, but otherwise overall coloration is as adult (and very different to Common Kingfisher). Streams in dense forest.

4 Stork-billed Kingfisher *Halcyon capensis* 38 cm

ADULT Frequent and quite widespread resident; below 760 m (–1830 m). Huge size and massive red bill. Has brown cap, orange-buff collar and underparts, and blue upperparts. Has an explosive laugh *ke-ke-ke-ke-ke*; song is a long series of paired melancholy whistles. Shaded slow-moving rivers and streams.

5 Ruddy Kingfisher *Halcyon coromanda* 26 cm

ADULT Rare and local resident in the Churia hills, Chitwan; 305 m. Rufous-orange with violet iridescence on upperparts, and striking coral-red bill. Flashes bluish-white rump in flight. Song is a soft and trilling *tyuur-rrrr*, incessantly repeated. Dense, broadleaved, evergreen forest.

6 White-throated Kingfisher *Halcyon smyrnensis* 28 cm

ADULT Widespread resident, common below 1000 m; rarely above 1800 m (–3050 m). White throat and centre of breast, brown head and most of underparts, and turquoise upperparts. Shows prominent white wing patch in flight. Call is a loud rattling laugh; song is drawn-out musical whistle, *kililili*. Cultivation, forest edges, gardens and wetlands.

7 Black-capped Kingfisher *Halcyon pileata* 30 cm

ADULT Rare and irregular visitor; below 300 m. Black cap, white collar, purplish-blue upperparts, and pale-orange underparts. Shows white wing patch in flight. Call is a ringing cackle *kikikikikiki*. Wetlands.

8 Crested Kingfisher *Megaceryle lugubris* 41 cm

ADULT Frequent and widespread resident; 250–1800 m (–3000 m). Much larger than the Pied Kingfisher, with evenly barred wings and tail. Lacks supercilium, and has spotted breast which is sometimes mixed with rufous. Mountain rivers, large rivers in foothills.

9 Pied Kingfisher *Ceryle rudis* 31 cm

a MALE and **b** FEMALE Common and widespread resident; below 915 m. Smaller than Crested Kingfisher, with white supercilium, white patches on wings, and black band(s) across breast. Female has single breast-band (double in male). Slow-moving rivers and streams and lakes and pools in open country.

Pied Cuckoo *Clamator jacobinus* 33 cm

ADULT Uncommon summer visitor; mainly below 365 m (–3660 m). Adult is black and white with prominent crest. Crest smaller, upperparts browner and underparts more buffish on juvenile. Call is metallic, pleasant *piu…piu…pee-pee piu, pee-pee piu*. Broadleaved forest and well-wooded areas.

Chestnut-winged Cuckoo *Clamator coromandus* 47 cm

ADULT Very local summer visitor; mainly 250–365 m (75–1370 m). Prominent crest, whitish collar, and chestnut wings. Immature has rufous fringes to upperparts. Makes a series of double metallic whistles, *breep breep*. Broadleaved forest.

Large Hawk Cuckoo *Hierococcyx sparverioides* 38 cm

a ADULT and **b** JUVENILE Widespread, fairly common March–October, 1830–3000 m; a few winter records 1800–2460 m. Larger than Common Hawk Cuckoo, with browner upperparts, strongly barred underparts, and broader tail banding. Juvenile has barred flanks and broad tail banding; head dark grey on older birds. Call is a shrill *pee-pee-ah…pee-pee-ah*, which is repeated, rising in pitch and momentum, climaxing in hysterical crescendo. Broadleaved forest.

Common Hawk Cuckoo *Hierococcyx varius* 34 cm

a ADULT and **b** JUVENILE Common and widespread resident; below 1000 m (–1500 m). Smaller than Large Hawk Cuckoo, with grey upperparts, more rufous on underparts, indistinct barring on belly and flanks, and narrow tail banding. Juvenile has spotted flanks and narrow tail banding. Call like that of Large Hawk Cuckoo. *See* Appendix 1 for comparison with Hodgson's Hawk Cuckoo. Well-wooded country.

Indian Cuckoo *Cuculus micropterus* 33 cm

a ADULT and **b** JUVENILE Widespread, recorded February–September; common in spring and summer below 2100 m (–3800 m). Brown coloration to grey upperparts and tail, broad barring on underparts, and pronounced white barring and spotting on tail. Juvenile has broad and irregular white tips to feathers of crown and nape, and white tips to scapulars and wing coverts. Call a descending, four-noted whistle, *kwer-kwah…kwah-kurh*. Forest and well-wooded country.

Eurasian Cuckoo *Cuculus canorus* 32–34 cm

a MALE and **b** HEPATIC FEMALE Widespread, recorded March–October; common in spring and summer 915–3800 m (–4250 m); uncommon lower down. Finer barring on whiter underparts than Oriental. Male's call is a loud repetitive *cuck-oo…cuck-oo*; both sexes have a bubbling call. Forest, well-wooded country and scrub.

Oriental Cuckoo *Cuculus saturatus* 30–32 cm

a MALE and **b** HEPATIC FEMALE Fairly common summer visitor, recorded mid-March–September; 1525–3355 m (–250 m). Broader barring on buffish-white underparts compared with Eurasian; upperparts are a shade darker; paler head. Hepatic female is slightly more heavily barred than Eurasian. Call a resonant *ho…ho…ho…ho* easily confused with the call of Common Hoopoe. Forest and well-wooded country.

Lesser Cuckoo *Cuculus poliocephalus* 25 cm

a MALE and **b** HEPATIC FEMALE Locally common summer visitor, recorded mainly April–August; 1500–3660 m. Smaller than Oriental; hepatic female can be bright rufous and indistinctly barred on crown and nape. Call is a strong, cheerful *pretty-peel-lay-ka-beet*. Forest, well-wooded country.

Banded Bay Cuckoo *Cacomantis sonneratii* 24 cm

ADULT Uncommon resident; mainly below 250 m (–2440 m). White supercilium, finely barred white underparts, and fine and regular dark barring on upperparts. Song is a shrill, whistled *pi-pi-pew-pew*, the first two notes at the same pitch, the last two descending. Dense broadleaved forest.

Grey-bellied Cuckoo *Cacomantis passerinus* 23 cm

a ADULT, **b** HEPATIC FEMALE and **c** JUVENILE Frequent summer visitor; below 1400 m (–2135 m). Adult is grey with white vent and undertail-coverts. On hepatic female, base colour of underparts is mainly white, upperparts are bright rufous with crown and nape only sparsely barred, and tail is unbarred. Juvenile is either grey, with pale barring on underparts, or similar to hepatic female, or intermediate. Song is a clear, interrogative *pee-pipee-pee...pipee-pee*, ascending in scale and pitch; also a single plaintive repeated whistle. Groves and open forest.

Plaintive Cuckoo *Cacomantis merulinus* 23 cm

a ADULT, **b** HEPATIC FEMALE and **c** JUVENILE Rare summer visitor. Adult has orange underparts. On hepatic female, base colour of underparts is pale rufous, and upperparts and tail are strongly barred. Juvenile has bold streaking on rufous-orange head and breast. Song is a mournful *tay...ta...tee.* Forest and wooded country.

Asian Emerald Cuckoo *Chrysococcyx maculatus* 18 cm

a MALE, **b** FEMALE and **c** JUVENILE Rare summer visitor, recorded April–September; 250 m and 1280–1800 m. Male is mainly emerald-green, with barred upperparts. Female has rufous-orange crown and nape, and unbarred bronze-green mantle and wings. Juvenile has unbarred rufous-orange crown and nape, rufous-orange barring on mantle and wing coverts, and rufous-orange wash to barred throat and breast. Song is a loud descending *kee-kee-kee-kee* and a sharp *chweek* uttered in flight. Broadleaved evergreen forest.

Drongo Cuckoo *Surniculus lugubris* 25 cm

a ADULT and **b** JUVENILE Local summer visitor, recorded March–early November; mainly below 1500 m (–2000 m). Black, with white-barred undertail-coverts. Bill fine and downcurved, and tail has indentation. Juvenile is spotted with white. Song is an ascending series of repeated whistles, *pee-pee-pee-pee-pee-pee.* Edges and clearings of forest and groves.

Asian Koel *Eudynamys scolopacea* 43 cm

a MALE and **b** FEMALE Common and widespread resident; below 1370 m, locally to 1800 m. Male is greenish-black, with green bill. Female is spotted and barred with white. Song is a loud rising, repeated *ko-el...ko-el...ko-el...ko-el.* Open woodland, gardens and cultivation.

Green-billed Malkoha *Phaenicophaeus tristis* 38 cm

ADULT Fairly common resident below 700 m; uncommon up to 2000 m. Greyish-green coloration, green and red bill, red eye-patch, white-streaked supercilium, and white-tipped tail. Dense forest and thickets.

Sirkeer Malkoha *Phaenicophaeus leschenaultii* 42 cm

ADULT Resident, frequent in the far west, uncommon farther east; below 915 m (–1370 m). Sandy coloration, yellow-tipped red bill, dark mask with white border, and bold white tips to tail. Thorn scrub and acacia trees in dry areas.

Greater Coucal *Centropus sinensis* 48 cm

a ADULT and **b** JUVENILE Common and widespread resident below 365 m, also very locally at 900 m in summer. Larger than Lesser, with brighter and more uniform chestnut wings and black underwing-coverts. Juvenile is heavily barred. Call is a deep primate-like *hoop-hoop-hoop-hoop-hoop-hoop-hoop*, descending and then rising towards the end of the series. Tall grassland and thickets near cultivation.

Lesser Coucal *Centropus bengalensis* 33 cm

a ADULT BREEDING and **b** IMMATURE Local and frequent resident below 365 m; very locally summers up to 1400 m. Smaller than Greater Coucal, with duller chestnut wings, and chestnut underwing-coverts; often with buff streaking on scapulars and wing coverts. Non-breeding has pronounced buff shaft-streaking on head and body, chestnut wings, and black tail; immature similar but with barred wings and tail. Song is a series of deep, resonant *pwoop-pwoop-pwoop* notes; similar to Greater Coucal, but usually slightly faster and more interrogative. Tall grassland, reedbeds and scrub.

Vernal Hanging Parrot *Loriculus vernalis* 14 cm

MALE Very rare and local resident; below 275 m. Small green parrot. Adult with red bill and red rump. Call is a distinctive rasping *de-zeez-zeet*. Moist broadleaved forest.

Alexandrine Parakeet *Psittacula eupatria* 53 cm

a MALE and **b** FEMALE Common and quite widespread resident; below 365 m (–1380 m). Very large, with maroon shoulder patch. Male has black chin stripe and pink collar. Call is a loud, guttural *keeak* or *kee-ah*, much deeper than Rose-ringed Parakeet. Sal and riverine forest.

Rose-ringed Parakeet *Psittacula krameri* 42 cm

a MALE and **b** FEMALE Common and widespread resident; below 365 m (–1370 m). Green head and blue-green tip to tail. Male has black chin stripe and pink collar. Call is a loud, shrill *kee-ah*. Broadleaved forest, wooded areas and cultivation.

Slaty-headed Parakeet *Psittacula himalayana* 41 cm

a MALE, **b** FEMALE and **c** IMMATURE Fairly common and quite widespread resident; usually summers up to 2135 m and winters down to 1000 m (75–3260 m). Dark-grey head, dark-green upperparts, red-and-yellow bill, and yellow-tipped tail. Female lacks maroon shoulder patch of male. Immature lacks slaty head. Call is a shrill *tooi-tooi*. Broadleaved forest and well-wooded areas.

Plum-headed Parakeet *Psittacula cyanocephala* 36 cm

a MALE, **b** FEMALE and **c** IMMATURE Widespread resident; fairly common below 500 m; frequent up to 1525 m. Head is plum-red on male, pale grey on female. Yellow upper mandible, and white-tipped blue-green tail. Head of female is paler grey than Slaty-headed Parakeet, and lacks black chin stripe and half collar of that species; shows yellow collar and upper breast. Call higher-pitched than Slaty-headed Parakeet. Broadleaved forest and well-wooded areas.

Blossom-headed Parakeet *Psittacula roseata* 36 cm

a MALE and **b** FEMALE Status uncertain, probably resident; recorded in nineteenth century and recently recorded at Chitwan and Koshi; below 250 m. Head is pinkish on male, pale bluish-grey on female. Yellow upper mandible and yellow-tipped tail. Open forest and well-wooded areas.

Red-breasted Parakeet *Psittacula alexandri* 38 cm

a MALE, **b** FEMALE and **c** IMMATURE Locally fairly common and quite widespread resident; below 365 m (–1370 m). Lilac-grey head with broad black chin stripe, pink underparts, and yellowish-green patch on wing coverts. Female has all-black bill. Immature has green underparts. Call is a sharp, nasal *kaink*. Open broadleaved forest and secondary growth.

Himalayan Swiftlet *Collocalia brevirostris* 14 cm
a b ADULT Fairly common and quite widespread resident; summers up to 4575 m, usually winters 915–2745 m, sometimes in the terai. Stocky brownish swiftlet with paler grey-brown underparts and diffuse greyish rump band. Shows distinct indentation to tail. Banking and gliding flight, interspersed with bat-like fluttering. Open areas near forest.

White-rumped Needletail *Zoonavena sylvatica* 11 cm
a b ADULT Local and uncommon, possibly resident; 150–250 m. Small and stocky, with oval-shaped wings. Has white rump, and whitish belly and undertail-coverts help distinguish from House Swift. Flight is fast with rapid wing beats, much banking from side to side, interspersed with short glides on slightly bowed wings. Broadleaved forest.

White-throated Needletail *Hirundapus caudacutus* 20 cm
a b ADULT Fairly common summer visitor, recorded mainly March–June; below 3200 m. Large swift, with very fast and powerful flight. Has striking white throat and white horseshoe crescent on underparts. Also shows prominent pale 'saddle' and white patch on tertials. Ridges, cliffs, upland grassland and river valleys.

Silver-backed Needletail *Hirundapus cochinchinensis* 20 cm
a b ADULT Status and movements are poorly understood, several records March–July; 250–2400 m. Similar to White-throated Needletail but has poorly-defined pale throat, and lacks white patch on tertials. Broadleaved forest.

Common Swift *Apus apus* 17 cm
a b ADULT Local summer visitor, recorded mainly mid March–July; 2000–3795 m. Uniform dark brown swift, with white throat; lacks white rump. Has prominently forked tail. Chiefly mountains.

Asian Palm Swift *Cypsiurus balasiensis* 13 cm
a b ADULT Uncommon resident from Central Terai eastwards; 75–120 m. Small and very slim, with scythe-shaped wings and long, forked tail (which is usually held closed). Fluttering flight, interspersed with short glides. Mainly brown with paler throat. Open country and cultivation with palms.

House Swift *Apus affinis* 15 cm
a b ADULT Common and widespread resident below 2100 m; below 915 m all year, descends from higher levels in cold weather. Small blackish swift with broad white rump band. Compared with Fork-tailed Swift is rather stocky, with comparatively short wings, and tail has only a slight fork. Towns and villages.

Fork-tailed Swift *Apus pacificus* 15–18 cm
a b ADULT Fairly common and quite widespread, possibly resident; mainly winters below 365 m, summers up to 3800 m. Blackish swift with white rump and white scaling on underparts. Slimmer bodied and longer winged than House Swift with deeply forked tail. Open ridges and hilltops.

Alpine Swift *Tachymarptis melba* 22 cm
a b ADULT Fairly common and widespread, probably resident; summers mainly below 2200 m (–3700 m), winters chiefly below 915 m. Large, powerful swift with white throat, brown breast-band, and white patch on belly. Mainly hills and mountains.

Crested Treeswift *Hemiprocne coronata* 23 cm
a b ADULT MALE and **c** FEMALE Locally common resident; below 365 m (–1280 m). Large size and long, forked tail. Blue-grey upperparts and paler underparts, becoming whitish on belly and vent. Male has dull orange ear-coverts (dark grey in female). Forest.

Barn Owl *Tyto alba* 36 cm

ADULT Uncommon and very local resident; 1320 m. Unmarked white face, whitish underparts, and golden-buff and grey upperparts. Eyes are dark. Utters a variety of eerie screeching and hissing noises. Generally nocturnal. Usually hunts in flight, quartering the ground and often banking or hovering to locate prey. Roosts in old buildings and hunts in cultivation.

Grass Owl *Tyto capensis* 36 cm

a **b** ADULT Rare and very local resident; 250 m. Similar to Barn Owl with whitish face and underparts, but upperparts are darker and heavily marked with dark brown. Also shows dark barring on flight feathers, golden-buff patch at base of primaries contrasting with dark primaries and dark-barred tail. Mottled rather than streaked upperparts, lack of prominent streaking on breast, and black eyes, are useful features from Short-eared Owl, which may be found in similar habitat. Generally nocturnal, and usually seen when flushed. Tall grassland.

Brown Hawk Owl *Ninox scutulata* 32 cm

ADULT Locally fairly common resident; below 1500 m. Hawk-like profile. Dark face, and rufous-brown streaking on underparts. Nocturnal, often hunting from prominent perch. Call is a repeated, soft, pleasant *oo...ok, oo...ok, ...* Forest and well-wooded areas.

Short-eared Owl *Asio flammeus* 37–39 cm

a **b** ADULT Uncommon winter visitor and passage migrant; up to 3350 m on passage. Streaked underparts and short ear-tufts. Buffish facial discs and yellow eyes. In flight, rather long and narrow wings shows buffish patch at base of primaries and dark carpal patches. Often seen hunting during the day, quartering low over the ground in a leisurely manner, when often hovering or gliding with wings in V. *See* Appendix 1 for comparison with Long-eared Owl. Grassland and open scrub country.

Mountain Scops Owl *Otus spilocephalus* 20 cm

a ADULT *O. s. spilocephalus* and **b** ADULT *O. s. huttoni* Locally fairly common resident; 1830–2590 m (1525–2745 m). Very small ear-tufts. Upperparts mottled with buff and brown; underparts indistinctly spotted with buff and barred with brown. It is likely that two intergrading races occur; western *huttoni* is grey or fulvous-brown; eastern *spilocephalus* is rufous. Call is a double whistle, *toot-too*. Dense broadleaved forest.

Oriental Scops Owl *Otus sunia* 19 cm

a ADULT RUFOUS and **b** BROWN MORPHS Fairly common resident; below 365 m (–1525 m). Prominent ear-tufts. Prominent white scapular spots, streaked underparts and upperparts; lacks prominent nuchal collar. Occurs as rufous, grey and brown morphs. Iris yellow. Nocturnal. Call is frog-like *wut-chu-chraaii*. Forest, secondary growth and groves.

Collared Scops Owl *Otus bakkamoena* 23–25 cm

ADULT Local resident; 150–1525 m. Larger than other scops owls, with buff nuchal collar, finely streaked underparts and indistinct buffish scapular spots. Iris dark orange or brown. Nocturnal. Call is a subdued, frog-like *whuk*, repeated at irregular intervals. Forest, well-wooded areas and groves.

Eurasian Eagle Owl *Bubo bubo* 56–66 cm

ADULT Local and frequent resident; below 1800 m (–3415 m). Very large owl, with upright ear-tufts. Upperparts mottled dark brown and tawny-buff; underparts heavily streaked. Mainly nocturnal, but usually perches before sunset, and after sunrise, in a prominent position on cliff or rock. Call is a resonant *tu-whooh*. Cliffs, rocky hills, ravines and wooded areas.

Spot-bellied Eagle Owl *Bubo nipalensis* 63 cm

a ADULT and **b** IMMATURE Rare and local resident; 150–2135 m. Very large owl, with prominent ear-tufts, and bold chevron-shaped spots on underparts. Upperparts dark brown, barred with buff. Eyes dark brown. Juvenile is striking with much white in underparts. Nocturnal. Call is a deep hoot and a mournful scream. Dense broadleaved forest.

Dusky Eagle Owl *Bubo coromandus* 58 cm

ADULT Rare and local resident; below 250 m. Large grey owl with prominent ear-tufts. Upperparts greyish-brown with fine whitish vermiculations and diffuse darker brown streaking. Underparts greyish-white with brown streaking. Call is a deep, resonant *wo,wo,wo,wo-o-o-o-o*. Generally nocturnal, but emerges from roost about an hour before sunset; sometimes hunts during day in cloudy weather. Often calls during the day. Well-watered areas with extensive tree cover.

Brown Fish Owl *Ketupa zeylonensis* 56 cm

ADULT Uncommon resident; 75–1525 m. Compared with Tawny Fish Owl, has close dark barring on dull buff underparts, which also show finer streaking, and upperparts are duller brown with finer streaking. Partly diurnal, emerging from roost long before sunset; sometimes hunts during the day. Calls include a soft, deep *hup-hup-hu* and a wild *hu-hu-hu-hu...hu ha*. Forest and well-wooded areas near water.

Tawny Fish Owl *Ketupa flavipes* 61 cm

ADULT Very rare and local resident; 250–365 m. Larger and more richly coloured than Brown Fish Owl. Upperparts are pale orange with bold black streaking; wing coverts and flight feathers have bold orange-buff barring. Shows broad black streaking on pale rufous-orange underparts, which lack fine, dark cross-barring shown by Brown Fish Owl. Has prominent whitish patch on forehead that is generally lacking in the Brown Fish Owl. Mainly nocturnal, but sometimes fishes during the day. Call is a deep *whoo-hoo* and a cat-like mewing. Ravines in broadleaved forest near water.

Brown Wood Owl *Strix leptogrammica* 47–53 cm

ADULT Uncommon resident; 250–2700 m. Uniform facial discs, uniform brown upperparts with fine white barring on scapulars, and buffish-white underparts with fine brown barring. Nocturnal. Calls include a *hoo-hoohoohoo(hoo)* and a loud eerie scream. Dense broadleaved forest.

Tawny Owl *Strix aluco* 45–47 cm

a ADULT *S. a. nivicola* and **b** ADULT *S. a. biddulphi* Frequent and quite widespread resident; 2000–4000 m. Rufous to dark-brown, with heavily streaked underparts, white markings on scapulars, dark centre to crown, and pale forecrown stripes. The larger and greyer West Himalayan form *biddulphi* possibly occurs. Nocturnal. Call is a *too-tu-whoo*, sometimes shortened to a two-noted *turr-whooh*; also a low-pitched *ku-wack-ku-wack*. Oak/rhododendron and coniferous forest.

Collared Owlet *Glaucidium brodiei* 17 cm
ADULT Fairly common, but local resident; 1350–2900 m (610–3050 m). Very small and heavily barred. Spotted crown, streaking on flanks, and owl-face pattern on upper mantle. Diurnal and crepuscular. Call is a repeated bell-like whistle *toot...tootoot...toot*. Broadleaved forest.

Asian Barred Owlet *Glaucidium cuculoides* 23 cm
ADULT Common and quite widespread resident; 245–2440 m (–2745 m). Heavily barred. Best told from Jungle Owlet by larger size, buff (rather than rufous) barring on wing coverts and flight feathers, and streaked flanks. Mainly diurnal, and often perching in prominent position during day. Open forest.

Jungle Owlet *Glaucidium radiatum* 20 cm
ADULT Common and quite widespread resident; below 915 m (–1600 m). Small and heavily barred. Smaller than Asian Barred Owlet, with more closely barred upperparts and underparts, and with rufous barring on wings, and barred flanks. Mainly crepuscular. Open forest and secondary growth.

Little Owl *Athene noctua* 23 cm
ADULT Scarce resident in Tibetan plateau country in the northwest; 2715–4155 m. Sandy-brown, with streaked breast and flanks, and streaked crown. Crepuscular and partly diurnal; often perching prominently in daylight. Cliffs and ruins in semi-desert.

Spotted Owlet *Athene brama* 21 cm
ADULT Common and quite widespread resident; below 1525 m (–2745 m). White spotting on upperparts, including crown, and diffuse brown spotting on underparts. Mainly crepuscular and nocturnal. Call is a harsh, screechy *chirurr-chirurr-chirurr...* followed by/alternated with *cheevak, cheevak, cheevak*. Habitation and cultivation.

Grey Nightjar *Caprimulgus indicus* 27–32 cm
a b MALE and c FEMALE Fairly common and quite widespread resident; summers up to 2895 m, winters 180–915 m. Grey-brown, heavily marked with black. Compared with Large-tailed Nightjar, lacks pale rufous-brown nuchal collar, and usually lacks buff or rufous edges to scapulars. Song is a loud, resonant *chunk-chunk-chunk-chunk...* Forest clearings and scrub-covered slopes.

Large-tailed Nightjar *Caprimulgus macrurus* 33 cm
a b MALE and c FEMALE Possibly resident; fairly common and quite widespread; below 915 m, uncommon up to 1525 m. More warmly coloured and strongly patterned than the Grey Nightjar, with longer and broader tail. Has diffuse, pale rufous-brown nuchal collar, well-defined buff edges to scapulars, and prominent buff tips to wing coverts. Song is a series of loud, resonant calls: *chaunk-chaunk-chaunk* notes, repeated at the rate of about 100 per minute. Edges and clearings of tropical and subtropical forest.

Indian Nightjar *Caprimulgus asiaticus* 24 cm
a b ADULT Rare, possibly resident; below 250 m. Like a small version of Large-tailed Nightjar. Has boldly streaked crown, rufous-buff nuchal collar, bold black centres and broad buff edges to scapulars, and relatively unmarked central tail feathers. Song is a far-carrying *chuk-chuk-chuk-chuk-tukaroo*; short sharp *qwit-qwit* in flight. Open scrub and cultivation.

Savanna Nightjar *Caprimulgus affinis* 23 cm
a b MALE and c FEMALE Common, but rather local, possibly resident; below 250 m (–915 m). Crown and mantle finely vermiculated, and often appears rather plain except for scapulars, which are edged with rufous-buff. Male has largely white outer tail feathers, although this can be difficult to see. Song is a strident *dheet*. Open forest and scrubby hillsides.

Rock Pigeon *Columba livia* 33 cm

  a **b** ADULT Common and widespread resident; summers up to 4270 m, winters up to at least 2810 m. Grey tail with blackish terminal band, and broad black bars across greater coverts and tertials/secondaries. Feral birds vary considerably in coloration and patterning. Often in large flocks. Feral birds live in villages and towns; wild birds around cliffs and ruins.

Hill Pigeon *Columba rupestris* 33 cm

  a **b** ADULT Common resident in trans-Himalayan areas in the northwest; usually summers 2900–5490 m, winters above 1650 m. Similar in appearance to Rock Pigeon, but has white band across tail contrasting with blackish terminal band. Often in large flocks. High-altitude villages and cliffs, mainly in Tibetan plateau country.

Snow Pigeon *Columba leuconota* 34 cm

  a **b** **c** ADULT Common and widespread resident; summers 3000–5200 m (–5700 m), winters above 1500 m. Slate-grey head, creamy-white collar and underparts, fawn-brown mantle, and white band across black tail. Keeps in pairs and small parties in summer and in large flocks in winter. Cliffs and gorges in mountains.

Common Wood Pigeon *Columba palumbus* 43 cm

  a **b** ADULT Erratic winter visitor; 950–2275 m. White wing patch and dark tail-band, buff neck patch, and deep vinous underparts. In flight, from below, shows greyish-white band across tail, blackish terminal band, and grey undertail-coverts are concolorous with base of tail. Wooded hillsides.

Speckled Wood Pigeon *Columba hodgsonii* 38 cm

  a MALE and **b** FEMALE Frequent and quite widespread resident; 1500–3050 m. Speckled underparts, and white spotting on wing coverts. Lacks buff patch on neck (prominent in both Common and Ashy Wood Pigeon). Male has maroon mantle and maroon on underparts, replaced by grey on female. In flight, from below, shows dark-grey undertail-coverts and underside to tail. Mainly oak/rhododendron forest.

Ashy Wood Pigeon *Columba pulchricollis* 36 cm

  a **b** ADULT Frequent resident from west-central areas eastwards; 1100–2440 m. Distinguished from Speckled Wood Pigeon by buff collar, slate-grey breast, buff belly and undertail-coverts, and uniform slate-grey upperparts. In flight, from below, buff undertail-coverts contrast with dark underside to tail. Dense broadleaved forest.

Mountain Imperial Pigeon *Ducula badia* 43–51 cm

  a **b** ADULT Rare and local, probably resident; 250–1250 m. Large size, brownish upperparts, dark-brown band across base of tail, and pale buff undertail-coverts. Dense broadleaved forest.

Oriental Turtle Dove *Streptopelia orientalis* 33 cm

a b ADULT *S. o. meena* and **c** ADULT *S. o. agricola* Common and widespread resident and winter visitor; summers 365–4570 m, winters mainly below 1370 m, occasionally up to 2000 m. Stocky dove with rufous-scaled scapulars and wing coverts, vinaceous-pink underparts, and black and bluish-grey barring on neck sides. Has dusky-grey underwing. Eastern race *agricola* has grey (rather than white) sides and tip to tail. Open forest, especially near cultivation.

Laughing Dove *Streptopelia senegalensis* 27 cm

a b ADULT Scarce, status and movements uncertain; 610–2440 m. Slim, small dove with fairly long tail. Brownish-pink head and underparts, uniform upperparts, and black stippling on upper breast. Dry cultivation and scrub-covered hills.

Spotted Dove *Streptopelia chinensis* 30 cm

a b ADULT Common and widespread resident below 1500 m; frequent up to 2000 m (–4000 m). Spotted upperparts, and black-and-white chequered patch on neck sides. Cultivation, habitation and open forest.

Red Collared Dove *Streptopelia tranquebarica* 23 cm

a MALE and **b** FEMALE Fairly common and quite widespread resident below 300 m; uncommon in summer up to 1370 m. Small, stocky dove, with shorter tail than Eurasian Collared Dove. Male has blue-grey head, pinkish-maroon upperparts, and pink underparts. Female similar to Eurasian Collared, but is more compact, with darker buffish-grey underparts, darker fawn-brown upperparts, and greyer underwing coverts. Light woodland and trees in open country.

Eurasian Collared Dove *Streptopelia decaocto* 32 cm

a b ADULT Fairly common and widespread resident; below 400 m (–2440 m). Sandy-brown with black half-collar. Larger and longer-tailed than Red Collared Dove. Plumage similar to female Red Collared Dove but with paler upperparts and underparts, and white underwing-coverts. Open dry country with cultivation and groves.

Barred Cuckoo Dove *Macropygia unchall* 41 cm

a MALE and **b** FEMALE Scarce resident from west-central areas eastwards; 250–2800 m. Long, graduated tail, slim body and small head. Upperparts and tail rufous, barred with dark brown. Male has unbarred head and neck, with extensive purple and green gloss. Female is heavily barred on head, neck and underparts. Dense broadleaved forest.

Emerald Dove *Chalcophaps indica* 27 cm

a MALE and **b c** FEMALE Locally common resident; mainly below 365 m (–1200 m). Stout and broad-winged dove, with very rapid flight. Upperparts green, with black-and-white banding on back. Male has grey crown and white shoulder patch. Moist tropical and subtropical broadleaved forest.

Orange-breasted Green Pigeon *Treron bicincta* 29 cm

a MALE and **b** FEMALE Local resident, common at Chitwan, uncommon or rare elsewhere; below 305 m. Central tail feathers of both sexes are grey. Male has orange breast, bordered above by lilac band, grey hind crown and nape, and green mantle. Female has yellow cast to breast and belly, and grey hind crown and nape. Sal and riverine forest.

Pompadour Green Pigeon *Treron pompadora* 28 cm

a MALE and **b** FEMALE Local resident; fairly common at Chitwan, uncommon or rare elsewhere; below 250 m. Both sexes told from Thick-billed Green Pigeon by thin blue-grey bill (without prominent red base) and lack of prominent greenish orbital skin. Also, male has orange patch on breast, yellow throat, and chestnut undertail-coverts, and female has streaked rather than barred appearance to undertail-coverts. Male has maroon mantle, female has green. Grey cap, and tail shape or pattern, help separate it from female Orange-breasted and Wedge-tailed Greens. Sal and riverine forest.

Thick-billed Green Pigeon *Treron curvirostra* 27 cm

a MALE and **b** FEMALE Scarce and local resident from west-central areas eastwards; below 455 m. Both sexes distinguished from Pompadour Green Pigeon by thick bill with red base and by prominent greenish orbital skin. Further, male has green breast without orange patch and different undertail-covert pattern. Inner undertail-coverts are tipped with white (giving rise to barred effect), and outer undertail-coverts are pale cinnamon. Male has maroon mantle, female has green. Sal and riverine forest.

Yellow-footed Green Pigeon *Treron phoenicoptera* 33 cm

ADULT Widespread and locally fairly common resident below 250 m; uncommon up to 1400 m. Large size, broad olive-yellow collar, pale greyish-green upperparts, mauve shoulder patch, and yellow legs and feet. Deciduous forest and fruiting trees around villages and cultivation.

Pin-tailed Green Pigeon *Treron apicauda* 42 cm

a MALE and **b** FEMALE Scarce resident; mainly below 305 m (–915 m). Both sexes have pointed central tail feathers, grey tail, green mantle, and lime-green rump. Male has pale-orange wash to breast. Sal and riverine forest.

Wedge-tailed Green Pigeon *Treron sphenura* 33 cm

a MALE and **b** FEMALE Locally fairly common resident; mainly 1525–200 m (–2800 m). Both sexes have long, wedge-shaped tail, indistinct yellow edges to wing coverts and tertials, and dark-green rump and tail. Male has maroon patch on upperparts (less extensive than on Pompadour Green Pigeon), and orange wash to crown and breast. Female has uniform green head (lacking grey crown of female Pompadour Green Pigeon). Mixed broadleaved forest.

Bengal Florican *Houbaropsis bengalensis* 66 cm

a **b** MALE and **c** **d** FEMALE Rare and local, probably resident; regularly recorded at Sukila Phanta, Chitwan and Bardia; below 305 m. Larger and stockier than Lesser Florican, with broader head and thicker neck. Male has black head, neck and underparts, and in flight wings are entirely white except for black tips. Female and immature are buff-brown to sandy-rufous, and have buffish-white wing coverts with fine dark barring. Mainly well-concealed in tall grassland. Males in breeding season perform striking display by leaping high into the air. Tall grassland with scattered bushes; sometimes in cultivation. Globally threatened.

Lesser Florican *Sypheotides indica* 46–51 cm

a **b** MALE BREEDING, **c** MALE NON-BREEDING and **d** **e** FEMALE Very rare late summer visitor; mainly below 250 m (–1310 m). Small, slim, long-necked bustard. Male breeding has spatulate-tipped head plumes, black head/neck and underparts, and white collar across upper mantle; white wing coverts show as patch on closed wing, but has less white on wing than Bengal Florican. Non-breeding male similar to female, but has white wing coverts. Female and immature are sandy or cinnamon-buff; separated from female/immature Bengal Florican by smaller size and slimmer appearance, heavily marked wing coverts, and rufous coloration to barred flight feathers. Grassland and cultivation. Globally threatened.

Sarus Crane *Grus antigone* 156 cm

a **b** ADULT and **c** IMMATURE Uncommon and local resident in west Terai. Adult is grey, with bare red head and upper neck and bare ashy-green crown. In flight, black primaries contrast with rest of wing. Immature has rusty-buff feathering to head and neck, and upperparts are marked with brown; older immatures are similar to adult but have dull-red head and upper neck and lack greenish crown of adult. Cultivation in well-watered country. Globally threatened.

Demoiselle Crane *Grus virgo* 90–100 cm

a **b** ADULT and **c** IMMATURE Uncommon passage migrant, April/May and October/November. Small crane. Adult has black head and neck with white tuft behind eye, and grey crown; black neck feathers extend as a point beyond breast, and elongated tertials project as shallow arc beyond body, giving rise to distinctive shape. Immature similar to adult, but head and neck are dark grey, tuft behind eye is grey and less prominent, and has grey-brown cast to upperparts. In flight, the Demoiselle Crane is best separated at a distance from the Common Crane by black breast. Cultivation and large rivers.

Common Crane *Grus grus* 110–120 cm

a **b** ADULT and **c** IMMATURE Scarce winter visitor below 250 m and passage migrant, March/April and October/November. Adult has mainly black head and foreneck, with white stripe behind eye extending down side of neck. Immature has brown markings on upperparts, with buff or grey head and neck. Adult head pattern apparent on some by first winter, and as adult by second winter. *See* Appendix 1 for comparison with Black-necked Crane. Cultivation, large rivers and marshes.

Size of illustrations:
1 & 2, 10% of actual size;
3–5, 5% of actual size.

Water Rail *Rallus aquaticus* 23–28 cm

ADULT Rare and local winter visitor; below 120 m (–1340 m). Slightly down-curved bill with red at base. Legs pinkish. Adult has streaked upperparts, greyish underparts, and barring on flanks. *See* Appendix 1 for comparison with Slaty-breasted Rail. Marshes and wet fields.

Brown Crake *Amaurornis akool* 28 cm

ADULT Local resident; common at Chitwan, rare elsewhere; below 365 m. Olive-brown upperparts, grey underparts, and olive-brown flanks and undertail-coverts; underparts lack barring. Has greenish bill and pinkish-brown to purple legs. Juvenile similar to adult. Marshes and vegetation bordering watercourses.

White-breasted Waterhen *Amaurornis phoenicurus* 32 cm

a ADULT and **b** JUVENILE Fairly common and widespread resident; below 1370 m (–3800 m). Adult has grey upperparts, and white face, foreneck and breast; undertail-coverts rufous-cinnamon. Juvenile has greyish face, foreneck and breast, and olive-brown upperparts. Marshes and thick cover close to pools, lakes and ditches.

Black-tailed Crake *Porzana bicolor* 25 cm

ADULT Possibly resident; rare and very local, an adult and three immatures recently recorded at Jiri, east-central Nepal, at 1925 m. Possibly overlooked. Red legs. Sooty-grey head and underparts, rufescent olive-brown upperparts, and sooty-black tail and undertail-coverts. Marshes.

Baillon's Crake *Porzana pusilla* 17–19 cm

a ADULT and **b** JUVENILE Scarce winter visitor and passage migrant, possibly breeds; mainly 75–120 m (–1370 m). Adult has rufous-brown upperparts, extensively marked with white. Flanks are barred. Bill and legs are green. Juvenile is similar but has buff underparts. Marshes, reedy lake edges and wet fields.

Ruddy-breasted Crake *Porzana fusca* 22 cm

a ADULT and **b** JUVENILE Local resident below 370 m, common at Chitwan and Koshi, uncommon elsewhere; uncommon visitor up to 1280 m. Red legs, chestnut underparts, and black-and-white barring on rear flanks and undertail-coverts. Juvenile is dark olive-brown, with white-barred undertail-coverts and fine greyish-white mottling/barring on rest of underparts. Marshes and wet paddy-fields.

Watercock *Gallicrex cinerea* M 43 cm, F 36 cm

a MALE BREEDING, **b** JUVENILE MALE and **c** FEMALE Rare monsoon visitor; below 1280 m. Male is mainly greyish-black, with yellow-tipped red bill and red shield and horn. Non-breeding male and female have buff underparts with fine barring, and buff fringes to dark-brown upperparts. Juvenile has uniform rufous-buff underparts, and rufous-buff fringes to upperparts. Male is much larger than female. Marshes and flooded fields.

Purple Swamphen *Porphyrio porphyrio* 45–50 cm

a ADULT and **b** JUVENILE Chiefly a winter visitor and passage migrant, also breeds; below 915 m (–1370 m). Large size, purplish-blue coloration, and huge red bill and red frontal shield. Juvenile greyer, with duller bill. Reedbeds and marshes.

Common Moorhen *Gallinula chloropus* 32–35 cm

a ADULT and **b** JUVENILE Locally common resident and winter visitor; mainly below 250 m (–4575 m on passage). White undertail-coverts and line along flanks. Adult has red bill with yellow tip and red shield. Juvenile has dull green bill, and is mainly brown. Marshes and reed-edged pools.

Common Coot *Fulica atra* 36–38 cm

ADULT Uncommon winter visitor and passage migrant; up to 3500 m (–5000 m). Blackish, with white bill and shield. Reed-edged lakes and pools.

Eurasian Woodcock *Scolopax rusticola* 33–35 cm

a b ADULT Locally fairly common and quite widespread resident; usually summers 1980–3900 m, winters down to 1350 m (–100 m). Bulky, with broad, rounded wings. Head banded black and buff; lacks sharply defined mantle and scapular stripes. Crepuscular and nocturnal. In breeding season, male has characteristic roding display flight at dawn and dusk, when it flies above the treetops with slow, deliberate wing beats, uttering *chiwich* call. Dense, moist forest.

Solitary Snipe *Gallinago solitaria* 29–31 cm

a b ADULT Uncommon and local winter visitor and passage migrant, probably also resident; mainly 2135–4000 m (–915 m). Large, dull-coloured snipe with long bill. Colder-coloured and less boldly marked than the Wood Snipe, with less striking head pattern, white spotting on ginger-brown breast, and rufous barring on mantle and scapulars (with finer white mantle and scapular stripes). Wings longer and narrower than Wood. In aerial display utters a deep *chok-achok* call, combined with a mechanical bleating produced by outer tail feathers. Marshy edges and beds of mountain streams.

Wood Snipe *Gallinago nemoricola* 28–32 cm

a b ADULT Rare summer visitor, possibly also resident; summers 3650–4900 m, winters 75–3050 m. Large snipe, with heavy and direct flight and broad wings. Bill relatively short and broad-based. More boldly marked than Solitary Snipe, with buff and blackish head stripes, broad buff stripes on blackish mantle and scapulars, and warm buff neck and breast with brown streaking. Legs greenish. In aerial display, flying in a wide circle, it utters a nasal *che-dep, che-dep, che-dep, ip-ip-ip, ock, ock*. Breeds in alpine meadows and dwarf scrub; winters in forest marshes. Globally threatened.

Pintail Snipe *Gallinago stenura* 25–27 cm

a ADULT and **b c** IN FLIGHT Frequent winter visitor and passage migrant; below 1370 m. More rounded wings than the Common Snipe, and slower and more direct flight. Lacks white trailing edge to secondaries, and has densely barred underwing-coverts and pale (buff-scaled) upperwing-covert panel (more pronounced than shown). Feet project noticeably beyond tail in flight. *See* Appendix 1 for comparison with Swinhoe's Snipe. Flight call is a rasping *tetch*. Marshes and wet paddy-fields.

Common Snipe *Gallinago gallinago* 25–27 cm

a ADULT and **b c** IN FLIGHT Locally fairly common winter visitor and passage migrant; below 1500 m (–4700 m on passage). Compared with the Pintail Snipe, wings are more pointed, and has faster and more erratic flight; shows prominent white trailing edge to wing and white banding on underwing-coverts. Flight call is a grating *scaaap*, higher-pitched and more anxious than the Pintail Snipe. Marshes and wet paddy stubbles.

Jack Snipe *Lymnocryptes minimus* 17–19 cm

a ADULT and **b c** IN FLIGHT Rare passage migrant and winter visitor; below 1500 m. Small, with short bill. Flight weaker and slower than that of the Common Snipe, with rounded wing-tips. Has divided supercilium but lacks pale crown stripe. Mantle and scapular stripes very prominent. If flushed, flies off silently and without zig-zagging flight. Marshes and wet paddy stubbles.

Greater Painted-snipe *Rostratula benghalensis* 25 cm

a ADULT MALE, **b** ADULT FEMALE and **c** JUVENILE Uncommon resident; mainly below 350 m (–1370 m). Rail-like wader, with broad, rounded wings and longish, down-curved bill. White or buff 'spectacles' and 'braces'. Adult female has maroon head and neck and dark greenish wing coverts. Adult male and juvenile duller, and have buff spotting on wing coverts. When flushed, rises heavily with legs trailing. Has a roding display flight. Marshes, vegetated pools and stream banks.

Black-tailed Godwit *Limosa limosa* 36–44 cm
a MALE BREEDING, **b** NON-BREEDING, **c** JUVENILE and **d** FLIGHT Scarce and local passage migrant; below 1525 m. White wing-bars and white tail-base with black tail-band. In breeding plumage, male has rufous-orange neck and breast, with blackish barring on underparts and white belly; breeding female is duller. In non-breeding plumage, is uniform grey on neck, upperparts and breast. Juvenile has cinnamon underparts and cinnamon fringes to dark-centred upperparts. Banks and shallow waters of lakes and rivers.

Whimbrel *Numenius phaeopus* 40–46 cm
a **b** ADULT Scarce passage migrant; below 1350 m. Smaller than Eurasian Curlew, with shorter bill. Distinctive head pattern, with whitish supercilium and crown stripe, dark eyestripe, and dark sides of crown. Flight call distinctive, *he-he-he-he-he-he-he*. Banks of rivers and lakes, grassy areas.

Eurasian Curlew *Numenius arquata* 50–60 cm
a **b** ADULT Common winter visitor and passage migrant to Koshi, scarce passage migrant elsewhere; below 3050 m. Large size and long, curved bill. Rather plain head. Has distinctive mournful *cur-lew* call. Banks of rivers and lakes, grassy areas.

Spotted Redshank *Tringa erythropus* 29–32 cm
a ADULT BREEDING, **b** **c** ADULT NON-BREEDING and **d** JUVENILE Local and frequent winter visitor and passage migrant; below 1350 m. Red at base of bill, and red legs. Longer bill and legs than the Common Redshank, and upperwing uniform. Non-breeding plumage is paler grey above and whiter below than Common Redshank. Underparts mainly black in breeding plumage. Juvenile has grey barring on underparts. Has distinctive *tu-ick* flight call. Banks and shallow waters of rivers and lakes.

Common Redshank *Tringa totanus* 27–29 cm
a ADULT BREEDING, **b** **c** ADULT NON-BREEDING and **d** JUVENILE Local winter visitor and passage migrant; below 915 m (–4270 m). Orange-red at base of bill, and orange-red legs. Shorter bill and legs than the Spotted Redshank, and with broad white trailing edge to wing. Non-breeding plumage is grey-brown above, with grey breast. Neck and underparts heavily streaked in breeding plumage. Juvenile has brown upperparts with buff spotting. Call is an anxious *teu-hu-hu*. Banks of rivers and lakes, marshes.

Marsh Sandpiper *Tringa stagnatilis* 22–25 cm
a ADULT BREEDING and **b** **c** ADULT NON-BREEDING Uncommon passage migrant and winter visitor; below 1300 m. Smaller and daintier than the Common Greenshank, with proportionately longer legs and finer bill. Legs greenish or yellowish. Upperparts are grey and foreneck and underparts white in non-breeding plumage. In breeding plumage, foreneck and breast streaked and upperparts blotched and barred. Juvenile has dark-streaked upperparts with buff fringes. Has an abrupt dull *yup* flight call. Banks of rivers and lakes, marshes.

Common Greenshank *Tringa nebularia* 30–34 cm
a ADULT BREEDING and **b** **c** NON-BREEDING Widespread; common winter visitor chiefly below 370 m; passage migrant up to 4800 m; a few summer records. Stocky, with long, stout bill and long, stout greenish legs. Upperparts are grey and foreneck and underparts white in non-breeding plumage. In breeding plumage, foreneck and breast streaked and upperparts untidily streaked. Juvenile has dark-streaked upperparts with fine buff or whitish fringes. Call is a loud, ringing and very distinctive *tu-tu-tu*. Wetlands.

Green Sandpiper *Tringa ochropus* 21–24 cm

a **b** **c** ADULT NON-BREEDING Widespread; fairly common winter visitor below 470 m; common passage migrant up to 4250 m. Greenish legs. White rump; dark upperwing and underwing. Compared with the Wood Sandpiper, has indistinct (or non-existent) supercilium behind eye and darker upperparts. *Tluee-tueet* flight call. Wetlands.

Wood Sandpiper *Tringa glareola* 18–21 cm

a **b** **c** ADULT NON-BREEDING and **d** JUVENILE Uncommon winter visitor, frequent on passage; below 3780 m. Yellowish legs. White rump, and upperwing lacks wing-bar. Compared with the Green Sandpiper, shows prominent supercilium, more heavily spotted upperparts, and paler underwing. Flight call is a soft *chiff-if-if*. Banks of rivers and lakes, marshes.

Common Sandpiper *Actitis hypoleucos* 19–21 cm

a **b** ADULT and **c** JUVENILE Widespread; common winter visitor and passage migrant, possibly breeds; winters below 1370 m (–5400 m on passage). Horizontal stance and constant bobbing action. In flight, rapid shallow wing beats are interspersed with short glides. Juvenile has buff fringes to upperparts. Flight call is an anxious *wee-wee-wee*. Wetlands.

Little Stint *Calidris minuta* 13–15 cm

a ADULT BREEDING, **b** **c** ADULT NON-BREEDING and **d** **e** JUVENILE Uncommon winter visitor and passage migrant; mainly below 1370 m (–3050 m). More rotund than Temminck's Stint with dark legs. Grey sides to tail; has weak *pi-pi-pi* flight call. Adult breeding has pale mantle V, rufous wash to face, neck sides and breast, and rufous fringes to upperpart feathers. Non-breeding has untidy, mottled/streaked appearance, with grey breast sides. Juvenile has whitish mantle V, greyish nape, and rufous fringes to upperparts. Muddy edges of lakes, streams and rivers.

Temminck's Stint *Calidris temminckii* 13–15 cm

a **b** ADULT BREEDING, **c** **d** ADULT NON-BREEDING and **e** JUVENILE Common and widespread winter visitor and passage migrant; below 1370 m (–4710 m on passage). More elongated and horizontal than the Little Stint. White sides to tail in flight; flight call a purring trill. Legs yellowish. In all plumages, lacks mantle V and is usually rather uniform, with complete breast-band and indistinct supercilium. *See* Appendix 1 for comparison with Long-toed Stint. Wetlands.

Dunlin *Calidris alpina* 16–22 cm

a ADULT BREEDING, **b** **c** ADULT NON-BREEDING and **d** JUVENILE Scarce passage migrant and winter visitor; below 1370 m. Dark centre to rump. Adult breeding has black belly. Adult non-breeding darker grey-brown than the Curlew Sandpiper, with less distinct supercilium. Juvenile has streaked belly, rufous fringes to mantle, and buff mantle V. Flight call is a slurred *screet*. Banks of rivers and lakes.

Curlew Sandpiper *Calidris ferruginea* 18–23 cm

a ADULT BREEDING, **b** **c** ADULT NON-BREEDING and **d** JUVENILE Rare passage migrant; below 1370 m (–3750 m). White rump. More elegant than the Dunlin, with longer and more down-curved bill. Adult breeding has chestnut-red underparts. Adult non-breeding paler grey than the Dunlin, with more distinct supercilium. Juvenile has strong supercilium, buff wash to breast, and buff fringes to upperparts. Flight call is a purring *prrriit*. River banks.

Ruff *Philomachus pugnax* M 26–32 cm, F 20–25 cm

a **b** **c** MALE BREEDING, **d** **e** NON-BREEDING and **f** JUVENILE Scarce passage migrant; below 1310 m. Males larger than females. Non-breeding and juvenile have neatly fringed upperparts. Breeding male has variable ruff. Marshes, wet fields, banks of rivers and lakes.

Indian Courser *Cursorius coromandelicus* 23 cm
a b ADULT Very rare and local resident; below 245 m. Grey-brown upperparts and orange underparts, with dark belly. Has chestnut crown, prominent white supercilium, and dark eye-stripe. In flight, shows white band across uppertail-coverts; underwing very dark, and wings broad with rounded wing tips. Juvenile has brown barring on chestnut-brown underparts. Open dry country and dry river beds.

Eurasian Thick-knee *Burhinus oedicnemus* 40–44 cm
a b ADULT Frequent and quite widespread resident; below 915 m (–1310 m). Sandy-brown and streaked. Short yellow-and-black bill, striking yellow eye, and long yellow legs. Call is a loud *cur-lee*. Mainly active at dusk and during night, and spends day sitting in shade. Desert, stony hills, open dry forest and fields.

Great Thick-knee *Esacus recurvirostris* 49–54 cm
a b ADULT Frequent and local resident and winter visitor; below 245 m (–1310 m). Upturned black-and-yellow bill, and white forehead and 'spectacles' and dark mask. Dark bar across coverts very prominent at rest. In flight, shows grey mid-wing panel and white patches in primaries. Mainly active at dusk and during the night, but often observable during the day, especially when disturbed. Stony banks of larger rivers and lakes.

Ibisbill *Ibidorhyncha struthersii* 38–41 cm
a b ADULT Frequent resident; breeds 3800–4200 m, winters mainly below 915 m. Adult has black face, down-curved dark red bill, and black and white breast-bands. Juvenile has brownish upperparts with buff fringes, faint breast-band, and dull legs and bill. Mountain streams and rivers with shingle beds.

Black-winged Stilt *Himantopus himantopus* 35–40 cm
a b ADULT and **c** IMMATURE Uncommon passage migrant; mainly below 1380 m (–3355 m). Black-and-white, slender appearance, long pinkish legs, and fine straight bill. Upperwing black and legs extend a long way behind tail in flight. Juvenile has browner upperparts with buff fringes. Shallow waters in marshes, pools and lakes.

Pied Avocet *Recurvirostra avosetta* 42–45 cm
a b ADULT Rare passage migrant; below 275 m. Upward kink to black bill. Distinctive black-and-white patterning. Juvenile has brown and buff mottling on mantle and scapulars. Marshes and banks of rivers and lakes.

Pheasant-tailed Jacana *Hydrophasianus chirurgus* 31 cm
a b ADULT BREEDING and **c** NON-BREEDING Mainly a summer visitor, although recorded in all months, fairly widespread; breeds up to 1525 m (–3050 m on passage); fairly common in the terai at Koshi and in the west. Extensive white on upperwing, and white underwing. Yellowish patch on sides of neck. Adult breeding has brown underparts and long tail. Adult non-breeding and juvenile have white underparts, with dark line down side of neck and dark breast-band (which are too distinct in plate). Marshes, lakes and ponds with floating vegetation.

Bronze-winged Jacana *Metopidius indicus* 28–31 cm
a b ADULT and **c** IMMATURE Widespread resident; fairly common in lowlands, uncommon up to 915 m. Dark upperwing and underwing. Adult has white supercilium, bronze-green upperparts, and blackish underparts. Juvenile has orange-buff wash on breast, short white supercilium, and yellowish bill. Marshes, pools and lakes with floating vegetation.

Pacific Golden Plover *Pluvialis fulva* 23–26 cm

a **b** ADULT BREEDING and **c** **d** ADULT NON-BREEDING Common winter visitor and passage migrant in the terai at Koshi, rare elsewhere (–2950 m on passage). A slim-bodied, long-necked and long-legged plover. In all plumages, has golden-yellow markings on upperparts, and dusky grey underwing-coverts and axillaries. In flight shows narrower white wing-bar and dark rump. In non-breeding plumage, usually shows prominent pale supercilium and dark patch at rear of ear-coverts (not depicted well in plate). Black underparts with white border striking in breeding plumage. Calls is a plaintive *tu-weep. See* Appendix 1 for comparison with Grey Plover. Mudbanks of wetlands, ploughed fields and grassland.

Long-billed Plover *Charadrius placidus* 19–21 cm

a ADULT BREEDING and **b** **c** NON-BREEDING Rare winter visitor and passage migrant; below 1380 m. Like a large Little Ringed Plover, but has longer tail with clearer dark subterminal bar, and more prominent white wing-bar (although wing-bar is still narrow). In breeding plumage, shows a combination of black band across forecrown, brownish ear-coverts (ear-coverts black in breeding Little Ringed Plover), and black breast-band, and has less distinct eye-ring than Little Ringed. Compared with Little Ringed, white forehead and supercilium more prominent in non-breeding plumage. Flight call is a clear *piwee*. Shingle banks of large rivers.

Little Ringed Plover *Charadrius dubius* 14–17 cm

a ADULT BREEDING and **b** **c** NON-BREEDING Common and widespread resident, also winter visitor; below 1500 m (–2745 m). Small size, elongated and small-headed appearance, and uniform upperwing with only a narrow wing-bar. Legs yellowish or pinkish. Adult breeding has striking yellow eye-ring. Adult non-breeding and juvenile have less distinct head pattern. Flight call is a clear *peeu*. Shingle and mudbanks of rivers, pools and lakes.

Kentish Plover *Charadrius alexandrinus* 15–17 cm

a ADULT MALE BREEDING and **b** **c** NON-BREEDING Locally common winter visitor and passage migrant, possibly breeds; below 1380 m. Small size and stocky appearance. White hind collar and usually small, well-defined patches on sides of breast. Male has rufous cap. Flight call is a soft *pi…pi...pi*, or a rattling trill. Banks of rivers and lakes.

Lesser Sand Plover *Charadrius mongolus* 19–21 cm

a MALE BREEDING, **b** FEMALE BREEDING and **c** **d** ADULT NON-BREEDING Rare winter visitor and spring passage migrant; mainly below 275 m (–3050 m). Larger and longer-legged than the Kentish Plover, lacking white hind collar. Very difficult to identify from Greater Sand Plover (*see* Appendix 1), although is smaller and has stouter bill (with blunt tip), and shorter dark grey or dark greenish legs. In flight, feet do not usually extend beyond tail and white wing-bar is narrower across primaries. Breeding male typically shows full black mask and forehead and more extensive rufous on breast compared with Greater Sand Plover (although variation exists in these characters). Flight call is a hard *chitik* or *chi-chi-chi*. Banks of rivers and lakes.

Oriental Pratincole *Glareola maldivarum* 23–24 cm

a **b** **c** ADULT BREEDING, **d** ADULT NON-BREEDING and **e** JUVENILE Rare passage migrant; below 1310 m. Adult breeding has black-bordered creamy-yellow throat and peachy-orange wash to underparts (patterning much reduced in non-breeding plumage). Shows red underwing-coverts in flight. Very graceful, feeding mainly by hawking insects on the wing in tern-like manner. Dry bare ground near wetlands.

Small Pratincole *Glareola lactea* 16–19 cm

a **b** **c** ADULT BREEDING and **d** NON-BREEDING Locally common resident and local migrant; below 305 m. Small size, with sandy-grey coloration, and shallow fork to tail. In flight, shows white panel across secondaries, blackish underwing-coverts, and black tail-band. Also hawks insects on the wing, often in large groups. Large rivers and lakes with sand or shingle banks.

Northern Lapwing *Vanellus vanellus* 28–31 cm

a **b** ADULT NON-BREEDING Uncommon winter visitor; below 1380 m (–2700 m). Black crest, white (or buff) and black face pattern, black breast-band, and dark green upperparts. Shows all-dark upperwing, and whitish rump and blackish tail-band in flight. Has very broad, rounded wing-tips, with distinctive slow-flapping flight with rather erratic wing beats. Wet grassland, marshes, fallow fields, and wetland edges.

Yellow-wattled Lapwing *Vanellus malarbaricus* 26–28 cm

a **b** ADULT Mainly a rare winter visitor to the terai, but recorded in all months. Yellow wattles and legs. White supercilium, dark cap, and brown breast-band. Wing and tail pattern much as the Red-wattled Lapwing. Call is a strident *chee-eet* and a hard *tit-tit-tit*. Dry river beds and open dry country.

River Lapwing *Vanellus duvaucelii* 29–32 cm

a **b** ADULT Common and widespread resident below 915 m; occasionally summers locally up to 1380 m. Black cap and throat, grey sides to neck, and black bill and legs. Black patch on belly. Call is a high-pitched *did,did,did*. Sand and shingle banks of rivers.

Grey-headed Lapwing *Vanellus cinereus* 34–37 cm

a **b** ADULT NON-BREEDING Winter visitor and passage migrant; uncommon in the Kathmandu Valley at 1310 m, rare elsewhere below 275 m. Yellow bill with black tip, and yellow legs. Grey head, neck and breast, latter with diffuse black border, and black tail-band. In flight, secondaries are all-white. Call is a plaintive *chee-it, chee-it*. River banks, marshes and wet fields.

Red-wattled Lapwing *Vanellus indicus* 32–35 cm

ADULT Common and widespread resident; below 1050 m (–1340 m). Black cap and breast, red bill with black tip, and yellow legs. Wing and tail pattern much as the Yellow-wattled Lapwing. Call is an agitated *did he do it*, *did he do it*. Open flat ground near water.

Size of illustrations:
1 & 2, 25% of actual size;
3–7, 15% of actual size.

1

Caspian Gull *Larus cachinnans* 55–65 cm

a ADULT NON-BREEDING, **b** 1ST-WINTER and **c** 2ND-WINTER Probably an uncommon passage migrant and winter visitor; recorded mainly below 915 m, immatures found at up to 4725 m on passage (although some reports may be referable to Heuglin's Gull). Much larger and broader-winged than Mew Gull (*see* Appendix 1). Adult has paler grey upperparts than Heuglin's Gull. Adult may show faint streaking on head in non-breeding plumage, but head is generally less heavily marked than in non-breeding Heuglin's Gull. First-winter from Heuglin's Gull by paler inner primaries, and much paler underwing-coverts with dark barring; brown mottling on mantle best distinction from first-winter Pallas's Gull. Second-year has paler grey mantle than second-year Heuglin's Gull; diffusely barred tail, dark greater-covert bar, and lack of distinct mask help separate it from first-year Pallas's Gull. Lakes and large rivers.

2

Heuglin's Gull *Larus heuglini* 58–65 cm

a ADULT NON-BREEDING, **b** 1ST-WINTER and **c** 2ND-WINTER Status uncertain; probably a rare passage migrant. Darkest large gull of region. Adult has darker grey upperparts than Yellow-legged Gull. First-winter from Yellow-legged Gull by dark inner primaries and darker underwing-coverts, and usually broader dark tail-band. Second-year has darker grey mantle and darker upperwing and underwing than second-year Yellow-legged Gull. Lakes and large rivers.

3

Pallas's Gull *Larus ichthyaetus* 69 cm

a ADULT BREEDING, **b** ADULT NON-BREEDING, **c** 1ST-WINTER and **d** 2ND-WINTER Locally fairly common winter visitor and passage migrant; mainly in lowlands (–3050 m on passage). Angular head with gently sloping forehead, crown peaking behind eye. Bill large, 'dark-tipped', with bulging gonys. Adult breeding has black hood with bold white eye-crescents, and distinctive wing pattern. Adult non-breeding has largely white head with variable black mask. First-winter has grey mantle and scapulars; told from second-winter Yellow-legged Gull by head pattern (as adult non-breeding), absence of dark greater-covert bar, and more pronounced dark tail-band. Second-winter has largely grey upperwing, with dark lesser-covert bar and extensive black on primaries and primary coverts. Lakes and large rivers.

4

Brown-headed Gull *Larus brunnicephalus* 42 cm

a ADULT BREEDING, **b** ADULT NON-BREEDING and **c** 1ST-WINTER Winter visitor and passage migrant, fairly common at Koshi Barrage, uncommon elsewhere; mainly in lowlands (–5490 m on passage). Larger than Black-headed Gull, with more rounded wing-tips, and broader bill. Adult has broad black wing tips (broken by white 'mirrors') and white patch on outer wing; underside to primaries largely black; iris pale yellow (rather than brown as in adult Black-headed Gull). In breeding plumage, hood paler brown than Black-headed's. First-winter have broad black wing-tips. Lakes and rivers.

5

Black-headed Gull *Larus ridibundus* 38 cm

a ADULT BREEDING, **b** ADULT NON-BREEDING and **c** 1ST-WINTER Winter visitor and passage migrant, fairly common at Koshi Barrage, uncommon elsewhere; mainly in lowlands (–5490 m on passage). White 'flash' on primaries of upperwing. In non-breeding and first-winter, bill tipped black and head largely white with dark ear-covert patch. Lakes and rivers.

6

Slender-billed Gull *Larus genei* 43 cm

a ADULT BREEDING, **b** ADULT NON-BREEDING and **c** 1ST-WINTER Rare and irregular winter visitor, recorded only at Koshi Barrage at 75 m. Head white throughout year, although may show grey ear-covert spot in winter. Gently sloping forehead and longish neck. Iris pale, except in juvenile. Adult has variable pink flush on underparts. Large rivers.

Gull-billed Tern *Gelochelidon nilotica* 35–38 cm

a ADULT BREEDING and **b** ADULT NON-BREEDING Fairly common winter visitor and passage migrant to Koshi Barrage at 75 m ; rare on passage elsewhere (–3050 m). Stout, gull-like black bill and gull-like appearance. Grey rump and tail concolorous with back. Black half-mask in non-breeding and immature plumages. Lakes and large rivers.

Caspian Tern *Sterna caspia* 47–54 cm

a ADULT BREEDING and **b** ADULT NON-BREEDING Winter visitor and passage migrant; fairly common at Koshi Barrage at 75 m, rare elsewhere. Large size with huge red bill. Lakes and large rivers.

River Tern *Sterna aurantia* 38–46 cm

a **b** ADULT BREEDING, **c** ADULT NON-BREEDING and **d** JUVENILE Locally common resident and partial migrant; mainly below 610 m (–1310 m). Adult breeding has orange-yellow bill, black cap, greyish-white underparts, and long tail. Large size, stocky appearance and stout yellow bill (with dark tip) help separate adult non-breeding and immature from Black-bellied Tern. Marshes, streams and rivers.

Common Tern *Sterna hirundo* 31–35 cm

a **b** ADULT BREEDING, **c** ADULT NON-BREEDING and **d** JUVENILE Uncommon passage migrant; 75–4000 m. In breeding plumage, has orange-red bill with black tip, pale grey wash to underparts, and long tail streamers. Has dark bill, whitish forehead and dark lesser-covert bar in non-breeding plumage. Lakes and large rivers.

Little Tern *Sterna albifrons* 22–24 cm

a **b** ADULT BREEDING, **c** ADULT NON-BREEDING and **d** JUVENILE Fairly common summer visitor to Chitwan and Koshi, regular at Bardia, mainly single reports from elsewhere; below 120 m (–1280 m). Fast flight with rapid wing beats, and narrow-based wings. Adult breeding has white forehead and black-tipped yellow bill. Adult non-breeding has blackish bill, black mask and nape band, and dark lesser-covert bar. Lakes and rivers.

Black-bellied Tern *Sterna acuticauda* 33 cm

a **b** ADULT BREEDING, **c** ADULT NON-BREEDING and **d** JUVENILE Locally fairly common resident and partial summer visitor; below 730 m. Much smaller than the River Tern, with orange bill (with variable black tip) in all plumages. Adult breeding has black belly and vent. Adult non-breeding and juvenile have white underparts, and black mask and streaking on crown. Marshes, lakes and rivers.

Whiskered Tern *Chlidonias hybridus* 23–25 cm

a **b** ADULT BREEDING, **c** **d** ADULT NON-BREEDING and **e** JUVENILE Irregular and uncommon winter visitor and spring passage migrant to Koshi Barrage, rare passage migrant elsewhere; 75–915 m. In breeding plumage, white cheeks contrast with grey underparts; lacks greatly elongated outer tail feathers. In non-breeding and juvenile plumages, distinguished from the White-winged Tern by larger bill, grey rump concolorous with back and tail, and different patterning of black on head. Marshes, lakes and rivers.

White-winged Tern *Chlidonias leucopterus* 20–23 cm

a ADULT BREEDING, **b** **c** ADULT NON-BREEDING and **d** JUVENILE Rare spring passage migrant; below 1350 m. In breeding plumage, black head and body contrast with pale upperwing coverts, and has black underwing-coverts. In non-breeding and juvenile plumages, smaller bill, whitish rump contrasting with grey tail, and different patterning of black on head are distinctions from the Whiskered Tern. Marshes, lakes and rivers.

Indian Skimmer *Rynchops albicollis* 40 cm

a ADULT and **b** JUVENILE An irregular and rare visitor, chiefly to Koshi at 75 m. Large, drooping orange-red bill. Juvenile has whitish fringes to upperparts. Large rivers. Globally threatened.

Osprey *Pandion haliaetus* 55–58 cm

a b ADULT Fairly common and widespread winter visitor, resident and passage migrant; below 915 m (–3965 m on passage). Long wings, typically angled at carpals, and short tail. Has whitish head with black stripe through eye, white underbody and underwing-coverts, and black carpal patches. Frequently hovers over water when fishing. Lakes and rivers.

Jerdon's Baza *Aviceda jerdoni* 46 cm

a b ADULT and **c** JUVENILE Very rare and local, possibly breeds; recorded near Dharan in the east at 250 m. Long and erect, white-tipped crest. Long, broad wings (pinched in at base) and fairly long tail. Adult has pale rufous head, indistinct gular stripe, rufous-barred underparts and underwing-coverts, and broad barring across primary tips. At rest, closed wings extend well down tail. Juvenile has whitish head. Broadleaved evergreen forest.

Black Baza *Aviceda leuphotes* 33 cm

a b c ADULT Scarce and local summer visitor, from west-central areas eastwards; 245–450 m (–1280 m). Largely black, with long crest, white breast-band, and greyish underside to primaries contrasting with black underwing-coverts. Broadleaved evergreen forest.

Black-shouldered Kite *Elanus caeruleus* 31–35 cm

a b ADULT and **c** JUVENILE Fairly common and widespread resident, mainly in the terai; summer visitor to Kathmandu Valley at 1370–1550 m. Small size. Grey and white with black 'shoulders'. Flight buoyant, with much hovering. Juvenile has brownish-grey upperparts with pale fringes, with less distinct shoulder patch. Grassland with cultivation and open scrub.

Black Kite *Milvus migrans* 55–68.5 cm

a b c ADULT and **d e** JUVENILE Common and widespread; resident and winter visitor below 2300 m, summer visitor up to 4900 m, also a passage migrant. Shallow tail-fork. Much manoeuvring of arched wings and twisting of tail in flight. Dark rufous-brown, with variable whitish crescent at primary bases on underwing, and pale band across median coverts on upperwing. Juvenile has broad whitish or buffish streaking on head and underparts. Mainly around habitation, also mountains.

Brahminy Kite *Haliastur indus* 48 cm

a b ADULT and **c d** JUVENILE Uncommon and widespread resident, occurs most frequently in eastern lowlands, especially on Koshi marshes; mainly below 360 m (–1370 m). Small size and kite-like flight. Wings usually angled at carpals. Tail rounded. Adult mainly chestnut, with white head, neck and breast. Juvenile mainly brown, with pale streaking on head, mantle and breast, large whitish patches at bases of primaries on underwing, and cinnamon-brown tail. Wetlands.

Pallas's Fish Eagle *Haliaeetus leucoryphus* 76–84 cm

a **b** ADULT and **c** **d** JUVENILE Scarce; recorded in all months, but mainly a winter visitor and passage migrant; below 305 m (–2745 m). Soars and glides with wings flat. Long, broad wings and protruding head and neck. Adult has pale head and neck, dark-brown upperwing and underwing, and mainly white tail with broad black terminal band. Juvenile less bulky, looks slimmer-winged, longer-tailed and smaller-billed than juvenile White-tailed Eagle; has dark mask, pale band across underwing-coverts, pale patch on underside of inner primaries, all-dark tail, and pale crescent on uppertail-coverts. Large rivers and lakes. Globally threatened.

White-tailed Eagle *Haliaeetus albicilla* 70–90 cm

a **b** ADULT **c** **d** JUVENILE Scarce but regular winter visitor; below 915 m (–1370 m on passage). Huge, with broad parallel-edged wings, short wedge-shaped tail, and protruding head and neck. Soars and glides with wings level. Adult has large yellow bill, pale head, and white tail. Juvenile has whitish centres to tail feathers, pale patch on axillaries, and variable pale band across underwing-coverts. Catches fish and waterfowl by flying low over the water surface. Large rivers and lakes.

Grey-headed Fish Eagle *Ichthyophaga ichthyaetus* 69–74 cm

a **b** ADULT **c** **d** JUVENILE Rare and local resident, mainly recorded at Chitwan; below 250 m (–915 m). Adult distinguished from Lesser Fish Eagle by largely white tail with broad black subterminal band, darker and browner upperparts, and rufous-brown breast. Juvenile has pale supercilium, boldly streaked head and underparts, diffuse brown tail barring, and whitish underwing with pronounced dark trailing edge. Spends most of the day perched in regularly-used trees above the water. Very noisy during the breeding season, a far-carrying *tiu-weeeu*. Slow-running waters and lakes in wooded country.

Lesser Fish Eagle *Ichthyophaga humilis* 64 cm

a **b** ADULT and **c** **d** JUVENILE Rare and local resident, mainly recorded at Chitwan; below 250 m. Adult differs from the Grey-headed Fish Eagle in smaller size, greyish tail, paler grey upperparts, white patch at base of outer primaries on underwing, and greyer underparts. Juvenile browner than adult, with paler underwing and paler base to tail; lacks prominent streaking of the juvenile Grey-headed Fish Eagle, and has clear-cut white belly and different tail pattern. As with the Grey-headed Fish Eagle, it is usually seen perched above the water, and rarely soars above the tree canopy. Forested streams and lakes.

1 Lammergeier *Gypaetus barbatus* 100–115 cm

a b ADULT and **c d** IMMATURE Common and widespread resident; 1200–4100 m (305–7500 m). Huge size, long and narrow pointed wings, and large wedge-shaped tail. Adult has blackish upperparts, wings and tail, and cream or rufous-orange underparts contrasting with black underwing-coverts. Immature has blackish head and neck and grey-brown underparts. Has unique habit of splitting bones for the marrow by dropping them from a great height. Open country in mountains.

2 Egyptian Vulture *Neophron percnopterus* 60–70 cm

a b c ADULT, **d e** IMMATURE and **f** JUVENILE Resident, also a passage migrant; fairly common in the centre and west, uncommon in the east; up to 915 m all year, summers regularly to 2000 m (–3810 m). Small vulture with long, pointed wings, small and pointed head, and wedge-shaped tail. Adult mainly dirty white, with bare yellowish face and black flight feathers. Juvenile blackish-brown with bare grey face. With maturity, tail, body and wing coverts become whiter and face yellower. Open country around habitation.

3 White-rumped Vulture *Gyps bengalensis* 75–85 cm

a b c ADULT and **d e f** JUVENILE Formerly common and widespread resident below 1000 m; summers up to 1800 m (–3100 m). Has sharply declined recently. Smallest of the *Gyps* vultures. Adult mainly blackish, with white rump and back, and white underwing-coverts. Key features of juvenile are dark brown coloration, streaking on underparts and upperwing-coverts, dark rump and back, whitish head and neck, and all-dark bill; in flight, underbody and lesser underwing-coverts distinctly darker than on the Long-billed Vulture. Juvenile is similar in coloration to the juvenile Himalayan Griffon, but much smaller and less heavily built, with narrower-looking wings and shorter tail, underparts less heavily streaked, and lacks prominent streaking on mantle and scapulars. Around habitation. Globally threatened.

4 Slender-billed Vulture *Gyps tenuirostris* 80–95 cm

a b ADULT and **c d** JUVENILE 'Long-billed Vulture' was previously recognised as two distinct subspecies *indicus* and *tenuirostris*, but recent studies have demonstrated that they are better treated as separate species, Indian and Slender-billed. Indian Vulture has not been recorded from Nepal. Distinguishing features from Eurasian Griffon (and Indian) are as follows. Bill, head and neck are more slender, and has angular crown (and prominent ear canals). Body appears more slender. Is colder brown in coloration, with striking white thighs (especially prominent in flight). In flight, the trailing edges of the wings appear rounded and pinched in at the body, and the outer primaries appear noticeably longer than the inner primaries. The underside of the flight feathers are uniformly dark. The undertail-coverts appear dark and in flight the feet reach the tip of the tail. Adult has dark bill and cere with pale culmen, lacks any down on head and neck, has dirty white ruff that is rather small and ragged. Juvenile has mainly dark bill, some white down on head and neck, and pale streaking on underparts. Open forests. Up to 1500 m. Globally threatened (Critical).

Himalayan Griffon *Gyps himalayensis* 115–125 cm

a b c ADULT and **d e f** JUVENILE Widespread and locally common resident; 900–4000 m (75–6100 m). Larger than the Eurasian Griffon, with broader body and slightly longer tail. Wing coverts and body pale buffish-white, contrasting strongly with dark flight feathers and tail; underparts lack pronounced streaking; legs and feet pinkish with dark claws, and has yellowish cere. Immature has brown feathered ruff, with bill and cere initially black (yellowish on adult), and has dark brown body and upperwing-coverts boldly and prominently streaked with buff (wing coverts almost concolorous with flight feathers), and back and rump also dark brown; streaked upperparts and underparts and pronounced white banding across underwing-coverts are best distinctions from the Cinereous Vulture; very similar in plumage to the juvenile White-rumped Vulture, but much larger and more heavily built, with broader wings and longer tail, underparts more heavily streaked, and streaking on mantle and scapulars. Open country in mountains.

Eurasian Griffon *Gyps fulvus* 95–105 cm

a b c ADULT and **d e f** JUVENILE Widespread resident; frequent below 915 m, summers locally up to 3050 m. Larger than the Long-billed Vulture, with stouter bill. Key features of adult are blackish cere, whitish head and neck, rufescent-buff upperparts, rufous-brown underparts and thighs with prominent pale streaking, and dark grey legs and feet; rufous-brown underwing-coverts usually show prominent whitish banding (especially across medians). Immature richer rufous-brown on upperparts and upperwing-coverts (with prominent pale streaking) than adult; has rufous-brown feathered neck ruff, more whitish down covering grey head and neck, blackish bill (yellowish on adult), and dark iris (pale yellowish-brown in adult). Open country.

Cinereous Vulture *Aegypius monachus* 100–110 cm

a b ADULT and **c** JUVENILE Mainly an uncommon winter visitor; below 2900 m (–4900 m on passage). Very large vulture with broad, parallel-edged wings. Soars with wings flat. At a distance appears typically uniformly dark, except for pale areas on head and bill. Adult blackish-brown with paler brown ruff; may show paler band across greater underwing-coverts, but underwing darker and more uniform than on *Gyps* species. Juvenile blacker and more uniform than adult. Open country.

Red-headed Vulture *Sarcogyps calvus* 85 cm

a b c ADULT and **d e f** IMMATURE Uncommon resident, formerly widespread, current distribution is uncertain; usually below 2000 m (–3100 m). Comparatively slim and pointed wings. Adult has bare reddish head and cere, white patches at base of neck and upper thighs, and reddish legs and feet; in flight, greyish-white bases to secondaries show as broad panel. Juvenile has white down on head; pinkish coloration to head and feet, white patch on upper thighs, and whitish undertail-coverts are best features. Open country near habitation, and well-wooded hills.

Short-toed Snake Eagle *Circaetus gallicus* 62–67 cm

a **b** **c** PALE PHASE, **d** DARK PHASE and **e** SOARING Scarce, possibly a passage migrant, may also breed; mainly in the terai (–2130 m). Long and broad wings, pinched in at base, and rather long tail. Head broad and rounded. Soars with wings flat or slightly raised; frequently hovers. Pattern variable, often with dark head and breast, barred underbody, dark trailing edge to underwing, and broad subterminal tail-band; can be very pale on underbody and underwing. Open dry country.

Crested Serpent Eagle *Spilornis cheela* 56–74 cm

a **b** ADULT, **c** **d** JUVENILE and **e** SOARING Fairly common and widespread resident; summers below 2100 m (–3350 m) and winters below 915 m. Broad, rounded wings. Soars with wings held forward and in pronounced V. Adult has broad white bands across wings and tail; hooded appearance at rest, with yellow cere and lores, and white spotting on brown underparts. Juvenile has blackish ear-coverts, yellow cere and lores, whitish head and underparts, narrower barring on tail (than adult), and largely white underwing with fine dark barring and dark trailing edge. Frequently soars above forest, often in pairs, uttering loud whistling cry. Forest and well-wooded country.

Black Eagle *Ictinaetus malayensis* 69–81 cm

a **b** ADULT and **c** **d** JUVENILE Fairly common resident from west-central areas eastwards, frequent in the west; usually 1000–3100 m (75–4000 m). In flight has distinctive wing shape, and long tail. Flies with wings raised in V, with primaries upturned. At rest, long wings extend to tip of tail. Adult dark brownish-black, with striking yellow cere and feet; in flight, shows whitish barring on uppertail-coverts, and faint greyish barring on tail and underside of remiges (compare with dark morph of the Changeable Hawk Eagle). Juvenile has dark-streaked buffish head, underparts and underwing-coverts. Hunts by sailing buoyantly and slowly over the canopy, sometimes weaving in and out of tree-tops. Broadleaved forest in hills and mountains.

Eurasian Marsh Harrier *Circus aeruginosus* 48–58 cm

a **b** **c** ADULT MALE, **d** **e** **f** ADULT FEMALE and **g** JUVENILE Fairly common and widespread winter visitor and passage migrant; winters below 915 m (–3050 m on passage). Broad-winged and stocky. As with other harriers, glides and soars with wings in noticeable V, quartering the ground a few metres above it, occasionally dropping to catch prey. Male has pale head, brown mantle and upperwing-coverts contrasting with grey secondaries/inner primaries; female mainly dark brown, except for cream on head and on leading edge of wing. Juvenile may be entirely dark. Marshes, lakes and grasslands.

Pied Harrier *Circus melanoleucos* 41–46.5 cm

a **b** **c** ADULT MALE, **d** **e** **f** ADULT FEMALE and **g** **h** **i** JUVENILE Widespread winter visitor, mainly uncommon, but fairly common at Chitwan, Lumbini and Koshi; below 350 m (–3810 m on passage). Male has black head, upperparts and breast, white underbody and forewing, and black median-covert bar. Female has white uppertail-covert patch, dark-barred greyish remiges and rectrices, pale leading edge to wing, pale underwing, and whitish belly. Juvenile has pale markings on head, rufous-brown underbody, white uppertail-covert patch, and dark underwing with pale patch on primaries. Open grassland and cultivation.

Hen Harrier *Circus cyaneus* 44–52 cm

a **b** **c** ADULT MALE and **d** **e** **f** FEMALE Fairly common and widespread winter visitor and passage migrant; often up to 3000 m in winter (–5400 m on passage). Comparatively broad-winged and stocky. Male has dark grey upperparts, extensive black wing-tips and lacks black secondary bars. Female has broad white band across uppertail-coverts and rather plain head pattern (usually lacking dark ear-covert patch). Juvenile has streaked underparts as female, but with rufous-brown coloration. Open country.

Pallid Harrier *Circus macrourus* 40–48 cm

a **b** **c** ADULT MALE, **d** **e** **f** FEMALE and **g** **h** JUVENILE Uncommon and quite widespread winter visitor and passage migrant; below 2200 m (–3350 m). Slim-winged and fine-bodied, with buoyant flight. As with other harriers glides and soars with wings in noticeable V, quartering the ground a few metres above it, occasionally dropping to catch prey. Folded wings fall short of tail-tip, and legs longer than on Montagu's Harrier. Male has pale grey upperparts, dark wedge on primaries, very pale grey head and underbody, and lacks black secondary bars. Female has distinctive underwing pattern: pale primaries, irregularly barred and lacking dark trailing edge, contrast with darker secondaries which have pale bands narrower than on the female Montagu's Harrier and tapering towards body (although the first-summer Montagu's are more similar in this respect), and lacks prominent barring on axillaries. Typically, female has stronger head pattern than the Montagu's Harrier, with more pronounced pale collar, dark ear-coverts and dark eye-stripe, and upperside of flight feathers darker and lacking banding; told from the female Hen Harrier by narrower wings with more pointed hand, stronger head pattern, and patterning of underside of primaries. Juvenile has primaries evenly barred (lacking pronounced dark fingers), without dark trailing edge, and usually with pale crescent at base; head pattern more pronounced than Montagu's Harrier, with narrower white supercilium, more extensive dark ear-covert patch, and broader pale collar contrasting strongly with dark neck sides. Open country.

Montagu's Harrier *Circus pygargus* 43–47 cm

a **b** **c** ADULT MALE, **d** **e** **f** FEMALE and **g** **h** JUVENILE Scarce winter visitor and passage migrant; below 250 m (–2650 m on passage). Folded wings reach tail-tip, and legs shorter than on the Pallid Harrier. Male has black band across secondaries, extensive black on underside of primaries, and rufous streaking on belly and underwing-coverts. Female differs from female Pallid Harrier in distinctly and evenly barred underside to primaries with dark trailing edge, broader and more pronounced pale bands across secondaries, barring on axillaries, less pronounced head pattern, and distinct dark banding on upperside of remiges. Juvenile has unstreaked rufous underparts and underwing-coverts, and darker secondaries than female; differs from the juvenile Pallid Harrier in having broad dark fingers and dark trailing edge to hand on underwing, and paler face with smaller dark ear-covert patch and less distinct collar. Open country.

Northern Goshawk *Accipiter gentilis* 50–61 cm

a b FEMALE and **c** JUVENILE Widespread and frequent presumably resident in the north, a rare winter visitor to Chitwan; 1370–4880 m (250–6100 m). Very large, with heavy, deep-chested appearance. Wings comparatively long, with bulging secondaries. Male has grey upperparts (greyer than female Eurasian Sparrowhawk), white supercilium, and finely barred underparts. Female considerably larger, with browner upperparts. Juvenile has heavy streaking on buff-coloured underparts. Forest.

Crested Goshawk *Accipiter trivirgatus* 30–46 cm

a b MALE and **c** JUVENILE Uncommon resident, mainly from west-central areas and eastwards; below 1370 m (–2100 m). Larger size and crest are best distinctions from the Besra. Short and broad wings, pinched in at base. Wing-tips barely extend beyond tail-base at rest. Male has dark grey crown and paler grey ear-coverts, black submoustachial and gular stripes, and rufous-brown streaking on breast, and barring on belly and flanks. Female has browner crown and ear-coverts, and browner streaking and barring on underparts. Juvenile has rufous or buffish fringes to crown, crest and nape feathers, streaked ear-coverts, and buff/rufous wash to streaked underparts (barring restricted to lower flanks and thighs). Mainly forest; also hunts above the tree-line.

Shikra *Accipiter badius* 30–36 cm

a MALE, **b c** FEMALE and **d e** JUVENILE Fairly common and widespread resident; usually below 1370 m (–2250 m). Adults paler than the Besra and the Eurasian Sparrowhawk. Underwing pale, with fine barring on remiges, and slightly darker wing-tips. Male has pale blue-grey upperparts, indistinct grey gular stripe, fine brownish-orange barring on underparts, unbarred white thighs, and only lightly barred central tail feathers. Upperparts of female are more brownish-grey. Juvenile has pale-brown upperparts, more prominent gular stripe, and streaked underparts; distinguished from juvenile Besra by paler upperparts and narrower tail barring, and from the Eurasian Sparrowhawk by streaked underparts. Open woods and groves.

Besra *Accipiter virgatus* 29–36 cm

a MALE, **b c** FEMALE and **d e** JUVENILE Frequent resident, mainly recorded from west-central areas eastwards; summers 1350–2800 m (–3440 m), winters down to 75 m. Small. Upperparts darker than the Shikra, and prominent gular stripe and streaked breast should separate it from the Eurasian Sparrowhawk; underwing strongly barred compared with the Shikra. In all plumages, resembles the Crested Goshawk, but considerably smaller, lacks crest, and has longer and finer legs. Male has dark slate-grey upperparts, broad blackish gular stripe, and bold rufous streaking on breast and barring on belly. Female browner on upperparts, with blackish crown and nape. Juvenile told from the juvenile Shikra by darker, richer brown upperparts, broader gular stripe, and broader tail barring. Breeds in dense broadleaved forest; also open country in winter.

Eurasian Sparrowhawk *Accipiter nisus* 31–36 cm

a b MALE, **c d** FEMALE and **e** JUVENILE Fairly common resident and winter visitor; summers mainly at 2440–4200 m (–5180 m on passage), winters 250–1450 m (down to 75 m). Upperparts of adult darker than the Shikra, with prominent tail barring, and strongly barred underwing. Uniform barring on underparts and absence of prominent gular stripe should separate it from the Besra. Male has dark slate-grey upperparts and reddish-orange barring on underparts. Female is dark-brown on upperparts, with dark-brown barring on underparts. Juvenile has dark-brown upperparts and barred underparts. Well-wooded country and open forest.

Oriental Honey-buzzard *Pernis ptilorhyncus* 57–60 cm

a **b** **c** MALE and **d** FEMALE Fairly common and widespread resident and passage migrant; below 1700 m (–3050 m on passage). Long and broad wings and tail, narrow neck and small head with small crest. Soars with wings flat. Very variable in plumage; often shows dark moustachial stripe and gular stripe, and patch of streaking across lower throat. Lacks dark carpal patch. Male has grey face, greyish-brown upperparts, two black tail-bands, usually three black bands across underside of remiges, and dark brown iris. Female has browner face and upperparts, three black tail-bands, four narrower black bands across remiges, and yellow iris. Well-wooded country, usually of broadleaves.

White-eyed Buzzard *Butastur teesa* 43 cm

a **b** **c** ADULT and **d** **e** JUVENILE Fairly common and widespread resident; below 300 m (–1500 m). Longish, rather slim wings, long tail, and buzzard-like head. Pale median-covert panel. Flight *Accipiter*-like. Adult has black gular stripe, white nape patch, barred underparts, dark wing-tips, and rufous tail; iris yellow. Juvenile has buffish head and breast streaked with dark brown, with moustachial and throat stripes indistinct or absent; rufous uppertail more strongly barred; iris brown. Dry open country, scrub and open dry forest.

Common Buzzard *Buteo buteo* 51–56 cm

a **b** **c** **d** ADULT *B. b. japonicus* and **e** **f** ADULT *B. b. refectus* Fairly common and widespread winter visitor and passage migrant, mainly 1000–4300 m (down to 250 m); possibly breeds, small numbers summer from 3350 m up to at least 3800 m. Stocky, with broad wings and moderate-length tail. Soars with wings held in V shape. Variable; some very similar to the Long-legged and Upland Buzzards. *B. b. japonicus* typically has rather pale head and underparts, with variable dark streaking on breast and brown patch on belly/thighs; tail dark-barred grey-brown. *B. b. refectus* is dark brown to rufous-brown, with variable amounts of white on underparts; tail dull brown with some dark barring, or uniform sandy-brown. Open country.

Long-legged Buzzard *Buteo rufinus* 61 cm

a **b** **c** **d** ADULT Widespread and frequent winter visitor and passage migrant; below 2755 m (–5000 m on passage). Larger and longer-necked than the Common Buzzard, with longer wings and tail (appears more eagle-like); soars with wings in deeper V. Variable in plumage. Most differ from the Common Buzzard in having combination of paler head and upper breast, rufous-brown lower breast and belly, more uniform rufous underwing-coverts, more extensive black carpal patches, larger pale primary patch on upperwing, and unbarred pale orange uppertail. Rufous and black morphs are similar to some plumages of the Common Buzzard. Open country.

Upland Buzzard *Buteo hemilasius* 71 cm

a **b** **c** **d** ADULT Uncommon winter visitor, possibly also a resident breeder; winters down to 250 m, summers up to 4420 m. Larger, longer-winged and longer-tailed than the Common Buzzard (appearing more eagle-like); soars with wings in deeper V. Tarsus always at least three-quarters feathered, often entirely feathered (half-feathered or less on Common and Long-legged Buzzards). Plumage variable. Pale morph has combination of large white primary patch on upperwing, greyish-white tail (with fine bars towards tip), whitish head and underparts with dark-brown streaking, brown thighs forming dark U-shape on underparts, and extensive black carpal patches (the *japonicus* race of the Common Buzzard can be very similar); never has rufous tail or rufous thighs as the Long-legged Buzzard. Dark morph probably not distinguishable on plumage from that of the Common and Long-legged Buzzards. Open country.

Indian Spotted Eagle *Aquila hastata* 60–65 cm

a b c ADULT and **d e f** JUVENILE Now recognised, once again, as a distinct species from Lesser Spotted Eagle *Aquila pomarina* (which is now best considered extralimital). As Greater Spotted, Indian Spotted is a stocky, medium-sized eagle with rather short and broad wings, buzzard-like head with comparatively fine bill, and a rather short tail. The wings are angled down at carpals when gliding and soaring. Adult is similar in overall appearance to Greater Spotted, and field characters are poorly understood. Has a wider gape than Greater Spotted, with thick 'lips', with gape-line extending well behind eye (reaching to below centre of eye in Spotted). A possible additional feature of the adult in the field is the paler brown lesser underwing-coverts, which contrast with rest of underwing (Greater Spotted typically has uniform dark underwing-coverts). Juvenile is more distinct from juvenile Greater Spotted. Spotting on upperwing coverts is less prominent, tertials are pale brown with diffuse white tips (dark with bold white tips in Greater Spotted), uppertail coverts are pale brown with white barring (white in Greater Spotted), and underparts are paler light yellowish brown with dark streaking. In some plumages can resemble Steppe Eagle – differences mentioned below for Greater Spotted are likely to be helpful for separation (although gape-line is also long in Steppe). Wooded areas in plains to the edge of the hills.

Greater Spotted Eagle *Aquila clanga* 65–72 cm

a b c ADULT, **d e f** JUVENILE and **g h** JUVENILE *'fulvescens'* Uncommon winter visitor, mainly below 250 m; passage migrant up to 3840 m. Medium-sized eagle with rather short and broad wings, stocky head, and short tail. Wings distinctly angled down at carpals when gliding, almost flat when soaring. Heavier than the Lesser Spotted Eagle, with broader wings and squarer hand, and shorter tail; dark-brown upperwing- and underwing-coverts show little contrast with flight feathers (although some can be similar to Lesser Spotted), and usually lacks second whitish carpal crescent on underwing. Compared with the Steppe Eagle, has less protruding head in flight, with shorter wings and less deep-fingered wing-tips; at rest, trousers less baggy, and bill smaller with rounded (rather than elongated) nostril and shorter gape; lacks adult Steppe's barring on underside of flight and tail feathers, and dark trailing edge to wing, and has a dark chin. Pale variant *'fulvescens'* distinguished from the juvenile Imperial Eagle by structural differences, lack of prominent pale wedge on inner primaries on underwing, and unstreaked underparts. Juvenile has bold whitish tips to dark-brown coverts. Large rivers and lakes; prefers wooded areas near water. Globally threatened.

Golden Eagle *Aquila chrysaetos* 75–88 cm

a b c ADULT and **d e** JUVENILE Uncommon and widespread resident; mainly 2745–4575 m (75–6190 m). Large eagle, with long and broad wings (with pronounced curve to trailing edge), long tail, and distinctly protruding head and neck. Wings clearly pressed forward and raised (with upturned fingers) in pronounced V when soaring. Adult has pale panel across upperwing coverts, gold crown and nape, and two-toned tail. Juvenile has white base to tail and white patch at base of flight feathers. Rugged mountains above tree-line.

Tawny Eagle *Aquila rapax* 63–71 cm

a **b** **c** **d** **e** ADULT, **f** **g** JUVENILE and **h** SUB-ADULT Widespread and rare resident; below 250 m. Compared with the Steppe Eagle, hand of wing does not appear so long and broad, tail slightly shorter, and looks smaller and weaker at rest; gape-line ends level with centre of eye (extends to rear of eye in the Steppe Eagle), and adult has yellowish iris. Differs from the spotted eagles in more protruding head and neck in flight, baggy trousers, yellow iris, and oval nostril. Adult extremely variable, from dark brown through rufous to pale cream, and unstreaked or streaked with rufous or dark brown. Dark morph very similar to the adult Steppe Eagle (which shows much less variation); distinctions include less pronounced barring and dark trailing edge on underwing, dark nape, and dark chin. Varying from rufous to pale cream-coloured, Tawny are uniformly pale from uppertail-coverts to back, with undertail-coverts same colour as belly (contrast often apparent on similar species). Pale adults also lack prominent whitish trailing edge to wing, tip to tail and greater-covert bar (present on immatures of similar species). Characteristic, if present, is distinct pale inner-primary wedge on underwing. Juvenile also variable, with narrow white tips to unbarred secondaries; otherwise as similar-plumaged adult. Many (possibly all) non-dark Tawny Eagles have distinctive immature/sub-adult plumage: dark throat and breast contrasting with pale belly. They can show dark banding across underwing-coverts; and the whole head and breast may be dark. Cultivation and open wooded country.

Steppe Eagle *Aquila nipalensis* 76–80 cm

a **b** **c** ADULT, **d** **e** **f** JUVENILE and **g** **h** IMMATURE Widespread and common winter visitor and passage migrant; mainly below 2200 m (–7925 m on passage). Broader and longer wings than the Greater and Lesser Spotted Eagles, with more pronounced and spread fingers, and more protruding head and neck; wings flatter when soaring, and less distinctly angled down at carpals when gliding. When perched, clearly bigger and heavier, with heavier bill and baggy trousers. Adult separated from adult spotted eagles by underwing pattern (dark trailing edge, distinct barring on remiges, indistinct/non-existent pale crescents in carpal region), pale rufous nape patch and pale chin. Juvenile has broad white bar across underwing, double white bar on upperwing, and white crescent across uppertail-coverts; prominence of bars on upperwing and underwing much reduced on older immatures, and such birds are very similar to some Lesser Spotted Eagles (*see* that species). Wooded hills, open country and lakes.

Imperial Eagle *Aquila heliaca* 72–83 cm

a **b** **c** ADULT and **d** **e** **f** JUVENILE Regular winter visitor to Koshi Tappu at 75 m in small numbers, a few winter records elsewhere below 1370 m; also a scarce passage migrant below 3900 m. Large, stout-bodied eagle with long and broad wings, longish tail, and distinctly protruding head and neck. Wings flat when soaring and gliding. Adult has almost uniform upperwing, small white scapular patches, golden-buff crown and nape, and two-toned tail. Juvenile has pronounced curve to trailing edge of wing, pale wedge on inner primaries, streaked buffish body and wing coverts, uniform pale rump and back (lacking distinct pale crescent shown by other species except the Tawny Eagle), and white tips to median and greater upperwing-coverts. Large rivers and lakes, open country. Globally threatened.

1a

1c

1h

1e

1b

1d

1g

1f

2b

2c

2f

2a

2e

2h

2d

2g

3c

3e

3a

3b

3d

3f

Bonelli's Eagle *Hieraaetus fasciatus* 65–72 cm

a **b** **c** ADULT and **d** **e** **f** JUVENILE Frequent but local resident; 1400–2600 m (100–3050 m). Medium-sized eagle with long and broad wings, distinctly protruding head, and long square-ended tail. Soars with wings flat. Adult has pale underbody and forewing, blackish band along underwing-coverts, whitish patch on mantle, and pale greyish tail with broad dark terminal band. Juvenile has ginger-buff to reddish-brown underbody and underwing-coverts (with variable dark band along greater underwing-coverts), uniform upperwing, and pale crescent on uppertail-coverts and patch on back. Well-wooded country.

Booted Eagle *Hieraaetus pennatus* 45–53 cm

a **b** **c** PALE MORPH and **d** **e** DARK MORPH Mainly an uncommon winter visitor and passage migrant, 75–4000 m; also a rare resident, has bred at 3200 m and 3850 m. Smallish eagle with long wings and long square-ended tail. Glides and soars with wings flat or slightly angled down at carpal. Always shows white shoulder patches, pale median-covert panel, pale wedge on inner primaries, white crescent on uppertail-coverts, and greyish undertail with darker centre and tip. Head, body and wing coverts whitish, brown or rufous respectively in pale, dark and rufous morphs. Well-wooded country.

Rufous-bellied Eagle *Hieraaetus kienerii* 53–61 cm

a **b** ADULT and **c** **d** JUVENILE Scarce resident recorded from east to west; 200–305 m. Smallish, with buzzard-shaped wings and tail. At rest, wing-tips extend well down tail. Glides and soars with wings flat. Adult has blackish hood and upperparts, white throat and breast, and (black-streaked) rufous rest of underparts. Juvenile has white underparts and underwing-coverts, dark mask and white supercilium, and dark patches on breast and flanks. Moist broadleaved forest.

Changeable Hawk Eagle *Spizaetus cirrhatus* 61–72 cm

a **b** ADULT PALE MORPH, **c** **d** DARK MORPH and **e** **f** JUVENILE Scarce resident recorded from east to west; below 360 m (75–1050 m). Narrower, more parallel-edged wings than the Mountain Hawk Eagle. Soars with wings flat (except in display, when both wings and tail raised). Adult lacks prominent crest, and has boldly streaked underparts and narrower tail barring compared with the Mountain Hawk Eagle; dark morph differentiated from the Black Eagle by structural differences, greyish undertail with diffuse dark terminal band, and extensive greyish bases to underside of remiges. Juvenile generally whiter on head than juvenile Mountain Hawk Eagle. Broadleaved forest and well-wooded country.

Mountain Hawk Eagle *Spizaetus nipalensis* 70–72 cm

a **b** ADULT and **c** **d** JUVENILE Widespread resident, locally frequent; mainly 1500–2835 m, scarce below 250 m in winter. Prominent crest. Wings broader than on the Changeable Hawk Eagle, with more pronounced curve to trailing edge. Soars with wings in shallow V. Distinguished from the Changeable Hawk Eagle by extensive barring on underparts, whitish-barred rump, and stronger dark barring on tail. Juvenile told from juvenile Changeable Hawk Eagle by more extensive dark streaking on crown and sides of head, white-tipped black crest, buff-barred rump, and fewer, more prominent tail-bars. Forested hills and mountains.

Collared Falconet *Microhierax caerulescens* 18 cm

a **b** **c** ADULT Uncommon resident, mainly from west-central areas and eastwards; below 915 m. Very small. Rather shrike-like when perched. Flies with rapid beats interspersed with long glides. Adult has white collar, black crown and eye-stripe, and rufous-orange underparts. Juvenile has rufous-orange on forehead and supercilium, and white throat. Edges and clearings of broadleaved tropical forest.

Lesser Kestrel *Falco naumanni* 29–32 cm

a **b** **c** MALE and **d** **e** **f** FEMALE Mainly an uncommon passage migrant in October and November below 2745 m; a few spring and several winter records, noted at 3700 m in February. Slightly smaller and slimmer than the Common Kestrel. Flapping shallower and stiffer. Claws whitish (black on the Common Kestrel). Compared with the Common Kestrel, male lacks dark moustachial stripe, has unmarked upperparts, blue-grey greater coverts, and plainer orange-buff underparts. In flight, underwing whiter with more clearly pronounced darker tips to primaries; tail often looks more wedge-shaped. First-year male more like the Common Kestrel, but has unmarked rufous mantle and scapulars. Female and juvenile have less distinct moustachial stripe than the Common Kestrel, and lack any suggestion of dark eye-stripe; underwing tends to be cleaner and whiter, with primary bases unbarred (or only lightly barred) and coverts less heavily spotted, and dark primary tips more pronounced. Open grassland and cultivation. Globally threatened.

Common Kestrel *Falco tinnunculus* 32–35 cm

a **b** **c** MALE and **d** **e** **f** FEMALE Common and widespread resident, winter visitor and passage migrant; up to 5200 m. Long, rather broad tail; wing-tips more rounded than on most falcons. Frequently hovers. Male has grey head and tail, and rufous upperparts heavily marked with black. Female and juvenile have rufous crown and nape streaked with black, diffuse and narrow dark moustachial stripe, rufous upperparts heavily marked with black, and dark barring on rufous tail. Open country.

Red-necked Falcon *Falco chicquera* 31–36 cm

a **b** **c** ADULT Resident, generally rare, but regular and uncommon at Koshi; 75–1370 m. Powerful falcon with pointed wings and longish tail. Flight usually fast and dashing. Has rufous crown and nape, pale blue-grey upperparts, white underparts finely barred with black, and grey tail with broad black subterminal band. Open country.

Amur Falcon *Falco amurensis* 28–31 cm

a **b** MALE and **c** **d** FEMALE Chiefly an uncommon passage migrant in October and November; 915–2900 m (from 250 m in winter to 4420 m in summer). In all plumages, has red to pale-orange cere, eye-ring, legs and feet. Frequently hovers. Male dark grey, with rufous undertail-coverts and white underwing-coverts. Female has dark grey upperparts, short moustachial stripe, whitish underparts with some dark barring and spotting, and orange-buff thighs and undertail-coverts; uppertail barred; underwing white with strong dark barring. Juvenile has rufous-buff fringes to upperparts, rufous-buff streaking on crown, and boldly streaked underparts. Open country.

Merlin *Falco columbarius* 25–30 cm

a **b** MALE and **c** **d** FEMALE Rare winter visitor and possibly also a passage migrant; 75–4000 m. Small and compact, with short, pointed wings. Flight typically swift, with rapid beats interspersed with short dashing glides, when wings often closed into body. Male has blue-grey upperparts, broad black subterminal tail-band, weak moustachial stripe, and diffuse patch of rufous-orange on nape. Female and juvenile have weak moustachial stripe, brown upperparts with variable rufous/buff markings, and strongly barred uppertail. Open country.

Eurasian Hobby *Falco subbuteo* 30–36 cm

a **b** ADULT and **c** JUVENILE Widespread resident, partial migrant, winter visitor and passage migrant; up to 4200 m. Slim, with long pointed wings and medium-length tail. Hunting flight swift and powerful, with stiff beats interspersed with short glides. Adult has broad black moustachial stripe, cream underparts with bold blackish streaking, and rufous thighs and under-tail-coverts. Juvenile has dark-brown upperparts with buffish fringes, pale buffish underparts that are more heavily streaked, and lacks rufous thighs and undertail-coverts. Well-wooded areas; also open country in winter.

Oriental Hobby *Falco severus* 27–30 cm

a **b** ADULT and **c** IMMATURE Rare, status uncertain; formerly bred in Kathmandu Valley; up to 1525 m. Similar to the Eurasian Hobby in structure and flight action. Adult has complete blackish hood, bluish-black upperparts, and unmarked rufous underparts. Juvenile has browner upperparts, and heavily streaked rufous-buff underparts. Open wooded hills.

Laggar Falcon *Falco jugger* 43–46 cm

a **b** ADULT and **c** **d** JUVENILE Rare, possibly resident; up to 1980 m, mainly in the terai. Large falcon, although smaller, slimmer-winged and less powerful than the Saker Falcon. Adult has rufous crown, fine but prominent dark moustachial stripe, dark-brown upperparts, and rather uniform uppertail; underparts and underwing-coverts vary in extent of streaking, but lower flanks and thighs usually wholly dark brown; may show dark panel across underwing-coverts. Juvenile similar to adult, but crown duller and underparts very heavily streaked, and has greyish bare parts; differs from the juvenile Peregrine Falcon in paler crown, finer moustachial stripe, and unbarred uppertail. Open dry country and cultivation.

Saker Falcon *Falco cherrug* 50–58 cm

a **b** ADULT Rare and local winter visitor and passage migrant; 1525–3795 m. Large falcon with long wings and long tail. Wing beats slow in level flight, with lazier flight action than the Peregrine Falcon. At rest, tail extends noticeably beyond closed wings (wings fall just short of tail-tip on the Laggar Falcon and are equal to tail on the Peregrine Falcon). *F. c. milvipes*, which is the race recorded in Nepal, has broad orange-buff barring on upperparts and is rather different in plumage from the Laggar Falcon. Additional differences include paler crown, less distinct moustachial stripe, and less heavily-marked underparts (with flanks and thighs usually clearly streaked and not appearing wholly brown – although some overlap exists). Semi-desert in hills and mountains and open dry scrubby areas.

Peregrine Falcon *Falco peregrinus* 38–48 cm

a **b** ADULT and **c** JUVENILE *F. p. peregrinator*; **d** **e** ADULT *F. p. calidus* Shahin *F. p. peregrinator* Fairly common resident; usually summers 1500–3000 m (–4200 m) and winters down to 75 m; *F. p. calidus* Winter visitor; from 75 m up to at least 1370 m. Heavy-looking falcon with broad-based and pointed wings and short, broad-based tail. Flight strong, with stiff, shallow beats and occasional short glides. *F. p. calidus* has slate-grey upperparts, broad black moustachial stripe and whitish underparts with narrow blackish barring; Juvenile *calidus* (not illustrated) has browner upperparts, heavily streaked underparts, broad moustachial stripe, and barred uppertail. *F. p. peregrinator* has darker upperparts with more extensive black hood, and rufous underparts; juvenile *peregrinator* has darker browner upperparts than adult, and paler underparts with heavy streaking. *F. p. babylonicus* ('Barbary Falcon') has occurred as a vagrant; has pale blue-grey upperparts, buffish underparts with only sparse markings, rufous on crown and nape, and finer moustachial stripe; juvenile *babylonicus* has darker brown upperparts, heavily streaked underparts, and only a trace of rufous on forehead and supercilium. Breeds in open rugged country, also around lakes and large rivers in winter.

Little Grebe *Tachybaptus ruficollis* 25–29 cm

a ADULT BREEDING and **b** **c** NON-BREEDING Fairly common resident, winter visitor and passage migrant; mainly below 1370 m (–3050 m). Small size, often with puffed-up rear end. In breeding plumage, has rufous cheeks and neck sides and yellow patch at base of bill. In non-breeding plumage, has brownish-buff cheeks and flanks. Juvenile is similar to non-breeding but has brown stripes across cheeks. Lakes and pools.

Great Crested Grebe *Podiceps cristatus* 46–51 cm

a ADULT BREEDING and **b** **c** NON-BREEDING Locally frequent winter visitor, possibly breeds; mainly below 1370 m (–4800 m). Large and slender-necked. Has white cheeks and fore-neck in non-breeding plumage. Rufous-orange ear-tufts and white cheeks and foreneck in breeding plumage. Lakes and large rivers.

Black-necked Grebe *Podiceps nigricollis* 28–34 cm

a ADULT BREEDING and **b** NON-BREEDING Scarce and local visitor, mainly in winter; up to 3050 m. Steep forehead, and bill appears up-turned. Dusky ear-coverts contrast with white throat and sides of head in non-breeding plumage. Yellow ear-tufts, black neck and breast and rufous flanks in breeding plumage. Lakes and large rivers.

Darter *Anhinga melanogaster* 85–97 cm

a **b** **c** ADULT MALE BREEDING and **d** IMMATURE Uncommon resident and non-breeding visitor, recorded from east to west; below 300 m (–1370 m). Long, slim head and neck, dagger-like bill, and long tail. Often swims with most of body submerged. In flight, neck is only part-ly outstretched with kink at base. As with other cormorants, frequently perches with wings held outstretched to dry. Adult has white stripe down side of neck, lanceolate white scapular streaks, and white streaking on wing coverts. Juvenile buffish-white below, with buff fringes to coverts forming pale panel on upperwing. Lakes, pools and slow-moving rivers.

Little Cormorant *Phalacrocorax niger* 51 cm

a **b** ADULT BREEDING, **c** NON-BREEDING and **d** IMMATURE Resident, also a winter visi-tor and passage migrant; common at Koshi Barrage, uncommon elsewhere, recorded from east to west; 250 m. Small size with short bill. Adult breeding all black, with a few white plumes on forecrown and sides of head. Non-breeding browner (and lacks white head plumes), with whitish chin. Immature has whitish chin and throat, and foreneck and breast a shade paler than upperparts, with some pale fringes. Lakes, pools and rivers.

Great Cormorant *Phalacrocorax carbo* 80–100 cm

a **b** ADULT BREEDING, **c** NON-BREEDING and **d** IMMATURE Fairly common and wide-spread non-breeding resident; mainly below 1000 m (–3960 m). Large with thick neck and stout bill. Adult breeding glossy black, with orange facial skin, white cheeks and throat, white head plumes and white thigh patch. Non-breeding more blackish-brown, and lacks white head plumes and thigh patch. Immature has whitish or pale buff underparts. Lakes and large rivers.

Size of illustrations:
1–3, 18% of actual size;
4–6, 9% of actual size.

Little Egret *Egretta garzetta* 55–65 cm

a ADULT BREEDING and **b** NON-BREEDING Fairly common and widespread resident; below 1525 m. Slim and graceful. Typically, has black bill, black legs with yellow feet, and greyish lores (lores reddish during courtship). Breeding plumage has prominent plumes on nape, breast and mantle. Wetlands.

Great Egret *Casmerodius albus* 65–72 cm

a ADULT BREEDING and **b** NON-BREEDING Widespread and locally fairly common resident; below 300 m (–3050 m). Large size, very long neck and large bill. Black line of gape extends behind eye. In breeding plumage bill is black, lores blue, and tibia reddish, and has prominent plumes on breast and mantle. In non-breeding plumage, bill yellow and lores pale green. Wetlands.

Intermediate Egret *Mesophoyx intermedia* 65–72 cm

a ADULT BREEDING and **b** NON-BREEDING Widespread and frequent, mainly resident; below 915 m (–1370 m). Smaller than the Great Egret, with shorter bill and neck. Black gape-line does not extend beyond eye. In breeding plumage, bill is black and lores yellow-green, and has breast- and mantle-plumes, and prominent crest. Has black-tipped yellow bill and yellow lores outside breeding season. Wetlands.

Cattle Egret *Bubulcus ibis* 48–53 cm

a **b** ADULT BREEDING and **c** NON-BREEDING Widespread and common resident; below 1525 m. Small stocky egret, with short yellow bill and short legs. Has orange-buff on head, neck and mantle in breeding plumage. Wetlands and grassland; often associated with livestock.

Grey Heron *Ardea cinerea* 90–98 cm

a **b** ADULT and **c** IMMATURE Widespread and frequent resident and winter visitor; below 915 m (–3050 m). In flight, black flight feathers contrast with grey upperwing- and underwing-coverts. Adult has yellow bill, whitish head and neck with black head plumes, and black patches on belly. Immature has dark cap with variable crest, greyer neck, and lacks or has reduced black on belly. *See* Appendix 1 for comparison with White-bellied Heron. Wetlands.

Purple Heron *Ardea purpurea* 78–90 cm

a **b** ADULT and **c** **d** JUVENILE Locally fairly common and widespread; mainly resident, also a monsoon visitor; below 300 m (–1370 m). Rakish, with long, thin neck. In flight, compared with the Grey Heron, bulge of recoiled neck is very pronounced, and protruding feet large. Adult has chestnut head and neck with black stripes, grey mantle and upperwing-coverts, and dark-chestnut belly and underwing-coverts. Juvenile has buffish neck and underparts, and brownish mantle and upperwing-coverts with rufous-buff fringes. Wetlands with tall cover.

Indian Pond Heron *Ardeola grayii* 42–45 cm

a **b** ADULT BREEDING and **c** NON-BREEDING Widespread and common resident; below 1525 m (–2745 m). Whitish wings contrast with dark saddle. Adult breeding plumage has yellowish-buff head and neck, white nape-plumes, and maroon-brown mantle/scapulars. Head, neck and breast streaked in non-breeding plumage. Wetlands.

Little Heron *Butorides striatus* 40–48 cm

a **b** ADULT and **c** JUVENILE Widespread and frequent resident and summer visitor; below 915 m. Small, stocky and short-legged heron. Adult has black crown and long crest, dark greenish upperparts, and greyish underparts. Juvenile has buff streaking on upperparts, and dark-streaked underparts. Wetlands with dense shrub cover.

Black-crowned Night Heron *Nycticorax nycticorax* 58–65 cm

a **b** ADULT and **c** JUVENILE Resident and summer visitor; locally common and widespread, but rather patchily distributed; below 1370 m. Stocky heron, with thick neck. Adult has black crown and mantle contrasting with grey wings and whitish underparts. Breeding plumage has elongated white nape plumes. Juvenile is boldly streaked and spotted. Immature resembles juvenile but has unstreaked brown mantle/scapulars. Wetlands, often with reedbeds.

Yellow Bittern *Ixobrychus sinensis* 38 cm

a **b** ADULT MALE and **c** JUVENILE Local and uncommon, mainly a summer visitor, a few winter records; below 250 m. Small size. Yellowish-buff wing coverts contrast with dark-brown flight feathers. Male has pinkish-brown mantle/scapulars, and face and sides of neck are wine-red coloured. Female is similar to male but with rufous streaking on black crown, rufous-orange streaking on foreneck and breast, and diffuse buff edges to rufous-brown mantle/scapulars. Juvenile appears buff with bold dark streaking to upperparts including wing coverts; foreneck and breast are heavily streaked. Reedbeds and marshes.

Cinnamon Bittern *Ixobrychus cinnamomeus* 38 cm

a **b** ADULT MALE, **c** FEMALE and **d** JUVENILE Frequent, mainly a summer visitor, but found in all months; chiefly below 250 m, has bred at 1370 m. Small size. Uniform-looking cinnamon-rufous flight feathers and tail in all plumages. Male has cinnamon-rufous crown, hindneck and mantle/scapulars. Female has dark-brown crown and mantle, and dark-brown streaking on foreneck and breast. Juvenile has buff mottling on dark-brown upperparts, and is heavily streaked with dark brown on underparts.

Black Bittern *Dupetor flavicollis* 58 cm

a **b** ADULT and **c** JUVENILE Rare, possibly resident, recorded from east to west; below 250 m. Blackish upperparts including wings, with orange-buff patch on side of neck. Juvenile has rufous fringes to upperparts. Forest pools, marshes and reed-edged lakes.

Great Bittern *Botaurus stellaris* 70–80 cm

a **b** ADULT Rare winter visitor and passage migrant; mainly in the terai (–3050 m). Stocky. Cryptically patterned with golden-brown, blackish and buff. Wet reedbeds.

Black-headed Ibis *Threskiornis melanocephalus* 75 cm

a ADULT BREEDING and **b** IMMATURE Frequent winter visitor, some birds resident, but no breeding records; recorded mainly in the east; below 275 m. Stocky, mainly white ibis with stout down-curved black bill. Adult breeding has naked black head, white lower-neck plumes, variable yellow wash to mantle and breast, and grey on scapulars and elongated tertials. Adult non-breeding has all-white body and lacks neck plumes. Immature has grey feathering on head and neck, and black-tipped wings. Flooded fields, marshes, rivers and pools.

Black Ibis *Pseudibis papillosa* 68 cm

ADULT Frequent and widespread resident; below 275 m (–915 m). Stocky, dark ibis with relatively stout down-curved bill. Has white shoulder patch and reddish legs. Adult has naked black head with red patch on rear crown and nape, and is dark-brown with green-and-purple gloss. Immature dark-brown, including feathered head. *See* Appendix 1 for comparison with Glossy Ibis. Marshes, lakes and fields, sometimes in dry cultivation.

Eurasian Spoonbill *Platalea leucorodia* 80–90 cm

a ADULT BREEDING and **b** JUVENILE Mainly a passage migrant and winter visitor, small numbers resident, flocks regularly recorded from Koshi marshes, rare elsewhere; 75–120 m (–915 m). White, with spatulate-tipped bill. Adult has black bill with yellow tip; has crest and yellow breast patch when breeding. Juvenile has pink bill; in flight, shows black tips to primaries. Marshes, lakes and large rivers.

Spot-billed Pelican *Pelecanus philippensis* 140 cm

a b ADULT, **c** IMMATURE and **d** JUVENILE Very local and uncommon non-breeding visitor, seen mainly March–May, all recent records are from Koshi; 75 m. Much smaller than Great White Pelican (*see* Appendix 1), with dingy appearance, rather uniform pinkish bill and pouch (except in breeding condition), and black spotting on upper mandible (except juveniles). Tufted crest/hindneck usually apparent even on young birds. Underwing pattern quite different from the Great White Pelican, showing little contrast between wing coverts and flight feathers and with paler greater coverts producing distinct central panel. Adult breeding has cinnamon-pink rump, underwing-coverts and undertail-coverts; head and neck appear greyish; has purplish skin in front of eye, and pouch is pink to dull purple and blotched with black. Adult non-breeding dirtier greyish-white, with pouch pinkish. Immature has variable grey-brown markings on upperparts. Juvenile has brownish head and neck, brown mantle and upper-wing coverts (fringed with pale buff), and brown flight feathers; spotting on bill initially lacking (and still indistinct at 12 months). Large rivers. Globally threatened.

Size of illustrations:
1–3, 12% of actual size;
4a, 8% of actual size.

Painted Stork *Mycteria leucocephala* 93–100 cm

a b ADULT and **c d** IMMATURE Rare, recorded from east to west, mainly a summer visitor, a few resident in the southwest; below 250 m. Adult has down-curved yellow bill, bare orange-yellow or red face, and red legs; white barring on mainly black upperwing-coverts, pinkish tertials, and black barring across breast. Juvenile dirty greyish-white, with grey-brown (feathered) head and neck and brown lesser coverts; bill and legs duller than adult's. Marshes and lakes.

Asian Openbill *Anastomus oscitans* 68 cm

a ADULT BREEDING and **b c** NON-BREEDING Widespread resident and summer visitor, common at Chitwan, frequent elsewhere; below 250 m. Stout, dull-coloured 'open bill'. Largely white (breeding) or greyish-white (non-breeding), with black flight feathers and tail; legs usually dull pink, brighter in breeding condition. Juvenile has brownish-grey head, neck and breast, and brownish mantle and scapulars slightly paler than the blackish flight feathers. At a distance in flight, best told from the White Stork by dull-coloured bill and black tail. Marshes and lakes.

Woolly-necked Stork *Ciconia episcopus* 75–92 cm

a b ADULT Frequent and widespread resident; mainly below 915 m, occasionally up to 1800 m. Stocky, largely blackish stork with 'woolly' white neck, black 'skullcap', and white vent and undertail-coverts. In flight, upperwing and underwing entirely dark. Juvenile is similar to adult but with duller brown body and wings and feathered forehead. Flooded fields, marshes and lakes.

White Stork *Ciconia ciconia* 100–125 cm

a b ADULT Rare passage migrant; below 305 m (–915 m). Mainly white stork, with black flight feathers, and striking red bill and legs. Generally has cleaner black-and-white appearance than the Asian Openbill Stork. Juvenile is similar to adult but with brown greater coverts and duller brownish-red bill and legs. Red bill and white tail help differentiate it from the Asian Openbill at a distance in flight. Wet grassland and fields.

Black Stork *Ciconia nigra* 90–100 cm

a b ADULT and **c** IMMATURE Frequent and widespread; a winter visitor below 1000 m, up to 2925 m on passage. Adult mainly glossy black, with white lower breast and belly, and red bill and legs; in flight, white underparts and axillaries contrast strongly with black neck and underwing. Juvenile has brown head, neck and upperparts flecked with white; bill and legs greyish-green. Marshes and rivers.

Black-necked Stork *Ephippiorhynchus asiaticus* 129–150 cm

a b ADULT and **c d** IMMATURE Rare resident and winter visitor, only in protected areas; below 305 m. Large, black-and-white stork with long red legs and huge black bill. In flight, wings white except for broad black band across coverts, and tail black. Male has brown iris; yellow in female. Juvenile has fawn-brown head, neck and mantle, mainly brown wing coverts, and mainly blackish-brown flight feathers; legs dark. Marshes and large rivers.

Lesser Adjutant *Leptoptilos javanicus* 110–120 cm

a ADULT BREEDING and **b c** NON-BREEDING Frequent and widespread resident; below 250 m (–1350 m). Flies with neck retracted, as the Greater Adjutant. Smaller than the Greater Adjutant, with slimmer bill that has straighter ridge to culmen. Compared with the Greater Adjutant, the adult shows a pale frontal plate on head, and denser feathering on the head and hindneck which forms small crest. Adult has glossy black mantle and wings, largely black underwing (with white axillaries), white undertail-coverts, and largely black neck ruff (appearing as a black patch on breast sides in flight); in breeding plumage, has narrow white fringes to scapulars and inner greater coverts, and copper spots on median coverts. Juvenile similar to adult, but upperparts dull black and head and neck more densely feathered. Marshes, pools and wet fields. Globally threatened.

Greater Adjutant *Leptoptilos dubius* 120–150 cm

a b c ADULT BREEDING and **d** IMMATURE Rare and erratic non-breeding visitor to the centre and east; below 250 m (–1500 m). Larger than the Lesser Adjutant, with stouter, conical bill with convex ridge to culmen. Adult breeding has bluish-grey mantle, silvery-grey panel across greater coverts, greyish or brownish underwing-coverts, grey undertail-coverts, and more extensive white neck ruff. Further, has blackish face and forehead (with appearance of dried blood) and has neck pouch (visible only when inflated). Adult non-breeding and immature have darker grey mantle and inner wing coverts, and brown greater coverts (which barely contrast with rest of wing); immature with brownish (rather than pale) iris. Marshes. Globally threatened.

Blue-naped Pitta *Pitta nipalensis* 25 cm

a MALE and **b** FEMALE Rare and very local, possibly resident, all recent records are from the hills surrounding the Kathmandu Valley; 1525 m. Large and stocky, with fulvous underparts. Male has glistening blue hindcrown and nape. Female has smaller greenish-blue patch on nape. Has a powerful double whistle. Broadleaved evergreen forest.

Hooded Pitta *Pitta sordida* 19 cm

ADULT Probably a summer visitor, very local, common at Chitwan, rare elsewhere; below 305 m. Black head with chestnut crown, green breast and flanks, and black belly patch. Song is an explosive double whistle, *wieuw-wieuw*. Calls include a *skyeew*. Broadleaved evergreen and moist deciduous forest with thick undergrowth.

Indian Pitta *Pitta brachyura* 19 cm

ADULT Local summer visitor, common at Chitwan, rare elsewhere; below 245 m (−1360 m). Bold black stripe through eye, white throat and supercilium, buff lateral crown stripes, and buff breast and flanks. Song is a sharp two-noted whistle, second note descending, *pree-treer*. Broadleaved forest with dense undergrowth.

Long-tailed Broadbill *Psarisomus dalhousiae* 28 cm

a ADULT and **b** JUVENILE Scarce and local resident; 275–1340 m. Long tail, which is often held cocked. Green, with black cap, and yellow 'ear' spot and throat. Juvenile has green cap. Has a loud, piercing *pieu-wieuw-wieuw-wieuw...*, usually five to eight notes on the same pitch. Moist broadleaved forest.

Asian Fairy Bluebird *Irena puella* 25 cm

a MALE and **b** FEMALE Rare and local resident, mainly in the southeast; below 365 m. Male has glistening violet-blue upperparts and black underparts. Female and first-year male entirely dull blue-green. Calls include a loud, liquid *tu-lip*. Moist broadleaved forest.

Golden-fronted Leafbird *Chloropsis aurifrons* 19 cm

ADULT Fairly common and widespread resident below 365 m; uncommon up to 915 m (−2285 m). Lacks blue on wings and tail. Adult has golden-orange forehead, yellowish border to black throat, and green underparts. Juvenile head green, with hint of turquoise moustachial stripe. Broadleaved forest and secondary growth.

Orange-bellied Leafbird *Chloropsis hardwickii* 20 cm

a MALE and **b** FEMALE Frequent and widespread resident; 250–2750 m, mainly 1300–2135 m. Male has orange belly, and black of throat extends to breast. Has purplish-blue edges to flight feathers and tail which appear blackish at distance. Female has orange belly centre and large blue moustachial stripe. Juvenile has green head; some with touch of orange on belly. Broadleaved forest.

Rufous-tailed Shrike *Lanius isabellinus* 18–19 cm

a MALE, **b** FEMALE and **c** 1ST-WINTER Very rare winter visitor; below 1340 m (–4050 m). Typically, has paler sandy-brown/grey-brown mantle and warmer rufous rump and tail than the Brown Shrike. Male has small white patch at base of primaries which is lacking in the Brown Shrike. Female is similar to male but lacks white patch in wing, and has grey-brown (rather than blackish) ear-coverts, and usually with some scaling on underparts. First-winter birds are similar to female but with pale fringes and dark subterminal lines to scapulars, wing coverts, and tertials. Open dry scrub country.

Brown Shrike *Lanius cristatus* 18–19 cm

a MALE and **b** 1ST-WINTER Fairly common winter visitor from central areas eastwards, uncommon farther west; mainly below 1525 m (–2700 m). Compared with the Rufous-tailed Shrike, typically has darker rufous-brown upperparts (lacking clear contrast between mantle and tail); also thicker bill and more graduated tail. Female has a darker mask than the female Rufous-tailed Shrike with more prominent white supercilium. Forest edges, scrub, open forest and bushy hillsides.

Bay-backed Shrike *Lanius vittatus* 17 cm

a ADULT, **b** IMMATURE and **c** JUVENILE Mainly a passage migrant, also recorded in summer and winter; below 335 m (–3965 m). Adult has black forehead and mask contrasting with pale-grey crown and nape, deep maroon mantle, whitish rump, and white patch at base of primaries. Juvenile told from juvenile Long-tailed Shrike by smaller size and shorter tail, more uniform greyish/buffish base colour to upperparts, pale rump, more intricately patterned wing coverts and tertials (with buff fringes and dark subterminal crescents and central marks), and primary coverts are prominently tipped with buff. First-year like washed-out version of adult; lacks black forehead. Open dry scrub, and bushes in cultivation.

Long-tailed Shrike *Lanius schach* 25 cm

a ADULT and **b** JUVENILE *L. s. erythronotus*; **c** ADULT *L. s. tricolor* Mainly resident, common and widespread; summers 300–3100 m, chiefly 1500–2700 m, sometimes winters in the foothills and terai. Two integrading races occur: *L. s. tricolor* chiefly in central areas and eastwards; *L. s. erythronotus* in the west. Adult has grey mantle, rufous scapulars and upper back, narrow black forehead, rufous sides to black tail, and small white patch on primaries. Juvenile has (dark-barred) rufous-brown scapulars, back and rump; dark greater coverts and tertials fringed rufous. Bushes in cultivation and in open country, lightly wooded areas and gardens.

Grey-backed Shrike *Lanius tephronotus* 25 cm

a ADULT and **b** JUVENILE Fairly common and widespread resident; summers 2200–4000 m (–4575 m), winters from 275 m to at least 2560 m. Adult has dark grey upperparts (no rufous on scapulars and upper back). Also usually lacks, or has only very indistinct, white patch at base of primaries, and lacks, or has very narrow, black forehead band. Juvenile has cold grey base colour to upperparts. Bushes in cultivation, scrub and secondary growth.

Southern Grey Shrike *Lanius meridionalis* 24 cm

a ADULT and **b** JUVENILE Local and mainly uncommon resident; 75–250 m. Narrow black forehead and broad black mask, grey mantle with white scapulars, broad white tips to secondaries, white sides and tip to tail, and white underparts. Juvenile has sandy cast to grey upperparts, buff tips to tertials and coverts, and grey mask. Open dry scrub country.

Eurasian Jay *Garrulus glandarius* 32–36 cm

ADULT Widespread, but local resident, fairly common in some places; mainly 1800–2440 m (900–2750 m). Reddish-brown head and body, black moustachial stripe, and blue barring on wings. White rump contrasts with black tail in flight. Broadleaved forest, mainly of oaks.

Black-headed Jay *Garrulus lanceolatus* 33 cm

ADULT Resident, common in the far west, uncommon farther east; 915–2500 m. Black face and crest, streaked throat, and pinkish-fawn body; blue barring on wings and tail. Oak and mixed broadleaved forest.

Yellow-billed Blue Magpie *Urocissa flavirostris* 61–66 cm

a ADULT *U. f. cucullata* and **b** ADULT *U. f. flavirostris* Common and widespread resident; mainly above 2440 m all year, summers up to 3660 m, sometimes winters down to 1850 m (–1300 m). Blue upperparts with very long, graduated, black-and-white-tipped tail. Differentiated from Red-billed Blue Magpie by yellow bill, and white on head restricted to crescent on nape. Nominate eastern race has yellow wash to underparts. Juvenile has olive-yellow bill. Broadleaved and coniferous forests.

Red-billed Blue Magpie *Urocissa erythrorhyncha* 65–68 cm

ADULT Common and widespread resident; chiefly 365–1525 m, occasionally to 2200 m in summer (150–3050 m). Differentiated from Yellow-billed Blue Magpie by red bill, and extensive white hindcrown and nape. Underparts are white. Juvenile has duller red bill and more extensive white crown compared with adult. Broadleaved and mixed forests.

Common Green Magpie *Cissa chinensis* 37–39 cm

ADULT Resident, locally fairly common in west-central areas and in the east; 245–1830 m, mainly below 1200 m (–2300 m). Green, with red bill and legs, black mask, chestnut wings, and white tips to tertials and tail feathers. Moist broadleaved forest.

Rufous Treepie *Dendrocitta vagabunda* 46–50 cm

ADULT Resident, widespread and common below 1050 m, uncommon up to 1370 m (–1800 m). Slate-grey hood, rufous-brown mantle, pale-grey wing panel, buffish underparts and rump, and whitish subterminal tail-band. Juvenile has brown hood. Open wooded country, groves and trees at edges of cultivation.

Grey Treepie *Dendrocitta formosae* 36–40 cm

ADULT Common and widespread resident; summers chiefly 1050–2150 m (–2590 m), winters 915–1525 m (–80 m). Dark grey face, grey underparts and rump, and black wings with white patch at base of primaries. Juvenile duller version of adult. Broadleaved forest and secondary growth.

Hume's Groundpecker *Pseudopodoces humilis* 19 cm

ADULT Frequent resident in the trans-Himalayan region in the north-west; 3965–5335 m. Down-curved black bill. Sandy-brown upperparts, buffish underparts, and white tail sides. Ground-dwelling and very active; flicking wings and moves quickly by bounding hops. Tibetan steppe country.

Spotted Nutcracker *Nucifraga caryocatactes* 32–35 cm

ADULT Common and widespread resident; summers mainly 2745–3660 m (–1500 m), winters from at least 2135–3050 m (–305 m). Mainly brown, with white spotting on head and body. In flight, shows white sides and tip to tail. Call is a far-carrying, dry and harsh *kraaaak*. Coniferous forest.

Red-billed Chough *Pyrrhocorax pyrrhocorax* 36–40 cm

ADULT Resident. Common and widespread resident; mainly above 2400 m, summers up to 5490 m (–7950 m), sometimes winters down to 2135 m (–1450 m). Curved red bill (shorter and orange-brown on juvenile). Call is a far-carrying, penetrating and nasal *chaow...chaow*. Gregarious throughout year, often in flocks of several hundred. High mountains, alpine pastures and cultivation.

Yellow-billed Chough *Pyrrhocorax graculus* 37–39 cm

ADULT Common and widespread resident; chiefly above 3500 m and up to at least 6250 m (2350–8235 m). Almost straight yellow bill (olive-yellow on juvenile). Call is a far-carrying, rippling *preeep*, and a decending whistled *sweeeoo*. Habits are similar to the Red-billed Chough, and often in mixed flocks, but generally occurs at higher altitude. High mountains, alpine pastures and cultivation.

House Crow *Corvus splendens* 40 cm

ADULT Common and widespread resident; below 1525 m (–2100 m). Two-toned appearance, with paler nape, neck and breast. Around human habitation and cultivation.

Large-billed Crow *Corvus macrorhynchos* 46–59 cm

a **b** ADULT *C. m. intermedius* and **c** **d** ADULT *C. m. culminatus* Common and widespread resident; below 1525 m (–2100 m). All black, lacking paler collar of the House Crow. Domed head, and large bill with arched culmen. Four races are known from Nepal. The two Himalayan forms (*intermedius* and *tibetosinensis*) are bigger and with heavier bill, wedge-shaped tail, and harsher calls, compared with the two races from the lowlands (*culminatus* and *levaillantii*). Himalayan forms are best differentiated from the Common Raven by absence of throat hackles, shorter and broader wings, less strongly wedge-shaped tail, squarer or domed crown, and dry *kaaa-kaaa* call. Forest, cultivation and open country above the treeline; usually associated with towns and villages.

Common Raven *Corvus corax* 58–69 cm

a **b** ADULT Fairly common resident in the trans- and High Himalayas; mainly from 3500 m up to at least 5000 m (2500–8235 m). Very large; long and angular wings, prominent throat hackles, and wedge-shaped tail. Call is a loud, deep resonant, croaking *wock...wock* call, different from other crows. Dry rocky areas above the tree-line.

Ashy Woodswallow *Artamus fuscus*   19 cm

   a   **b**   ADULT   Local resident; common in the east, fairly common in central areas, uncommon elsewhere; mainly below 365 m (– 2560 m). Slate-grey head, pinkish-grey underparts, and narrow whitish horseshoe-shaped band across uppertail-coverts. Spends much time hawking insect prey on the wing, with much gliding interspersed with short bouts of rapid wing-flapping. Open wooded country.

Eurasian Golden Oriole *Oriolus oriolus*   25 cm

   a   MALE,   **b**   FEMALE and   **c**   IMMATURE   Widespread summer visitor, common at Chitwan, frequent elsewhere; below 1830 m (–2600 m). Male golden-yellow, with black mask and mainly black wings. Female and immature variable, usually with streaking on underparts and yellowish-green upperparts. Song is a loud, fluty *weela-wheo-oh*. Open woodland, and trees in cultivation.

Slender-billed Oriole *Oriolus tenuirostris*   27 cm

   a   MALE,   **b**   FEMALE and   **c**   IMMATURE   Scarce from central areas eastwards, probably a winter visitor; below 2285 m. Long, slender, slightly downcurved bill. Adult has black stripe through eye and band across nape (diffuse or indistinct on immature). Utters mellow, fluty notes, *whee-ow* or *chuck, trarry-you*, and has woodpecker-like *kick* call. Trees in open country and groves.

Black-hooded Oriole *Oriolus xanthornus*   25 cm

   a   MALE,   **b**   FEMALE and   **c**   IMMATURE   Resident, widespread and common below 365 m; uncommon up to 915 m; rare to 1370 m. Adult has black head and breast; female's upperparts duller than male's. Immature has yellow forehead, and black-streaked white throat. Song is a mixture of mellow, fluty notes, *wye-you* or *wye-you-you*. Open broadleaved forest and well-wooded areas.

Maroon Oriole *Oriolus traillii*   27 cm

   a   MALE,   **b**   FEMALE and   **c**   IMMATURE   Locally fairly common and quite widespread resident; summers mainly 1500–2440 m, winters 1200–1800 m (–75 m). Maroon rump and tail. Male has maroon underparts. Female has whitish belly and flanks, streaked with maroon-grey. Immature has brown-streaked white underparts. Dense broadleaved forest.

Large Cuckooshrike *Coracina macei*   30 cm

   a   MALE and   **b**   FEMALE   Common and widespread resident; summers up to 2135 m (–2440 m), winters up to at least 1525 m. Large and mainly pale grey in coloration. Female has grey barring on underparts. Song is a rich, fluty *pi-io-io*. Open woodland, and trees in cultivation.

Black-winged Cuckooshrike *Coracina melaschistos*   24 cm

   a   MALE and   **b**   FEMALE   Fairly widespread resident; frequent up to 915 m all year, to 2400 m in summer. Male slate-grey, with black wings and bold white tips to tail feathers. Female paler grey, with faint barring on underparts. Open forest and groves.

Black-headed Cuckooshrike *Coracina melanoptera*   18 cm

   a   MALE and   **b**   FEMALE   Scarce, recorded mainly in spring and summer; below 275 m (–1430 m). Male has slate-grey head and breast, and pale-grey mantle. Female has whitish supercilium, barred underparts, pale-grey back and rump contrasting with blackish tail, and broad white fringes to coverts and tertials. Open broadleaved forest and secondary growth.

Rosy Minivet *Pericrocotus roseus*   20 cm
   a MALE and **b** FEMALE   Local, possibly resident, frequent at Chitwan, uncommon elsewhere; mainly below 245 m (–1370 m). Male has grey-brown upperparts, white throat, and pinkish underparts and rump. Female has greyish forehead, white throat, pale yellow underparts, and dull olive-yellow rump. Broadleaved forest.

Small Minivet *Pericrocotus cinnamomeus*   16 cm
   a MALE and **b** FEMALE   Frequent and widespread resident; below 290 m (–915 m). Small size. Male has grey upperparts, dark-grey throat, and orange underparts. Female has pale throat and orange wash on underparts. Open wooded areas.

Grey-chinned Minivet *Pericrocotus solaris*   18 cm
   a MALE and **b** FEMALE   Scarce resident from west-central areas eastwards; 250–2075 m. Male has grey chin, pale orange throat, grey ear-coverts, slate-grey upperparts, and orange-red underparts and rump. Female has grey forehead, supercilium and ear-coverts, whitish chin and whitish sides to yellow throat. Moist broadleaved forest.

Long-tailed Minivet *Pericrocotus ethologus*   20 cm
   a MALE and **b** FEMALE   Common and widespread resident; summers 1200–3500 m (–3965 m), winters 245–2135 m. Male has extension of red wing patch down secondaries. Female has narrow, indistinct yellow wash on forehead and supercilium, grey ear-coverts, and paler yellow throat than breast. Distinctive *pi-ru* whistle. Forest; also well-wooded areas in winter.

Short-billed Minivet *Pericrocotus brevirostris*   20 cm
   a MALE and **b** FEMALE   Scarce resident from west-central areas eastwards; 1005–2745 m. Male lacks extension of red wing patch down secondaries which is shown by the Long-tailed Minivet. Further, the male is more crimson-red (rather than scarlet-red) on underparts than the Long-tailed Minivet. The black on the throat extends further onto breast, and the Short-billed Minivet has glossier black upperparts (although these features are variable and often difficult to detect in the field). Female has yellow forehead and cast to ear-coverts, and deep-yellow throat concolorous with rest of underparts. Distinctive monotone whistle. Broadleaved forest and forest edges.

Scarlet Minivet *Pericrocotus flammeus*   20–22 cm
   a MALE and **b** FEMALE   Common and widespread resident; below 2200 m. Best recognised by large size and isolated patch of colour on secondaries, red in male and yellow in female. Male is more orange-red than the Long-tailed and Short-billed minivets. Head pattern of female closest to female Short-billed Minivet. Broadleaved and coniferous forests.

Bar-winged Flycatcher-shrike *Hemipus picatus*   15 cm
   a MALE and **b** FEMALE   Common and widespread resident; below 1830 m. Dark cap contrasts with white sides of throat; has white wing patch and white rump. Female's cap browner than male. Broadleaved forest and forest edges.

Yellow-bellied Fantail *Rhipidura hypoxantha*   13 cm
MALE   Common and widespread resident; summers chiefly 2440–4000 m; winters 1200–1800 m (150–2560 m). Long fanned tail, yellow supercilium, dark mask, and yellow underparts. Forests and high-altitude shrubberies.

White-throated Fantail *Rhipidura albicollis*   19 cm
ADULT   Fairly common and widespread resident up to 1500 m, sometimes to 2440 m. Narrow white supercilium and white throat; lacks spotting on wing coverts. Broadleaved forest and secondary growth.

White-browed Fantail *Rhipidura aureola*   18 cm
ADULT   Fairly widespread resident; uncommon in most areas; below 275 m. Broad white supercilia which meet over forehead, blackish throat, white breast and belly, and white spotting on wing coverts. Forest undergrowth.

Black Drongo *Dicrurus macrocercus* 28 cm

a IMMATURE and **b** ADULT Common and widespread resident; from 75 m up to at least 1525 m all year, in summer sometimes to 2000 m. Adult has glossy blue-black underparts and white rictal spot. Tail-fork may be lost during moult. Immature has black underparts with bold whitish fringes. Around habitation and cultivation.

Ashy Drongo *Dicrurus leucophaeus* 29 cm

a IMMATURE and **b** ADULT Common and widespread resident and partial migrant; summers 1220–2745 m, winters 1065–1525 m; also a locally common resident in the lowlands. Adult has dark-grey underparts and slate-grey upperparts with blue-grey gloss; iris bright red. Immature has brownish-grey underparts with indistinct pale fringes. Broadleaved and coniferous forests.

White-bellied Drongo *Dicrurus caerulescens* 24 cm

a IMMATURE and **b** ADULT Locally common and widespread resident; below 305 m. Similar to Ashy Drongo, but with white belly and shorter tail with shallower tail-fork. Immature is similar to adult but throat and breast is browner and border with white belly is less clearly defined. Open forest and well-wooded areas.

Crow-billed Drongo *Dicrurus annectans* 28 cm

a IMMATURE and **b** ADULT Probably a local and uncommon summer visitor; below 250 m. Adult has stout bill, and widely splayed tail with shallow tail-fork. Immature has white spotting on breast and belly. Moist broadleaved forest.

Bronzed Drongo *Dicrurus aeneus* 24 cm

ADULT Fairly common resident; summers mainly below 1600 m, sometimes to 2000 m, usually winters below 1220 m. Adult small, with shallow tail-fork. Heavily spangled. Clearings and edges of moist broadleaved forest.

Lesser Racket-tailed Drongo *Dicrurus remifer* 25 cm

a IMMATURE and **b** ADULT Local and frequent resident; 915–1800 m (150–2440 m). Tufted forehead without crest, square-ended tail, and smaller size and bill than Greater Racket-tailed Drongo. Tail-rackets are smaller, flattened and webbed on both sides of shaft, while the Greater Racket-tailed Drongo has longer tail-rackets that are twisted and webbed on only one side. Moist broadleaved forest.

Spangled Drongo *Dicrurus hottentottus* 32 cm

ADULT Fairly widespread resident; fairly common below 1050 m, uncommon up to 1525 m (–4115 m). Broad tail with upward-twisted corners, and long down-curved bill. Adult has extensive spangling, and hair-like crest. Moist broadleaved forest; associated with flowering trees, especially silk cotton.

Greater Racket-tailed Drongo *Dicrurus paradiseus* 32 cm

a IMMATURE and **b** ADULT, Fairly widespread resident; locally common below 150 m; uncommon up to 365 m (–1370 m). Larger and with larger bill than the Lesser Racket-tailed Drongo. Has prominent crest and forked tail; crest much reduced in immature. Open broadleaved forest.

Black-naped Monarch *Hypothymis azurea* 16 cm

a MALE and **b** FEMALE Local and frequent resident; below 365 m. Male mainly blue, with black nape and throat. Female lacks these features and is duller, with grey-brown mantle and wings. Middle storey of broadleaved forest.

Asian Paradise-flycatcher *Terpsiphone paradisi* 20 cm

a WHITE MALE, **b** RUFOUS MALE and **c** FEMALE Summer visitor, common at Chitwan, now uncommon elsewhere; below 1525 m. Male has black head and crest, with white or rufous upperparts and long tail-streamers. Female and immatures have reduced crest and lacks streamers. Open forest, groves and gardens.

Common Iora *Aegithina tiphia* 14 cm

a MALE BREEDING and **b** FEMALE Common and widespread resident below 365 m, frequent up to 1900 m; a summer visitor at higher altitudes. Green upperparts, yellow underparts and prominent white wing-bars. Male has black tail, and may have some black markings on crown and nape in breeding plumage. Female has a green tail. Open broadleaved forest and well-wooded areas.

Large Woodshrike *Tephrodornis gularis* 23 cm

a MALE and **b** FEMALE Resident, locally fairly common below 365 m; uncommon up to 1450 m. Male has black mask and grey crown and nape; mask, crown and nape browner in female. Larger than the Common Woodshrike; lacks white supercilium and white on tail. Broadleaved forest and well-wooded areas.

Common Woodshrike *Tephrodornis pondicerianus* 18 cm

ADULT Locally fairly common resident; below 455 m. Smaller than Large Woodshrike, with broad white supercilium and white tail sides. Open broadleaved forest, secondary growth and well-wooded areas.

White-throated Dipper *Cinclus cinclus* 20 cm

a ADULT and **b** JUVENILE Fairly common resident in the trans-Himalayan region; 3500–4800 m (–2590 m). Adult has white throat and breast. Juvenile has dark scaling on grey upperparts, and grey scaling on whitish underparts. Rocky fast-flowing mountain streams.

Brown Dipper *Cinclus pallasii* 20 cm

a ADULT and **b** JUVENILE Common and widespread resident 800–3100 m; frequent up to 4960 m in summer. Adult entirely brown. Juvenile has pale spotting on brown upperparts and underparts. Rocky fast-flowing mountain streams and small lakes.

Blue-capped Rock Thrush *Monticola cinclorhynchus* 17 cm

a MALE BREEDING, **b** FEMALE and **c** 1ST-WINTER MALE Frequent summer visitor; 1200–2135 m (–275 m on passage). Male has white wing patch, blue crown and throat, and orange rump and underparts; bright coloration obscured by pale fringes in non-breeding and first-winter plumages. Female has uniform olive-brown upperparts; lacks buff neck patch of Chestnut-bellied Rock Thrush. Open dry forest and rocky slopes with scattered trees.

Chestnut-bellied Rock Thrush *Monticola rufiventris* 23 cm

a MALE and **b** FEMALE Fairly common and widespread resident; summers mainly 1800–3400 m (–4460 m), winters 915–2380 m. Male has chestnut-red underparts and blue rump and uppertail-coverts; lacks white on wing. Female has orange-buff neck patch, dark barring on slaty olive-brown upperparts, and heavy scaling on underparts. Juvenile has pale spotting on upperparts; male with blue on wing. Open broadleaved and coniferous forests on rocky slopes.

Blue Rock Thrush *Monticola solitarius* 20 cm

a MALE BREEDING, **b** FEMALE and **c** 1ST-WINTER MALE Widespread resident; frequent in summer in the trans-Himalayan region, 2590–4880 m; winters below 1400 m. Male indigo-blue, with bright coloration obscured by pale fringes in non-breeding and first-winter plumages. Female has bluish cast to slaty-brown upperparts, and buff scaling on underparts. Breeds on open rocky slopes and cliffs; winters along streams, rivers and amongst old buildings.

Blue Whistling Thrush *Myophonus caeruleus* 33 cm

ADULT Common and widespread resident; summers from 1500 m up to the tree-line (470–4800 m), most frequent up to 3100 m, winters below 2745 m. Adult blackish, spangled with glistening blue; yellow bill. Juvenile browner, and lacks blue spangling. Forest and wooded areas, usually close to streams or rivers.

Pied Thrush *Zoothera wardii* 22 cm

a MALE and **b** FEMALE Widespread, but uncommon summer visitor; mainly 1500–2400 m (–3050 m). Male black and white, with white supercilium and wing-bars, and yellow bill. Female has buff supercilium, buff wing-bars and tips to tertials, and scaled underparts. Open broadleaved forest and secondary growth.

Orange-headed Thrush *Zoothera citrina* 21 cm

a MALE and **b** FEMALE Widespread and fairly common partial migrant, mainly a summer visitor; 250–1830 m, rare in winter below 250 m (–915 m). Adult has orange head and underparts; male with blue-grey mantle, female with olive-brown wash to mantle. Damp, shady places in forest, often in wet ravines.

Plain-backed Thrush *Zoothera mollissima* 27 cm

ADULT Fairly common resident; summers 3000–4000 m, winters 1500–2400 m (–2700 m). Best told from the Long-tailed Thrush by absent or indistinct wing-bars. Further subtle differences are more rufescent coloration to upperparts, less pronounced pale wing panel, more extensive black scaling on belly and flanks, and shorter-looking tail. Summers on rocky and grassy slopes with bushes; winters in forest and open country with bushes.

Long-tailed Thrush *Zoothera dixoni* 27 cm

ADULT Frequent resident; summers 2100–4520 m; winters 1500–2700 m. Adult has prominent wing-bars; belly and flanks more sparsely marked than on the Plain-backed Thrush, flanks more barred than scaled, and appears longer-tailed. Undergrowth in forests of birch, fir or juniper; thick forest, often near streams in winter.

Scaly Thrush *Zoothera dauma* 26–27 cm

ADULT Widespread and fairly common partial migrant; summers 2320–3300 m (–3540 m), winters 75–1500 m. Boldly scaled upperparts and underparts. Juvenile has spotted breast. Thick forest with dense undergrowth, often near streams.

Long-billed Thrush *Zoothera monticola* 28 cm

ADULT Resident; frequent in winter, 915–2500 m (– 75 m); summers 2285–3850 m. Huge bill and short tail. Differs from Dark-sided Thrush in larger bill with prominent hook, dark lores, dark slate-olive upperparts, darker and more uniform sides of head and underparts, and dark spotting on belly. Moist, dense forest, usually near streams.

Dark-sided Thrush *Zoothera marginata* 25 cm

ADULT Rare, possibly resident; 200–2440 m. Long bill and short tail. Differs from the Long-billed Thrush in rufescent-brown upperparts, pale lores, more strongly marked sides of head (dark ear-covert patch with pale crescent behind), paler underparts with more prominent scaling on breast and flanks, and rufous panel on wing. Moist, dense forest near streams.

Tickell's Thrush *Turdus unicolor* 21 cm

a MALE, **b** FEMALE and **c** 1ST-WINTER MALE Mainly a fairly common summer visitor, 1500–2450 m (–2745 m); several winter reports, 150–1280 m. Small thrush. Male is pale bluish-grey, with whitish belly and vent. Female and first-winter male have pale throat and submoustachial stripe, dark malar stripe, and often have spotting on breast. Open broadleaved forest.

White-collared Blackbird *Turdus albocinctus* 27 cm

a MALE and **b** FEMALE Fairly common and widespread resident; summers chiefly 2400–3445 m (–3750 m), winters 1525–3000 m, mainly above 2100 m (–80 m). Male black, with white collar. Female brown, with variable pale collar. Broadleaved and coniferous forests and forest edges.

Grey-winged Blackbird *Turdus boulboul* 28 cm

a MALE and **b** FEMALE Common and widespread resident; summers chiefly 2100–2745 m (1850–3300 m), winters 1400–1980 m (–75 m). Male black, with greyish wing panel. Female olive-brown, with pale rufous-brown wing panel. Moist broadleaved forest and forest edges.

Eurasian Blackbird *Turdus merula* 25–28 cm

a MALE and **b** FEMALE An erratic visitor, mainly in winter and spring, a few summer records; 3305–4800 m (–75 m). Male is entirely black and female mainly brown, lacking pale collar or pale wing panel which are shown by similar species. Juniper scrub.

Chestnut Thrush *Turdus rubrocanus* 27 cm

a MALE and **b** FEMALE *T. r. rubrocanus*; **c** MALE *T. r. gouldii* Uncommon and erratic winter visitor; mainly 2000–2745 m (915–3100 m). Chestnut upperparts and underparts. Male *rubrocanus* has pale collar; female has more uniform brownish-grey head/neck. *T. r. gouldii*, which is a vagrant, has darker head/neck and lacks collar. Open wooded areas with fruiting trees.

Kessler's Thrush *Turdus kessleri* 27 cm

a MALE and **b** FEMALE Scarce and erratic winter visitor; 3440–4330 m. Male has black head, creamy-white mantle and breast-band, and chestnut back and belly. Female has brownish head, pale mantle and breast-band, and ginger-brown belly. Mixed birch and rhododendron forest, juniper and *Berberis* shrubberies and cultivation.

Eyebrowed Thrush *Turdus obscurus* 23 cm

a MALE and **b** 1ST-WINTER FEMALE Scarce winter visitor to the east; 1500–2300 m. White supercilium, greyish crown and ear-coverts, and orange flanks. Open forest.

Dark-throated Thrush *Turdus ruficollis* 25 cm

a MALE, **b** FEMALE and **c** 1ST-WINTER FEMALE *T. r. ruficollis*; **d** MALE, **e** FEMALE and **f** 1ST-WINTER FEMALE *T. r. atrogularis* Common and widespread winter visitor; below 4200 m. Two races occur: *T. r. atrogularis* 75–4200 m; *T. r. ruficollis* mainly 2400–3900 m. Uniform grey upperparts and wings. *T. r. ruficollis* has red throat and/or breast, and red on tail; first-winter has rufous wash to supercilium and breast. *T. r. atrogularis* has black throat and/or breast; first-winter has grey streaking on breast and flanks. Forest, forest edges, cultivation and pastures with scattered trees.

Dusky Thrush *Turdus naumanni* 24 cm

a MALE and **b** 1ST-WINTER Scarce winter visitor; 75–3175 m. Prominent supercilium, spotting across breast and down flanks, and chestnut on wing. First-winter birds can be very dull, with chestnut in wings sometimes not apparent. Broader supercilium and spotting on flanks are best features from Dark-throated Thrush. Pastures with scattered trees and cultivation.

Mistle Thrush *Turdus viscivorus* 27 cm

ADULT Resident. Fairly common and widespread resident in the west; summers mainly 2400–3800 m, winters 2135–3050 m (down to 1525 m). Large size, pale grey-brown upperparts, whitish edges to wing feathers, and spotted breast. Summers in open coniferous forest and shrubberies; winters on grassy slopes and at forest edges.

1 Dark-sided Flycatcher *Muscicapa sibirica* 14 cm
ADULT Fairly common and widespread summer visitor, 2000–3300 m (–275 m on passage); one winter record at 915 m. Small dark bill, and long primary projection. Breast and flanks heavily marked, with narrow pale line down centre of belly. Canopy of open forest.

2 Asian Brown Flycatcher *Muscicapa dauurica* 13 cm
ADULT Mainly an uncommon passage migrant and summer visitor; summers 1000–1550 m; rare in winter. Large bill with prominent pale base to lower mandible. Shorter primary projection than the Dark-sided Flycatcher, and lores are more extensively pale than in that species. Pale underparts, with light brownish wash to breast and flanks. *See* Appendix 1 for comparison with Brown-breasted Flycatcher. Open broadleaved forest.

3 Rusty-tailed Flycatcher *Muscicapa ruficauda* 14 cm
ADULT Uncommon summer visitor and passage migrant; summers 2440–3655 m (–75 m). Rufous uppertail-coverts and tail, rather plain face, and pale orange lower mandible. Fir, birch and oak forests.

4 Ferruginous Flycatcher *Muscicapa ferruginea* 13 cm
ADULT Scarce summer visitor; 2000–3300 m (–1200 m). Rufous-orange uppertail-coverts and tail, rufous-orange flanks and undertail-coverts, and grey cast to head. Moist broadleaved forest.

5 Slaty-backed Flycatcher *Ficedula hodgsonii* 13 cm
a MALE and **b** FEMALE Scarce and local resident in west-central areas and eastwards; once sighted at 3450 m in summer, all other records at 245–2000 m in winter and early spring. Male has orange underparts, deep-blue upperparts (lacking any patches of glistening blue as in male *Cyornis* flycatchers), and black tail with white at base. Female has greyish-olive underparts, lacking well-defined white throat, and lacks rufous on tail. Fir forest in summer, moist broadleaved forest in winter.

6 Rufous-gorgeted Flycatcher *Ficedula strophiata* 14 cm
a MALE and **b** FEMALE Common and widespread resident; summers mainly 2440–3800 m, winters 915–1830 m (150–2135 m). Rufous throat, and white sides to black tail. Female duller than male. Broadleaved and coniferous forests.

7 Red-throated Flycatcher *Ficedula parva* 11.5–12.5 cm
a MALE and **b** FEMALE Common and widespread winter visitor; below 1830 m (–2590 m on passage). White sides to tail. Male has reddish-orange throat. Female and many males have whitish underparts with greyish breast-band. Open forest, bushes and wooded areas.

8 Kashmir Flycatcher *Ficedula subrubra* 13 cm
a MALE and **b** FEMALE Scarce passage migrant, mainly in spring; below 2135 m. Male has more extensive and deeper red on underparts than Red-throated Flycatcher, with diffuse black border to throat and breast. Female and first-winter male can rather resemble some male Red-throated Flycatchers, but coloration of throat is more rufous, and this coloration is often more pronounced on breast than throat and often continues as wash onto belly and/or flanks. Open broadleaved forest. Globally threatened.

9 White-gorgeted Flycatcher *Ficedula monileger* 13 cm
ADULT Rare, presumably resident, from west-central areas eastwards; 915–3000 m, but altitudinal movements are poorly known. White throat enclosed within black band, with orange-buff supercilium. Dense undergrowth in moist broadleaved forest.

Snowy-browed Flycatcher *Ficedula hyperythra* 11 cm

a MALE and **b** FEMALE Frequent resident; summers 2000–2440 m, sometimes up to 3000 m, winters 275–1525 m. Small size and short tail. Both sexes with rufous-brown wings. Male has short white supercilium, slaty-blue upperparts, and orange throat/breast. Female has orange-buff supercilium and eye-ring. Dense undergrowth in moist broadleaved forest.

Little Pied Flycatcher *Ficedula westermanni* 10 cm

a MALE and **b** FEMALE Uncommon resident; summers 1200–3000 m, winters from 275 m up to at least 915 m (−75 m). Male black and white, with broad white supercilium. Female has grey-brown upperparts, brownish-grey wash to breast, and rufous cast to rump/uppertail-coverts. Breeds in broadleaved forest; also winters in open wooded country.

Ultramarine Flycatcher *Ficedula superciliaris* 12 cm

a MALE and **b** FEMALE *F. s. superciliaris*; **c** MALE *F. s. aestigma* Common and widespread; mainly a summer visitor, 1800–3200 m, a few winter records below 1500 m (−75 m on passage). Male has deep-blue upperparts and sides of neck/breast, and white underparts. Female has greyish-brown breast side patches and lacks rufous on rump/uppertail-coverts. Two intergrading races occur; male *superciliaris* in West Nepal has white supercilium. Breeds in forest; winters in open woodland and wooded areas.

Slaty-blue Flycatcher *Ficedula tricolor* 13 cm

a MALE and **b** FEMALE Common and widespread resident; summers mainly 3050–3400 m (−4000 m), winters 75–2135 m. Male has white throat and white on tail; belly and flanks greyish. Female has white throat and rufous tail. Breeds in subalpine shrubberies, dense bushes and forest edges; winters in forest undergrowth, ravines

Sapphire Flycatcher *Ficedula sapphira* 11 cm

a MALE, **b** FEMALE and **c** IMMATURE MALE Rare, possibly resident; recorded mainly in the east, 2135–2800 m in April and May and 150 m in winter. Small flycatcher with slim appearance and tiny bill. Orange throat and breast contrast with white belly in all plumages. Male has blue breast sides and bright blue or brown-and-blue upperparts. Female has rufous uppertail-coverts and tail. Evergreen broadleaved forest.

Verditer Flycatcher *Eumyias thalassina* 15 cm

a MALE and **b** FEMALE Partial migrant; common and widespread in summer, 1200–2625 m, uncommon up to 3200 m and down to 1000 m; occasionally recorded in winter, mainly 75–350 m. Male greenish-blue to turquoise, with black lores; may be confused with male Pale Blue Flycatcher which, however, has a longer bill. Female duller and greyer, with dusky lores. Open forest and wooded areas, especially of broadleaves.

Grey-headed Canary Flycatcher *Culicicapa ceylonensis* 13 cm

ADULT Common and widespread partial migrant; summers 1200–3100 m, mainly 1500–2400 m, some birds remain to winter below 1800 m. Grey head and breast, yellow rest of underparts, and greenish upperparts. Forest and wooded areas.

Large Niltava *Niltava grandis* 20 cm

a MALE and **b** FEMALE Local and uncommon resident; 1525–2850 m. Large size. Male dark blue, with brilliant blue crown, neck patch and shoulder patch. Female has rufous-buff forecrown and lores, rufescent wings and tail, and buff throat patch; has glistening patch of blue on neck like female Rufous-bellied Niltava. Moist broadleaved forest, especially near streams.

Small Niltava *Niltava macgrigoriae* 11 cm

a MALE and **b** FEMALE Fairly common resident; winters 270–1400 m, summers up to 2200 m. Small size. Male dark blue, with brilliant blue forehead and neck patch. Female has indistinct blue neck patch and rufescent wings and tail; lacks oval throat patch of female Rufous-bellied Niltava. Bushes in broadleaved forest, along streams, edges of tracks and forest clearings.

Rufous-bellied Niltava *Niltava sundara* 18 cm

a MALE and **b** FEMALE Common and widespread resident; winters chiefly 800–1830 m, summers 2135–3200 m. Male has brilliant blue crown and neck patch, and orange on underparts extending to vent. Female has oval-shaped throat patch. Undergrowth in broadleaved forest and secondary growth.

Pale-chinned Flycatcher *Cyornis poliogenys* 18 cm

ADULT Locally common resident from west-central areas eastwards; below 455 m. Greyish head and well-defined cream throat; creamy-orange breast and flanks that merge with belly. Bushes and undergrowth in broadleaved forest.

Pale Blue Flycatcher *Cyornis unicolor* 18 cm

a MALE and **b** FEMALE Rare and local from west-central areas eastwards, presumably resident; 275–1525 m. Male confusable with Verditer Flycatcher but has longer bill, and is pale blue rather than turquoise in coloration with distinctly greyer belly. Has shining blue forecrown and dusky lores. Female very different from the Verditer Flycatcher and more like other *Cyornis*; best recognised by large size and uniform greyish underparts. Moist broadleaved forest.

Blue-throated Flycatcher *Cyornis rubeculoides* 14 cm

a MALE and **b** FEMALE Partial migrant; frequent summer visitor 365–1500 m (150–2135 m); rare in winter 75–300 m. Male has blue throat (some with orange wedge) and well-defined white belly and flanks. Female has poorly defined creamy-orange throat, orange breast well demarcated from white belly, and creamy lores (compare with the Pale-chinned and female Hill Blue flycatchers). Olive-brown head and upperparts and rufescent tail are best features from female Tickell's. Open forest and wooded areas.

Hill Blue Flycatcher *Cyornis banyumas* 14 cm

a MALE and **b** FEMALE Rare resident; central and eastern areas in May and August 1250–3350 m; central middle hills in winter. Long bill and long primary projection. On both sexes, orange of breast and flanks merges gradually with white of belly. Male has blackish ear-coverts. Female has dark lores (compared with Blue-throated and Tickell's Blue Flycatchers) and sharp demarcation between ear-coverts and creamy-orange throat. Dense, moist broadleaved forest.

Tickell's Blue Flycatcher *Cyornis tickelliae* 14 cm

a MALE and **b** FEMALE Scarce, possibly resident in the far west; below 305 m. Male has orange throat and breast with clear horizontal division from white flanks and belly. Female has greyish-blue upperparts (especially rump and tail). Open dry broadleaved forest.

Pygmy Blue Flycatcher *Muscicapella hodgsoni* 10 cm

a MALE and **b** FEMALE Scarce and local resident; 2100–3500 m in breeding season, down to 75 m in winter. Small size, short tail, fine bill, and flowerpecker-like appearance and behaviour. Underparts entirely orange on male and orange-buff on female. Dense, moist broadleaved forest.

Gould's Shortwing *Brachypteryx stellata*   13 cm

ADULT Scarce and very local, possibly resident; summers 3250–3900 m (–450 m on passage). Adult with chestnut upperparts, slate-grey underparts and white star-shaped spotting on belly and flanks. Breeds in rhododendron and juniper shrubberies near the tree-line; winters in forest.

Lesser Shortwing *Brachypteryx leucophrys*   13 cm

a MALE and **b** FEMALE Rare, possibly resident; 250–2135 m January–April. Smaller and shorter-tailed than the White-browed Shortwing, with pinkish legs. Male is pale slaty-blue with white throat and belly. Female is brown with white throat and belly. Both sexes have fine white supercilium that may be obscured. Immature male shows intermediate plumage. Undergrowth in moist broadleaved forest and secondary growth.

White-browed Shortwing *Brachypteryx montana*   15 cm

a MALE, **b** FEMALE and **c** IMMATURE MALE Very uncommon resident; summers 2560–3660 m, winters 245–2375 m. Larger than the Lesser Shortwing with longer tail and dark legs. Male dark slaty-blue, with fine white supercilium. Rufous-orange lores and more uniform brownish underparts of female are features which differentiate it from female Lesser Shortwing. Immature male has fine white supercilium. Dense undergrowth in moist forest, often near streams.

Siberian Rubythroat *Luscinia calliope*   14 cm

a MALE and **b** FEMALE Winter visitor and passage migrant; frequent below 1370 m. Olive-brown upperparts and tail, and white supercilium and moustachial stripe. Male has ruby-red throat and grey breast. Female has olive-buff wash to breast. Legs pale brown. Bushes and thick undergrowth, often near water.

White-tailed Rubythroat *Luscinia pectoralis*   14 cm

a MALE and **b** FEMALE *L. p. pectoralis*; **c** MALE *L. p. tschebaiewi* Frequent and widespread resident; breeds 3300–4800 m, winters 100–1340 m, locally common at 100 m; also a rare passage migrant. Male has ruby-red throat, black breast-band and white on tail. Female has grey upperparts, grey breast-band and white tip to tail. Legs black. *L. p. tschebaiewi* (vagrant to Nepal) has white moustachial stripe in male, sometimes shown also by female. Breeds in subalpine shrubberies, and on alpine slopes; winters in scrub and tall grass in marshes.

Bluethroat *Luscinia svecica*   15 cm

a MALE NON-BREEDING, **b** 1ST-WINTER FEMALE and **c** MALE BREEDING Fairly common and widespread winter visitor and passage migrant; below 1370 m (–3445 m on passage). White supercilium and rufous tail sides..Male has variable blue, black and rufous patterning to throat and breast (patterning obscured by whitish fringes in fresh plumage). Female is less brightly coloured but usually with blue and rufous breast-bands. First-winter female may have just black submoustachial stripe and band of black spotting across breast. Summers in scrub along streams and lakes; winters in scrub and tall grass.

Indian Blue Robin *Luscinia brunnea*   15 cm

a MALE and **b** FEMALE Fairly common and widespread summer visitor 2135–3445 m, mainly 2440–3355 m; two winter records, from foothills and at 3505 m (–75 m on passage). Male has blue upperparts and orange underparts, with white supercilium and black ear-coverts. Female has olive-brown upperparts, and buffish underparts with white throat and belly. Both sexes have light-coloured legs (compared with White-browed Bush Robin). Breeds in forest undergrowth; winters in forest, secondary scrub and plantations.

Orange-flanked Bush Robin *Tarsiger cyanurus* 14 cm

a MALE and **b** FEMALE Common and widespread resident; summers mainly 3000–4000 m, winters 1370–2745 m. White throat, orange flanks, blue tail, and redstart-like stance. Male has blue upperparts and breast sides. Female has olive-brown upperparts and breast sides. Forest understorey and bushes at clearings and edges of forest.

Golden Bush Robin *Tarsiger chrysaeus* 15 cm

a MALE and **b** FEMALE Frequent, locally fairly common resident; summers mainly 3500–4200 m, winters 1700–2800 m. Orange to orange-buff underparts, with orange tail sides. Pale legs. Male has broad orange supercilium, dark mask, and orange scapulars. Female duller, with less distinct supercilium. Summers in subalpine shrubberies and forest undergrowth; winters in forest undergrowth and dense scrub.

White-browed Bush Robin *Tarsiger indicus* 15 cm

a MALE and **b** FEMALE Resident, frequent in the centre and east, very uncommon in the west; summers 3000–4000 m, winters 2100–3050 m (–915 m). Upright stance, long tail, fine and down-curved supercilium, and dark legs (compared with Indian Blue Robin). Male has slaty-blue upperparts and rufous-orange underparts. Female has olive-brown upperparts and dirty orange-buff underparts. Subalpine shrubberies and bushes at forest edges.

Rufous-breasted Bush Robin *Tarsiger hyperythrus* 15 cm

a MALE and **b** FEMALE Locally frequent resident from west-central areas eastwards; summers 3200–4200 m, winters 2135–3050 m (–1500 m). Carriage and profile as Orange-flanked Bush Robin. Male has dark blue upperparts, blackish ear-coverts, glistening blue supercilium and shoulders, and rufous-orange underparts. Female has blue tail and orange-buff throat. Summers in bushes at forest edges; winters in moist forest undergrowth.

Oriental Magpie Robin *Copsychus saularis* 23 cm

a MALE and **b** FEMALE Widespread resident, common below 1525 m; frequent up to 2000 m (–3050 m in summer). Black/slate-grey and white, with white on wing and at sides of tail. Gardens, groves, open broadleaved forest and secondary growth.

White-rumped Shama *Copsychus malabaricus* 22 cm

a MALE and **b** FEMALE Locally fairly common and quite widespread resident; below 365 m. Long, graduated tail and white rump. Male has glossy blue-black upperparts and breast, and rufous-orange underparts. Female duller, with brownish-grey upperparts. Undergrowth in broadleaved forest.

Indian Robin *Saxicoloides fulicata* 19 cm

a MALE and **b** FEMALE Local resident, uncommon in the west, rare in the centre and east; below 760 m. Reddish vent and black tail in all plumages. Male has white shoulders and black underparts. Female has greyish underparts. Dry stony areas with scrub, and cultivation edges.

Rufous-backed Redstart *Phoenicurus erythronota* 16 cm

a MALE BREEDING, **b** 1ST-WINTER MALE and **c** FEMALE Winter visitor, locally fairly common in some years in the northwest; 2300–3300 m. Large size. Often holds tail slightly cocked. Male has rufous mantle and throat, white on wing, and black mask; plumage heavily obscured by pale fringes in non-breeding and first-winter plumages. Female has double buffish wing-bar. Scrub and stone walls bordering fields in dry habitats.

Blue-capped Redstart *Phoenicurus coeruleocephalus* 15 cm

a MALE BREEDING, **b** FEMALE and **c** 1ST-WINTER MALE Resident; fairly common on breeding grounds in the northwest, 2900–3700 m (–4270 m); in non-breeding season, frequent in the west and centre, rare in the east, 1370–2900 m (–150 m). Male has blue-grey cap, black tail, and white on wing; the dark areas have pale fringes in non-breeding and first-winter plumages. Female has grey underparts, prominent double wing-bar, blackish tail, and chestnut rump. Summers on rocky slopes with open forest; winters in open forest and secondary growth.

Black Redstart *Phoenicurus ochruros* 15 cm

a MALE and **b** FEMALE Resident; common in summer in the northwest and frequent in Khumbu, 2560–5200 m (–5700 m); fairly common below 700 m in winter. Male has black upperparts and breast, and rufous underparts. Female is similar to female Hodgson's Redstart but lacks whitish area on belly and has orange-buff wash to flanks and vent. Breeds in Tibetan steppe habitat; winters in cultivation, stony areas and thin scrub.

Hodgson's Redstart *Phoenicurus hodgsoni* 15 cm

a MALE BREEDING and **b** FEMALE Frequent and quite widespread winter visitor, locally common; mainly 760–2800 m (150–5030 m on passage). Male has grey upperparts, white wing patch, and black throat and breast. Female has dusky-brown upperparts, and grey underparts with white on belly. First-winter male is similar in plumage to female. Open forests, grassy areas and cultivation with bushes.

White-throated Redstart *Phoenicurus schisticeps* 15 cm

a MALE and **b** FEMALE Frequent and quite widespread resident and winter visitor; summers 3050–4400 m, from 2500 m up to at least 3150 m in winter (2200–3965 m). Both sexes with white throat, white wing patch, rufous rump and dark tail. Summers in shrubberies on rocky slopes and forest edges; winters in meadows and cultivation and on bush-covered slopes.

White-winged Redstart *Phoenicurus erythrogaster* 18 cm

a MALE and **b** FEMALE Resident and winter visitor; uncommon in summer 4900–5600 m; locally fairly common in some years in winter 2650–3965 m and probably higher. Large size and stocky appearance. Male has white cap and large white patch on wing. Female has buff-brown upperparts and buffish underparts. Breeds in rocky alpine meadows; winters in stony pastures and scrub patches.

Blue-fronted Redstart *Phoenicurus frontalis* 15 cm

a MALE and **b** FEMALE Common and widespread resident; summers chiefly 3350–4900 m, winters 1000–3050 m (–455 m). Orange rump and tail sides, with black centre and tip to tail. Male has blue head and upperparts and chestnut-orange underparts; plumage heavily obscured by rufous-brown fringes in non-breeding and first-winter plumage. Female has dark-brown upperparts and underparts, with orange wash to belly; tail pattern best feature from other female redstarts. Breeds in subalpine shrubberies; winters in bushes and open forest.

White-capped Water Redstart *Chaimarrornis leucocephalus* 19 cm
ADULT Common and widespread resident; summers 1830–5000 m (–5100 m), winters 915–1525 m (75–3500 m). White cap, and rufous tail with broad black terminal band. Mainly mountain streams and rivers.

Plumbeous Water Redstart *Rhyacornis fuliginosus* 12 cm
a MALE and **b** FEMALE Widespread resident; common in summer 1525–3750 m (–600 m), uncommon up to 4420 m, winters 75–2560 m. Male slaty-blue, with rufous-chestnut tail. Female and first-year male have black-and-white tail and white spotting on grey underparts. Mountain streams and rivers, also summers in alpine meadows and rocky areas far from water.

White-bellied Redstart *Hodgsonius phaenicuroides* 18 cm
a MALE and **b** FEMALE Frequent summer visitor, mainly 2900–4270 m (–2450 m); rare winter visitor to foothills, 915 m. Long, graduated tail that is often held cocked and fanned. Male has white belly, rufous tail sides, and white spots on alula. Female has white throat and belly, and chestnut on tail. Breeds in subalpine shrubberies; winters in thick undergrowth and forest edges at lower levels.

White-tailed Robin *Myiomela leucura* 18 cm
a MALE and **b** FEMALE Resident, generally uncommon, locally fairly common; summers 1900–2745 m, winters mainly below 915 m. White patches on tail. Male blue-black, with glistening blue forehead and shoulders. Female olive-brown, with whitish lower throat. Undergrowth in moist broadleaved forest, often near streams.

Little Forktail *Enicurus scouleri* 12 cm
ADULT Fairly common and widespread resident; summers chiefly 1830–4000 m (1150–4240 m), winters 900–1830 m (–400 m). Small and plump, with short tail. White forehead. Mountain streams; also slower-moving streams in winter.

Black-backed Forktail *Enicurus immaculatus* 25 cm
ADULT Resident; frequent from west-central areas eastwards, very uncommon in the west; below 1370 m. Black crown and mantle, and more white on forehead than Slaty-backed Forktail. Fast-flowing streams in moist broadleaved forest.

Slaty-backed Forktail *Enicurus schistaceus* 25 cm
ADULT Resident, generally uncommon, but fairly common locally; 900–1675 m (–450 m). Slaty-grey crown and mantle; less white on forehead and larger bill than Black-backed Forktail. Fast-flowing streams in forest and wooded lake margins.

Spotted Forktail *Enicurus maculatus* 25 cm
ADULT Fairly common and widespread resident; summers mainly 1370–3100 m, winters from 290 m up to at least 2745 m. Large size; white forehead, white spotting on mantle, and black breast. Rocky streams in forest.

Grandala *Grandala coelicolor* 23 cm

a MALE and **b** FEMALE Locally fairly common resident; summers 3900–5500 m; winters mainly 3000–3960 m (–1950 m). Slim and long-winged; a strong flier and often in flocks. Male purple-blue, with darker wings and tail. Female and immature male have white patches on wing, and streaked head and underparts. Rocky slopes and stony meadows; alpine zone in summer, lower altitudes in winter.

Purple Cochoa *Cochoa purpurea* 30 cm

a MALE and **b** FEMALE Rare, possibly resident in central and eastern areas, May–early November; 915–2255 m. Lilac crown, wing panelling and tail (the tail with a dark tip). Male purplish-brown. Female has rufous-brown upperparts and brownish-orange underparts. Song is a broad flute-like *peeeeee*; also *peee-you-peee*. *See* Appendix 1 for comparison with Green Cochoa. Mainly dense moist broadleaved forest.

Hodgson's Bushchat *Saxicola insignis* 17 cm

a MALE NON-BREEDING and **b** FEMALE Very local winter visitor, fairly common at Sukila Phanta, rare at Koshi Barrage; below 150 m (–1380 m). Large size. Male has white throat extending to form almost complete white collar, and more white on wing than the Common Stonechat. Female has broad buffish-white wing-bars and tips to primary coverts. Grassland and tall grasses and reeds along rivers. Globally threatened.

Common Stonechat *Saxicola torquata* 17 cm

a MALE BREEDING, **b** MALE NON-BREEDING and **c** FEMALE Common and widespread resident, winter visitor and passage migrant; summers 365–4880 m, winters below 1500 m. Male has black head, white patch on neck, orange breast, and whitish rump (features obscured in fresh plumage); lacks white in tail. Female has streaked upperparts and orange on breast and rump. Tail darker than in female White-tailed Stonechat. Summers in open country with bushes, including high-altitude semi-desert; winters in scrub, reedbeds and cultivation.

White-tailed Stonechat *Saxicola leucura* 12.5–13 cm

a MALE BREEDING and **b** FEMALE Local and fairly common resident; below 275 m (–915 m). Male has largely white inner webs to tail feathers. Female has greyer upperparts than the Common Stonechat, with diffuse streaking, and paler grey-brown tail. Reeds and tall grassland.

Pied Bushchat *Saxicola caprata* 13.5 cm

a MALE BREEDING, **b** FEMALE and **c** 1ST-WINTER MALE Common and widespread resident below 915 m; fairly common up to 1400 m, sometimes summers up to 2400 m (–2850 m). Male black, with white rump and wing patch; rufous fringes to body in non-breeding and first-winter plumages. Female has dark-brown upperparts and rufous-brown underparts, with rufous-orange rump. Mainly cultivation and open country with scattered bushes or tall grass.

Jerdon's Bushchat *Saxicola jerdoni* 15 cm

a MALE and **b** FEMALE Very rare and local resident, mainly recorded at Sukila Phanta; 75–150 m. Male has black upperparts, including rump and tail, and white underparts. Female similar to female Grey Bushchat, but lacks prominent supercilium, and has longer, more graduated tail lacking rufous at sides. Tall grassland.

Grey Bushchat *Saxicola ferrea* 15 cm

a MALE and **b** FEMALE Common and widespread resident; summers 1500–3355 m, most frequent above 1800 m, winters chiefly 150–2135 m (–75 m). Male has white supercilium and dark mask; upperparts grey to almost black, depending on extent of feather wear. Female has buff supercilium and rufous rump and tail sides. Secondary growth, forest edges and scrub-covered hillsides.

Brown Rock-chat *Cercomela fusca* 17 cm

ADULT Rare and very local resident in the terai; 75 m. Both sexes brown, with more rufescent underparts. Buildings in open country.

Variable Wheatear *Oenanthe picata* 14.5 cm

a MALE and **b** FEMALE Very rare and local winter visitor; below 760 m. Male has black head, breast and upperparts, and white underparts. Females has black of plumage replaced by grey. Both sexes show extensive white at sides of tail. *See* Appendix 1 for comparison with Pied Wheatear..Cultivation and rocky areas.

Desert Wheatear *Oenanthe deserti* 14–15 cm

a MALE BREEDING, **b** MALE NON-BREEDING and **c** FEMALE NON-BREEDING Scarce but regular summer visitor and passage migrant in the northwest; summers up to 4880 m (–150 m on passage). Sandy-brown upperparts, with largely black tail and contrasting white rump. Male has black throat (partly obscured by pale fringes in fresh plumage). Female has blackish centres to wing coverts and tertials in fresh plumage and largely black wings when worn (useful distinction from the Isabelline Wheatear). Dry semi-desert in Tibetan plateaux country.

Isabelline Wheatear *Oenanthe isabellina* 16.5 cm

ADULT Rare spring passage migrant; 1370–2590 m. Rather plain sandy-brown and buff. Tail shorter than in the Desert Wheatear with more white at base and sides. Has paler, sandy-brown wings with contrasting dark alula (lacking black centres to coverts and tertials/secondaries). *See* Appendix 1 for comparison with Northern Wheatear. Dry cultivation.

Spot-winged Starling *Saroglossa spiloptera* 19 cm

a MALE and **b** FEMALE Passage migrant and breeder, recorded in most months; frequent throughout below 915 m, uncommon up to 1830 m. White wing patch and whitish iris. Male has blackish mask, reddish-chestnut throat, and dark-scalloped greyish upperparts. Female has browner upperparts, and greyish-brown markings on throat and breast. Juvenile has buff wing-bars. Open broadleaved forest and well-wooded areas, favours flowering trees.

Chestnut-tailed Starling *Sturnus malabaricus* 20 cm

a ADULT and **b** JUVENILE Fairly common and widespread, recorded in all months, but has poorly understood migratory movements; below 1370 m. Adult has grey upperparts, rufous underparts, and chestnut tail. Juvenile is rather uniform with rufous sides and tips to outer tail feathers. Open wooded areas and groves.

Brahminy Starling *Sturnus pagodarum* 21 cm

a ADULT and **b** JUVENILE Resident, frequent in the west, uncommon in the centre and east, has poorly understood seasonal movements; mainly below 915 m (–3050 m). Adult has black crest, and rufous-orange sides of head and underparts. Juvenile lacks crest; has grey-brown cap and paler orange-buff underparts. Dry, well-wooded areas and thorn scrub.

Common Starling *Sturnus vulgaris* 21 cm

a ADULT BREEDING, **b** NON-BREEDING and **c** JUVENILE Uncommon and widespread, mainly a passage migrant, also a winter visitor to the far west; mainly below 1500 m (–2805 m). Adult metallic green and purple; heavily marked with buff and white in winter. Juvenile dusky brown with whiter throat. Cultivation and damp grassland.

Asian Pied Starling *Sturnus contra* 23 cm

a ADULT and **b** JUVENILE Fairly common and widespread resident; below 305 m (–1370 m, possibly escaped birds). Adult black and white, with orange orbital skin and large, pointed yellowish bill. Juvenile has brown plumage in place of black. Cultivation, damp grassland and habitation.

Common Myna *Acridotheres tristis* 25 cm

a b ADULT Common and widespread resident; regular up to at least 1830 m all year, occasionally summers up to 3050 m and winters to 2135 m. Brownish myna with yellow orbital skin, white wing patch and white tail-tip. Juvenile duller. Habitation and cultivation.

Bank Myna *Acridotheres ginginianus* 23 cm

a b ADULT Resident; fairly common and widespread but local, mainly 75–305 m (–1370 m, possibly escaped birds). Orange-red orbital patch, orange-yellow bill, and tufted forehead. Wing patch, underwing-coverts and tail-tip orange-buff. Adult is bluish-grey with blackish cap. Juvenile duller and browner than adult. Cultivation, damp grassland near villages, often associated with grazing animals.

Jungle Myna *Acridotheres fuscus* 23 cm

a ADULT and **b** JUVENILE Common and widespread resident; below 1525 m (–2200 m). Tufted forehead, and white wing patch and tail-tip; lacks bare orbital skin. Juvenile browner, with reduced forehead tuft. Cultivation near well-wooded areas, and edges of habitation.

Hill Myna *Gracula religiosa* 25–29 cm

ADULT Resident; frequent in the centre and east, rare in the west; mainly below 455 m (–1280 m). Large myna with yellow wattles, large orange-yellow bill, and white wing patches. Juvenile has duller bill, paler yellow wattles, and less gloss to plumage. Moist broadleaved forest.

Kashmir Nuthatch *Sitta cashmirensis* 12 cm

a MALE and **b** FEMALE Locally fairly common resident in the northwest; 2400–3505 m. Compared with female Chestnut-bellied Nuthatch, has uniform undertail-coverts and lacks clearly defined white cheeks. Appears larger and longer-billed than the White-tailed Nuthatch, with more pronounced white cheeks, no white at base of tail, and distinctive rasping jay-like call. Deciduous and broadleaved/coniferous forest.

Chestnut-bellied Nuthatch *Sitta castanea* 12 cm

a MALE and **b** FEMALE Common and widespread resident; below 1830 m. Male has deep chestnut underparts and white cheeks. Female paler cinnamon-brown on underparts, although white cheeks more pronounced than on similar species; has pale fringes to undertail-coverts. Calls include an explosive *siditit*. Broadleaved forest and groves.

White-tailed Nuthatch *Sitta himalayensis* 12 cm

ADULT Common and widespread resident; summers chiefly 1800–3140 m (–3400 m), sometimes descending in winter (down to 915 m). White at base of tail (difficult to see); less distinct white cheek patch than the Kashmir Nuthatch; uniform undertail-coverts. Calls include a hard *chak'kak* which may be repeated as a rattle. Mainly broadleaved forest.

White-cheeked Nuthatch *Sitta leucopsis* 12 cm

ADULT Locally fairly common resident in the northwest; 2745–3900 m. Black crown and nape, white face, and whitish underparts with rufous flanks and undertail-coverts. Call likened to bleating of a young goat. Coniferous and mixed forest.

Velvet-fronted Nuthatch *Sitta frontalis* 10 cm

a MALE and **b** FEMALE Locally fairly common resident; below 2015 m, most frequent up to 1800 m. Violet-blue upperparts, black forehead, black-tipped red bill, and lilac underparts. Female lacks black eye-stripe. Open broadleaved forest and well-wooded areas.

Wallcreeper *Tichodroma muraria* 16 cm

a ADULT MALE BREEDING and **b** ADULT NON-BREEDING Fairly common and widespread in winter 245–5000 m (–5730 m); has bred at 3350 m, 4400 m. Long, down-curved bill. Largely crimson wing coverts; shows white primary spots in flight. Breeding male has black throat. Rock cliffs and gorges; also stony river beds in winter.

Eurasian Treecreeper *Certhia familiaris* 12 cm

ADULT Fairly common and quite widespread resident; summers mainly 3000–4100 m, winters from 2000 m up to at least 3655 m. Unbarred tail, and whitish throat and breast. Mainly conifer/birch forest.

Bar-tailed Treecreeper *Certhia himalayana* 12 cm

ADULT Fairly common resident in the west; summers 2200–3660 m, winters down to 1800 m, occasionally to 305 m. Dark barring on tail, white throat, and dull whitish or dirty greyish-buff underparts. Mainly coniferous forest.

Rusty-flanked Treecreeper *Certhia nipalensis* 12 cm

ADULT Fairly common and quite widespread resident; summers chiefly 2550–3660 m, winters from 1830 m up to at least 3505 m. Buffish supercilium continues around dark ear-coverts, unbarred tail, white throat, and rufous flanks. Mainly oak, also coniferous/broadleaved forest.

Brown-throated Treecreeper *Certhia discolor* 12 cm

ADULT Locally fairly common resident; summers mainly 2000–2750 m, occasionally up to 3050 m, winters chiefly down to 1800 m (–305 m). Brownish-buff throat and breast; unbarred tail. Mainly broadleaved forest, especially mossy oak; also coniferous/broadleaved forest.

Fire-capped Tit *Cephalopyrus flammiceps* 10 cm
a MALE BREEDING and **b** FEMALE Uncommon resident and erratic visitor; mainly 2135–3000 m (–1280 m). Flowerpecker-like, with greenish upperparts and yellowish to whitish underparts. Lacks crest. Breeding male has bright orange-scarlet forecrown. Deciduous forest and deciduous/coniferous forest.

Rufous-naped Tit *Parus rufonuchalis* 13 cm
ADULT Fairly common resident in the northwest; 2600–4000 m. Large size, extensive black bib (to upper belly), and grey belly. Lacks wing-bars. Mainly coniferous forest.

Rufous-vented Tit *Parus rubidiventris* 12 cm
a ADULT *P. r. rubidiventris* and **b** ADULT *P. r. beavani* Common and widespread resident; summers 2550–4250 m, winters 2135–4270 m. Smaller than the Rufous-naped Tit, with smaller black bib, and (where ranges overlap) has rufous belly. Lacks wing-bars. The race *beavani*, which occurs east of the Langtang valley, has greyish belly. Coniferous forest and conifer/birch forest; also rhododendron shrubberies.

Spot-winged Tit *Parus melanolophus* 11 cm
ADULT Common resident in the west, hybridises with Coal Tit in west-central areas; summers 2800–4000 m (–2200 m); winter altitudes are poorly known. Small size, broad white tips to median and greater coverts, blue-grey mantle, rufous breast sides, and dark grey belly. Hybrids show a variety of intermediate features; some hybrids differ from either species in having a band of cinnamon-orange down centre of underparts. Mainly coniferous forest, also coniferous/broadleaved forest.

Coal Tit *Parus ater* 11 cm
ADULT Fairly common resident in the centre and east, hybridises with Spot-winged Tit in west-central areas; summers 2440–4000 m (–4250 m), winters from 2500 m up to at least 3050 m (1830–4270 m). Small size, whitish tips to median and greater coverts, olive-grey mantle, and creamy-buff underparts. Mainly coniferous forest, also fir/birch forest.

Grey-crested Tit *Parus dichrous* 12 cm
ADULT Fairly common and widespread resident; summers chiefly 2450–4000 m, winters 2000–3655 m (–4270 m). Greyish crest and upperparts, whitish collar, and orange-buff underparts. Mainly broadleaved, also coniferous/rhododendron and coniferous forests.

Great Tit *Parus major* 14 cm
ADULT Widespread resident; common up to 1525 m, frequent up to 1800 m (–3050 m). Black breast centre and line down belly, Greyish mantle, greyish-white breast sides and flanks, and white wing-bar. Juvenile has yellowish-white cheeks and underparts, and yellowish-olive wash to mantle. Open forest and well-wooded country, favours broadleaves.

Green-backed Tit *Parus monticolus* 12.5 cm
ADULT Widespread resident, common from 1370 m up to 3100 m, frequent up to 3660 m; replaces Great Tit altitudinally; breeds chiefly above 1525 m and winters below 2745 m. Green mantle and back, and yellow on underparts. Forest, prefers moister habitat than Great Tit.

Black-lored Tit *Parus xanthogenys* 13 cm

ADULT Resident, widespread and common, except in the far east, where uncommon; summers 850–2300 m (–2925 m), winters 915–2135 m (–75 m). Prominent black crest, and black centre to yellow throat and breast. Black forehead and lores, uniform greenish upperparts (with black streaking confined to scapulars), olive rump, and yellowish wing-bars. Open forest, forest edges and groves.

Yellow-cheeked Tit *Parus spilonotus* 14 cm

ADULT Uncommon and very local resident in the far east; 1980–2440 m (–450 m). Very similar to Black-lored Tit but has yellow forehead and lores, black streaking on greenish mantle, grey rump, and white wing-bars. Open broadleaved forest.

Yellow-browed Tit *Sylviparus modestus* 10 cm

ADULT Quite widespread resident, fairly common in centre and east, uncommon in west; summers 2135–3250 m (–3660 m), winters 1500–2800 m. Very small, with slight crest and rather stubby bill. Olive-green upperparts, yellowish eye-ring, fine yellow supercilium, and yellowish-buff underparts. Broadleaved forest, favours oaks.

Sultan Tit *Melanochlora sultanea* 20.5 cm

a MALE and **b** FEMALE Rare and local resident in the centre and east; 275–1370 m (–2500 m). Large, bulbul-like tit. Male blue-black, female blackish-olive, both with bright yellow crest and underparts. Edges of broadleaved forest, favours evergreens.

Black-throated Tit *Aegithalos concinnus* 10.5 cm

a ADULT and **b** JUVENILE Common and widespread resident; mainly 1400–2700 m all year, but occasionally down to 1065 m (–3000 m). Chestnut crown, white chin and black throat, white cheeks, and grey mantle. Juvenile has white throat and indistinct black-spotted breast-band. Broadleaved and broadleaved/coniferous forest and secondary growth.

White-throated Tit *Aegithalos niveogularis* 11 cm

a ADULT and **b** JUVENILE Frequent and local resident in the northwest; 2800–3965 m. White forehead and forecrown and whitish throat; iris brownish. Diffuse blackish mask and cinnamon underparts, with darker breast-band. Juvenile has dusky throat, more prominent breast-band, and paler lower breast and belly. Bushes in birch/coniferous forest and high-altitude shrubberies.

Rufous-fronted Tit *Aegithalos iouschistos* 11 cm

a ADULT and **b** JUVENILE Frequent resident from west-central areas eastwards; 2590–3700 m all year. Broad black mask (reaching nape), dusky throat, rufous-buff crown centre and cheeks, and rufous underparts. Juvenile has paler crown-stripe, cheeks and underparts. Broadleaved, coniferous and mixed forests, prefers drier habitats.

Winter Wren *Troglodytes troglodytes* 9.5 cm

ADULT Fairly common and widespread resident; chiefly 2500–4725 m (2135–5300 m). Small and squat, with stubby tail. Brown, with dark-barred wings, tail and underparts. High-altitude rocky and bushy slopes, also in forest undergrowth in winter.

Sand Martin *Riparia riparia* 13 cm
a **b** **c** ADULT Passage migrant; status uncertain. White throat and half-collar and brown breast-band. Very similar to Pale Martin; upperparts darker brown, breast-band clearly defined and tail-fork deeper. Rivers and lakes.

Pale Martin *Riparia diluta* 13 cm
a **b** **c** ADULT Status uncertain; recorded in March, May and December. Upperparts paler and greyer than on Sand and Plain Martins; throat greyish-white; breast-band not clearly defined; tail-fork very shallow. Rivers and lakes.

Plain Martin *Riparia paludicola* 12 cm
a **b** **c** ADULT Widespread and common resident; below 1500 m (–2900 m). Pale brownish-grey throat and breast, merging into dingy white rest of underparts; some with suggestion of breast-band. Underwing darker than on Sand and Pale Martins, flight weaker and more fluttering, and has shallower indent to tail. Upperparts darker than on the Pale Martin. Rivers and lakes.

Eurasian Crag Martin *Hirundo rupestris* 15 cm
a **b** **c** ADULT Widespread and locally fairly common resident; usually winters 915–2135 m, summers up to 4575 m. Larger and stockier than the *Riparia* martins. Dark underwing-coverts, dusky throat, brown flanks and undertail-coverts (latter with pale fringes). Lacks breast-band. Shows white spots in tail when spread. Rocky cliffs and gorges.

Barn Swallow *Hirundo rustica* 18 cm
a **b** **c** ADULT and **d** JUVENILE Widespread and common resident and summer visitor; mainly below 1830 m (–6400 m on passage). Reddish throat, long tail-streamers, and blue-black breast-band. Juvenile duller; lacks tail-streamers. Cultivation, habitation, lakes and rivers.

Wire-tailed Swallow *Hirundo smithii* 14 cm
a **b** **c** ADULT and **d** JUVENILE Uncommon and local in west terai, possibly resident; 75 m. Chestnut crown, white underparts, and fine tail projections. Juvenile has brownish cast to blue upperparts, and dull brownish crown. Open country and cultivation near fresh waters.

Red-rumped Swallow *Hirundo daurica* 16–17 cm
a **b** **c** ADULT and **d** JUVENILE Common and widespread resident; breeds below 2745 m, winters below 915 m; also a rare winter visitor. Rufous-orange neck sides and rump, finely streaked buffish-white underparts, and black undertail-coverts. Cultivation and upland pastures.

Streak-throated Swallow *Hirundo fluvicola* 11 cm
a **b** **c** ADULT and **d** JUVENILE Scarce visitor recorded December–May and August; below 1280 m. Small, with slight fork to long, broad tail. Chestnut crown, streaked throat and breast, white mantle streaks, and brownish rump. Juvenile is duller, with browner crown. Rivers and lakes.

Northern House Martin *Delichon urbica* 12 cm
a **b** **c** ADULT Probably a rare passage migrant; below 1470 m. From Asian by whiter underparts and underwing-coverts, longer deeply-forked tail, and whiter and more extensive rump patch. Mountain valleys.

Asian House Martin *Delichon dasypus* 12 cm
a **b** **c** ADULT Fairly common and widespread resident; below 4575 m, has bred at 3500 m and 4000 m. Dusky-white underparts and rump, shallow tail-fork, dusky underwing, and (not always) dusky centres to undertail-coverts. Grassy slopes with cliffs, forest, mountain villages.

Nepal House Martin *Delichon nipalensis* 13 cm
a **b** **c** ADULT Fairly common and widespread resident; summers up to 3500 m (–3865 m), winters 915–2135 m (–160 m). Square-cut tail, narrow white rump, blackish underwing-coverts and undertail-coverts, and blackish throat (just chin in some). Mountain ridges with cliffs, forest, villages.

Striated Bulbul *Pycnonotus striatus*   23 cm

ADULT Local and frequent resident from west-central areas eastwards; 1525–2690 m. Crested, green bulbul with boldly streaked underparts and finely streaked upperparts. Mainly broad-leaved evergreen forest.

Black-crested Bulbul *Pycnonotus melanicterus*   19 cm

ADULT Resident, common in the far east, frequent elsewhere; widespread below 365 m, uncommon up to 915 m (–1525 m). Crested black head, yellow underparts, and uniform greenish wings and tail. Moist broadleaved forest and thick secondary growth.

Red-whiskered Bulbul *Pycnonotus jocosus*   20 cm

ADULT Locally common and widespread resident; below 455 m. Black crest, red 'whiskers', white underparts with complete or broken breast-band, and red vent. Juvenile duller and lacks 'whiskers'. Open forest and secondary growth.

Himalayan Bulbul *Pycnonotus leucogenys*   20 cm

ADULT Common and widespread resident; 350–2400 m (250–3050 m). Brown crest and nape, white cheeks with black throat, and yellow vent. Dry scrub, secondary growth and bushes around habitation.

Red-vented Bulbul *Pycnonotus cafer*   20 cm

ADULT Resident; common and widespread below 1500 m, uncommon up to 2135 m. Blackish head with slight crest, scaled appearance to upperparts and breast, red vent, and white rump. Open deciduous forest, secondary growth and trees around habitation.

White-throated Bulbul *Alophoixus flaveolus*   22 cm

ADULT Resident, locally frequent in the far east, rare west to Chitwan; mainly below 455 m. Brownish crest, white throat, yellow breast and belly, and rufous cast to wings and tail. Undergrowth in broadleaved evergreen forest and secondary growth.

Ashy Bulbul *Hemixos flavala*   20 cm

ADULT Resident. Frequent and quite widespread resident; 305–1525 m. Grey crest and upperparts, black mask and tawny ear-coverts, and olive-yellow wing patch. Broadleaved forest; also forest edges in winter.

Mountain Bulbul *Hypsipetes mcclellandii*   24 cm

ADULT Fairly common and quite widespread resident; mainly 1830–2135 m (915–2285 m). Brown crest, greyish throat with white streaking, cinnamon-brown breast with buff streaking, and greenish upperparts. Forest and secondary growth.

Black Bulbul *Hypsipetes leucocephalus*   25 cm

ADULT Common and widespread resident; 75–3050 m. Slate-grey bulbul with black crest. Has shallow fork to tail, and red bill, legs and feet. Juvenile lacks crest; has whitish underparts with diffuse grey breast-band, and brownish cast to upperparts. Mainly broadleaved forest.

Hill Prinia *Prinia atrogularis* 17 cm
a ADULT BREEDING and **b** NON-BREEDING Frequent resident in the far east; 1400–2500 m.
Black throat and breast with white spotting in breeding plumage. White supercilium and buffish underparts in non-breeding plumage; upperparts are unstreaked (compare with Striated
Prinia). Scrub and grass hillsides and terraced cultivation.

Striated Prinia *Prinia criniger* 16 cm
a ADULT BREEDING and **b** NON-BREEDING Common and widespread resident; summers
chiefly 1220–2300 m (–3000 m), winters 915–2135 m (–75 m). Large size, streaked upperparts,
and stout bill. In breeding plumage has dark bill and lores, and indistinct streaking to grey-
brown upperparts. In non-breeding has prominently streaked, rufous-brown upperparts, and
buff lores. Scrub and grass hillsides and terraced cultivation.

Grey-crowned Prinia *Prinia cinereocapilla* 11 cm
ADULT Local resident, fairly common at Chitwan, uncommon elsewhere; below 1065 m
(–1600 m). Orange-buff supercilium, dark blue-grey crown and nape, and rufous-brown mantle and back. Grassland in forest clearings and at forest edges, and secondary growth. Globally
threatened.

Grey-breasted Prinia *Prinia hodgsonii* 11 cm
a ADULT BREEDING and **b** NON-BREEDING Widespread resident; common below 400 m, frequent up to 1200 m, locally to 1750 m. Small size. Diffuse grey breast-band in summer. In non-
breeding plumage has fine dark bill, fine whitish supercilium, brown upperparts with rufescent cast,
and greyish wash to sides of neck and breast. Bushes at forest edges, scrub and secondary growth.

Jungle Prinia *Prinia sylvatica* 13 cm
a ADULT BREEDING and **b** NON-BREEDING Frequent resident in the far west terai; 75–150 m.
Larger than the Plain Prinia, with stouter bill, and uniform wings. Song is a loud, pulsing *zong zee
chu*, repeated monotonously; calls include a dry rattle and a loud *tiu*. In breeding plumage has greyer upperparts, dark lores and bill, and shorter tail with prominent white outertail feathers. More
rufescent in non-breeding plumage, with prominent supercilium, and longer tail. Scrub and tall
grass in open dry areas.

Yellow-bellied Prinia *Prinia flaviventris* 13 cm
ADULT Local and fairly common resident; 75–250 m. White throat and breast and yellow belly.
Slate-grey cast to crown and olive-green cast to upperparts. Juvenile has uniform yellowish olive-
brown upperparts and yellow underparts. Tall grassland by wetlands.

Graceful Prinia *Prinia gracilis* 11 cm
ADULT Very local and fairly common resident in the terai; 75–150 m. Small, with fine bill and
streaked upperparts. Tall grass and scrub along river banks in the terai.

Plain Prinia *Prinia inornata* 13 cm
a ADULT BREEDING and **b** NON-BREEDING Frequent and widespread resident; below 305 m.
Smaller than the Jungle Prinia, with finer bill, and pale or rufous fringes to tertials. Song is a
rapid wheezy trill, *tlick-tlick-tlick* etc.; calls include a plaintive *tee-tee-tee* and nasal *beep*. In breeding plumage has greyer upperparts, dark bill, and shorter tail with prominent white outertail
feathers. More rufescent in non-breeding plumage, with longer tail. Reeds, grassland, edges of
cultivation, scrub and forest edges.

Ashy Prinia *Prinia socialis* 13 cm
a ADULT BREEDING and **b** NON-BREEDING Fairly common and widespread resident; below
305 m. Slate-grey crown and ear-coverts, red eyes, slate-grey or rufous-brown upperparts, and
orange-buff wash to underparts. Tall grass and scrub, open secondary growth, reedbeds and
forest edges.

Zitting Cisticola *Cisticola juncidis* 10 cm

a ADULT BREEDING and **b** NON-BREEDING Fairly common and widespread resident; below 1350 m, summers locally up to 1900 m. Small, with short tail that has prominent white tips. Bold streaking on buff upperparts, including nape, and thin whitish supercilium. Song, uttered in display flight, is a repetitive *pip pip pip…*; call is a single *plit*. Fields and grassland.

Bright-headed Cisticola *Cisticola exilis* 10 cm

a MALE BREEDING and **b** NON-BREEDING Local and fairly common resident; 75–150 m. Breeding males have unstreaked creamy-white crown. In other plumages very similar to the Zitting Cisticola; typically show unstreaked rufous nape, rufous supercilium and neck sides, blacker crown and mantle with less distinct streaking, and longer and more uniformly dark tail with narrow buff tips. Song is a *cheeezz…joo-ee, di-do*, given in display flight or from perch; the *cheeezz* often given alone. Tall grassland.

Oriental White-eye *Zosterops palpebrosus* 10 cm

ADULT Common and widespread resident; below 1370 m, summers up to 2440 m. Black lores and white eye-ring, bright yellow throat and breast, and whitish belly. Open broadleaved forest and wooded areas.

Chestnut-headed Tesia *Tesia castaneocoronata* 8 cm

ADULT Resident, fairly common and widespread in the centre and east, rare in the west; summers 2135–4000 m, winters mainly 800–1830 m (–250 m). Adult has chestnut head and yellow underparts. Juvenile lacks chestnut head and has dark rufous underparts. Thick undergrowth in moist forest.

Slaty-bellied Tesia *Tesia olivea* 9 cm

ADULT Rare and very local, probably resident; recorded in the Arun Valley 1000–1700 m in August and September and in upper Mai Valley 2200 m in April. Darker-grey underparts than the Grey-bellied Tesia. Crown often brighter than mantle. Bright-orange lower mandible lacks dark tip. Song is four to six whistles, followed by explosive jumble of tuneless notes. Thick undergrowth in moist, mainly evergreen forest.

Grey-bellied Tesia *Tesia cyaniventer* 9 cm

ADULT Frequent resident in the centre and east, uncommon in the west; summers mainly 1525–2440 m, winters from 1830 m to the foothills (–75 m). Paler grey underparts than Slaty-bellied Tesia, with almost whitish belly. Supercilium brighter than crown, and yellow lower mandible has dark tip. Song slower than Slaty-bellied Tesia, lacking explosive jumble of notes at end. Thick undergrowth in moist forest, favours streamsides.

Common Tailorbird *Orthotomus sutorius* 13 cm

a MALE and **b** FEMALE Common and widespread resident; below 1830 m. Rufous forehead, greenish upperparts, and whitish underparts including undertail-coverts. Bushes in gardens, cultivation edges and forest edges.

White-browed Tit Warbler *Leptopoecile sophiae* 10 cm

a MALE and **b** FEMALE Frequent resident in the trans-Himalayas; 2700–4575 m all year, mainly above 3500 m. Whitish supercilium, rufous crown, and lilac and purple in plumage. Dwarf scrub in semi-desert.

Pale-footed Bush Warbler *Cettia pallidipes*   11 cm

ADULT   Local resident, fairly common at Chitwan, mainly single records from elsewhere; chiefly below 250 m (–1830 m). Upperparts more rufescent, underparts whiter, and supercilium more prominent, compared with Brownish-flanked Bush Warbler. Pale pinkish legs and feet. Song is a loud, explosive *zip...zip-tschuck-o-tschuck*. Tall grass and bushes at forest edges.

Brownish-flanked Bush Warbler *Cettia fortipes*   12 cm

a ADULT *C. f. fortipes* and **b** ADULT *C. f. pallidus*   Resident, locally fairly common in far east, rare farther west; has uncertain seasonal movements; 1800–3200 m in summer, 1400–2135 m in December. Underparts duskier, and upperparts more olive-tinged, than Pale-footed Bush Warbler. Brownish legs and feet. Western *pallidus* is more olive-toned above, and more buffish-grey on the underparts, compared with the nominate form in the east. Song is a *weeee chiwiyou*. Open forest and thickets.

Chestnut-crowned Bush Warbler *Cettia major*   13 cm

ADULT   Rare resident; breeds in Central Himalayas 3550–3680 m, winters very locally below 250 m. Chestnut crown. Differentiated from the Grey-sided Bush Warbler by larger size, rufous-buff on fore supercilium, and whiter underparts. Song has an introductory note, then an explosive warble. Summers in rhododendron shrubberies and bushes in forest; winters in reedbeds.

Aberrant Bush Warbler *Cettia flavolivacea*   12 cm

ADULT   Resident, common in the centre and east, rare in the west; summers mainly 2440–3950 m, winters 915–1830 m (–100 m). Greenish upperparts, and yellowish supercilium and underparts. Song is short warble, followed by inflected whistle *dir dir-tee teee-wee*. Bushes at forest edges and shrubberies.

Yellowish-bellied Bush Warbler *Cettia acanthizoides*   9.5 cm

ADULT   Scarce and local, probably resident; 2000–3660 m in spring and summer. Small size, pale rufous-brown upperparts, whitish throat and breast, and yellowish belly and flanks. Song is a thin, high-pitched *see-saw see-saw see-saw* etc. Mainly bamboo stands.

Grey-sided Bush Warbler *Cettia brunnifrons*   10 cm

ADULT   Common and widespread resident; summers chiefly 2745–4000 m, winters 915–2135 m (–75 m). Chestnut crown. Differentiated from the Chestnut-crowned Bush Warbler by small size, shorter whitish supercilium, and greyer underparts. Song is a loud, wheezy, repeated *sip ti ti sip*. Summers in high-altitude shrubberies and bushes at forest edges; winters in scrub and forest undergrowth.

Spotted Bush Warbler *Bradypterus thoracicus*   13 cm

a   **b** ADULT   Rare resident; summers in central Himalayas, 3350–3850 m, winters locally below 250 m. Spotting on throat and breast (can be indistinct). Shortish bill, grey ear-coverts and breast, and olive-brown flanks; boldly patterned undertail-coverts. Song is a repeated *trick-i-di*. Summers in high-altitude shrubberies, winters in reedbeds and tall grass.

Chinese Bush Warbler *Bradypterus tacsanowskius*   14 cm

a 1ST-WINTER and **b** ADULT   Rare and very local winter visitor, mainly recorded at Koshi; 75 m. Grey-brown upperparts and pale tips to undertail-coverts; underparts often with yellowish wash. Some have fine spotting on lower throat. Compare with Brown Bush Warbler in Appendix 1. Song is a rasping, insect-like *dzzzeep-dzzzeep-dzzzeep* etc. Reedbeds.

Paddyfield Warbler *Acrocephalus agricola*   13 cm

a ADULT FRESH and **b** WORN   Local winter visitor, fairly common at Koshi, uncommon elsewhere; 75–150 m. Prominent white supercilium behind eye, and stout bill with dark tip. Often shows dark edge to supercilium. Rufous cast to upperparts in fresh plumage. Typically shows dark centres and pale edges to tertials (wings usually uniform in Blyth's Reed Warbler). *See* Appendix 1 for comparison with Black-browed Reed Warbler. Reedbeds and damp grassland.

Blyth's Reed Warbler *Acrocephalus dumetorum* 14 cm
a ADULT FRESH and **b** WORN   Fairly common and widespread winter visitor; below 1525 m (–2900 m on passage). Long bill, olive-brown to olive-grey upperparts, and uniform wings. Supercilium indistinct compared with the Paddyfield Warbler, barely apparent behind eye. Bushes and trees at edges of forest and cultivation.

Clamorous Reed Warbler *Acrocephalus stentoreus* 19 cm
ADULT   Local winter visitor and passage migrant, chiefly in the terai, frequent at Koshi, rare elsewhere; 75–150 m (–1340 m). Large size, long bill, short primary projection, and whitish supercilium. *See* Appendix 1 for comparison with Oriental Reed Warbler. Reedbeds and bushes around wetlands.

Thick-billed Warbler *Acrocephalus aedon* 19 cm
ADULT   Uncommon but regular winter visitor; below 1500 m. Large size. Short, stout bill and rounded head. 'Plain-faced' appearance, lacking prominent supercilium or eye-stripe. Tall grass, scrub, reeds and bushes at edges of forest and cultivation.

Striated Grassbird *Megalurus palustris* 25 cm
ADULT   Local resident, fairly common at Koshi Tappu, rare elsewhere; 75–305 m. Streaked upperparts, finely streaked breast and long, graduated tail. Has longer and finer bill and more prominent supercilium than Bristled Grassbird. Tall damp grassland and reedbeds.

Bristled Grassbird *Chaetornis striatus* 20 cm
ADULT   Status uncertain, mainly recorded April–October, only two winter records; recorded from west to east, but local, fairly common at Sukila Phanta and Chitwan; below 250 m. Streaked upperparts and fine streaking on lower throat. Has shorter, stouter bill and less prominent supercilium than the Striated Grassbird, also shorter and broader tail with buffish-white tips. Short grassland with scattered bushes and some tall vegetation. Globally threatened.

Rufous-rumped Grassbird *Graminicola bengalensis* 18 cm
ADULT   Very local resident, frequent at Chitwan and Sukila Phanta, rare elsewhere; below 250 m. Rufous and whitish streaking on black upperparts, white-tipped blackish tail, and white underparts with rufous-buff breast sides and flanks. Tall grass and reeds.

Booted Warbler *Hippolais caligata* 12 cm
ADULT   Scarce winter visitor and passage migrant; 75–2810 m. Small size and *Phylloscopus*-like behaviour. Tail looks long and square-ended, and undertail-coverts look short. Often shows faint whitish edges and tip to tail and fringes to tertials. Supercilium usually distinct, and often shows dark upper edge. Scrub and bushes at cultivation edges in dry habitats.

Lesser Whitethroat *Sylvia curruca* 13 cm
ADULT   Uncommon and widespread winter visitor and passage migrant; below 1500 m (–2750 m on passage). Brownish-grey upperparts, grey crown with darker ear-coverts, blackish bill, and dark grey legs and feet. *See* Appendix 1 for comparison with the Orphean Warbler. Scrub.

Common Chiffchaff *Phylloscopus collybita* 11 cm

ADULT Frequent and widespread winter visitor; below 1370 m (–2800 m on passage). Brownish to greyish upperparts; olive-green edges to wing coverts, remiges and rectrices. Black bill and legs. No wing-bar. Forest, bushes and secondary growth.

Dusky Warbler *Phylloscopus fuscatus* 11 cm

ADULT Frequent and widespread winter visitor; below 1600 m. Brown upperparts and whitish underparts, with buff flanks. Prominent supercilium, and hard *chack* call. Bushes and long grass, especially near water.

Smoky Warbler *Phylloscopus fuligiventer* 10 cm

ADULT Uncommon resident; summers 3900–5000 m, regular in winter below 915 m. Very dark, with short yellowish supercilium, and yellowish centre of throat and belly. Call is a throaty *thrup thrup*. Breeds in dwarf juniper and other shrubberies; winters in dense under-growth near water.

Tickell's Leaf Warbler *Phylloscopus affinis* 11 cm

FRESH Common and widespread resident; summers mainly 2550–4880 m, winters chiefly in the terai, occasionally up to 1190 m. Dark greenish to greenish-brown upperparts, and bright-yellow supercilium and underparts. *Chit* call. Breeds in open country with bushes; winters in bushes at edges of forest and cultivation.

Sulphur-bellied Warbler *Phylloscopus griseolus* 11 cm

FRESH Scarce passage migrant and winter visitor; below 1500 m. Dark greyish upperparts, bright-yellow supercilium, and dusky-yellow underparts strongly washed with buff. Soft *quip* call. Has distinctive habit of climbing about rocks and nuthatch-like on tree trunks and branch-es. Rocky areas and around old buildings.

Western Crowned Warbler *Phylloscopus occipitalis* 11 cm

FRESH Uncommon spring passage migrant and rare winter visitor, possibly breeds; 75–2900 m. Crown stripe, large size, greyish-green upperparts, and greyish-white underparts. Head and wing pattern tends to be less striking than on Blyth's Leaf Warbler. Broadleaved and conifer-ous forests.

Blyth's Leaf Warbler *Phylloscopus reguloides* 11 cm

FRESH Common and widespread resident; summers 1980–3800 m, winters mainly below 1500 m (–2750 m). Crown stripe, yellowish on underparts, and broad wing-bars with dark panel across greater coverts. Summers in broadleaved and coniferous forests, winters in bushes and open forest.

Yellow-vented Warbler *Phylloscopus cantator* 10 cm

FRESH Uncommon and very local in the east; probably mainly a winter visitor, possibly resi-dent, has bred; 75–1525 m. Yellow crown stripe with blackish at sides; yellow throat, white belly, and yellow undertail-coverts. Mainly evergreen broadleaved forest.

Buff-barred Warbler *Phylloscopus pulcher* 10 cm

FRESH Common and widespread resident; summers 3250–4300 m, winters 915–3050 m and possibly higher (–75 m). Buffish-orange wing-bars, yellowish supercilium and wash to under-parts, white on tail, and small yellowish rump patch. Breeds in subalpine shrubberies and forest; winters in broadleaved forest.

Ashy-throated Warbler *Phylloscopus maculipennis* 9 cm

FRESH Fairly common and widespread resident; summers chiefly 2440–3500 m, winters 1525–2900 m (–915 m). Small size, greyish throat and breast, yellow belly and flanks, white super-cilium and crown stripe, yellow rump, and white on tail. Broadleaved and broadleaved/conifer-ous forest; also secondary growth in winter.

Lemon-rumped Warbler *Phylloscopus chloronotus* 9 cm

FRESH Common and widespread resident; summers mainly 2750–4000 m, winters 275–2750 m. Yellowish crown stripe and rump band, dark crown-sides, dark panel across greater coverts, and whitish underparts. Forest; also secondary growth in winter.

Hume's Warbler *Phylloscopus humei* 10–11 cm

FRESH Widespread resident; common in summer 3280–3980 m, fairly common in winter below 2135 m (–2560 m). Lacks rump band and well-defined crown stripe. Has buffish or whitish wing-bars and supercilium. Bill appears all-dark, and legs are normally blackish-brown. Call is a rolling *whit-hoo*. Breeds in coniferous forest and subalpine shrubberies; winters in forest and secondary growth.

Yellow-browed Warbler *Phylloscopus inornatus* 10–11 cm

FRESH Uncommon winter visitor and passage migrant; 915–2590 m. Lacks rump band and well-defined crown stripe. Has yellowish wing-bars and supercilium (although these become whiter in worn plumage). Bill has orange at base. Call is a piercing *cheweest*. Groves and open forest.

Greenish Warbler *Phylloscopus trochiloides* 10–11 cm

a FRESH *P. t. viridanus,* **b** FRESH *P. t. trochiloides* and **c** FRESH *P. t. nitidus P. t. trochiloides* is a common summer visitor, chiefly 3000–4270 m, *P. t. viridanus* is a common winter visitor below 1830 m, and passage migrant. *P. t. nitidus* is a scarce and local spring passage migrant below 2135 m. Slurred, loud *chli-wee* call. No crown stripe; fine wing-bar (sometimes two). Breeds in forest and subalpine shrubberies; winters in well-wooded areas.

Large-billed Leaf Warbler *Phylloscopus magnirostris* 13 cm

FRESH Summer visitor, fairly common in the centre and east, uncommon in the west, 2440–3600 m; reported in winter up to 2750 m, but further confirmation is desirable. Clear, loud *der-tee* call is best feature from Greenish Warbler. Large, with large dark bill. Very bold yel-low-white supercilium and broad dark eye-stripe. Forest along mountain rivers and streams.

Tytler's Leaf Warbler *Phylloscopus tytleri* 11 cm

FRESH Rare, status uncertain, probably only a passage migrant; recorded 2135–3050 m in April. Slender, mainly dark bill, long fine supercilium, no wing-bars, shortish tail. Oak/rhodo-dendron forest and shrubberies at forest edges.

Golden-spectacled Warbler *Seicercus burkii*   10 cm

ADULT Common and widespread resident; altitudinal range uncertain, probably summers 1550–2050 m, winters down to 250 m, occasionally to 150 m. Yellow eye-ring, and yellowish-green face. Forest understorey and secondary growth.

Whistler's Warbler *Seicercus whistleri*   10 cm

ADULT Common and widespread resident; altitudinal range uncertain, probably summers 2130–3800 m, winters below 2135 m. Very similar in plumage to Golden-spectacled Warbler; dark sides of crown are not as black and are diffuse on forehead, and yellow eye-ring is broader at rear. Generally, upperparts are duller greyish-green, underparts are duller yellow, and wing-bar is usually more distinct. Shows more white in outertail feathers; especially there is much white on basal half of outer web of outermost tail feathers (generally lacking white in this area in Golden-spectacled Warbler). Song lacks tremelos and trills which are present in Golden-spectacled Warbler and this is best means of identification. Forest understorey, secondary growth and high altitude shrubberies.

Grey-hooded Warbler *Seicercus xanthoschistos*   10 cm

a   ADULT *S. x. xanthoschistos* from centre and east;   **b**   ADULT *S. x. albosuperciliaris* from far west Common and widespread resident; summers 1000–2750 m (–3050 m), winters down to 750 m (–245 m). *Phylloscopus*-like appearance. Whitish supercilium, and grey crown with pale central stripe; yellow underparts and no wing-bars. Lower canopy and bushes in forest and secondary growth.

Grey-cheeked Warbler *Seicercus poliogenys*   10 cm

ADULT Probably resident, rare in the centre and east; 2440–3200 m (–250 m). White eye-ring, and dark-grey head with poorly defined lateral crown stripes; grey ear-coverts, grey lores and white chin. Evergreen broadleaved forest.

Chestnut-crowned Warbler *Seicercus castaniceps*   9.5 cm

ADULT Frequent resident; summers 1800–2750 m, winters 250–2285 m. Chestnut crown, white eye-ring, and grey ear-coverts; white belly, yellow rump and wing-bars, and white on tail. Mainly oak forest.

Broad-billed Warbler *Tickellia hodgsoni*   10 cm

ADULT Probably resident, rare and local in the east; 2350 m (June), 2300 m (September), 2195 m (November). Chestnut crown and greyish-white supercilium; grey throat and breast, yellow belly, white on tail, and no wing-bars. Understorey in evergreen broadleaved forest.

Rufous-faced Warbler *Abroscopus albogularis*   8 cm

ADULT Very rare, possibly resident; recorded only in the far east below 1220 m. Rufous face, and black on throat; yellow breast and white belly, whitish rump, no wing-bars, no white on tail. Bamboo in moist broadleaved forest.

Black-faced Warbler *Abroscopus schisticeps*   9 cm

ADULT Local resident, fairly common in the centre and east, rare in the west; 1525–2700 m. Black mask, yellow supercilium and throat, and grey crown. Moist broadleaved forest.

Yellow-bellied Warbler *Abroscopus superciliaris*   9 cm

ADULT Resident from west-central areas eastwards; locally fairly common in the far east, uncommon farther west; mainly 245–1525 m (–2285 m). White supercilium and greyish crown; white throat and breast, yellow underparts, no wing-bars, no white on tail. Bamboo in moist broadleaved forest.

Goldcrest *Regulus regulus*   9 cm

ADULT Frequent resident; 2200–3050 m in winter, up to 4000 m in summer. Small size. Plain face, lacking supercilium, but with dark eye and pale eye-ring. Yellow centre to crown. Coniferous forest.

White-throated Laughingthrush *Garrulax albogularis* 28 cm

ADULT Common and widespread resident; summers chiefly 1800–2440 m, occasionally to 3500 m, winters from 1220 m up to at least 2255 m. White throat and upper breast, rufous-orange belly, and broad white tip to tail. Broadleaved and mixed forest and secondary growth.

White-crested Laughingthrush *Garrulax leucolophus* 28 cm

ADULT Common and widespread resident; 305–2135 m, mainly 800–1980 m. White crest and black mask, white throat and upper breast, and chestnut mantle. Broadleaved forest and secondary growth.

Lesser Necklaced Laughingthrush *Garrulax monileger* 27 cm

ADULT Resident from west-central areas eastwards, local and uncommon in central areas, becoming more frequent farther east; below 915 m. Smaller than Greater Necklaced Laughingthrush. Olive-brown primary coverts, narrow necklace thinning at centre, blackish lores, incomplete lower black border to ear-coverts. Moist broadleaved forest and secondary growth.

Greater Necklaced Laughingthrush *Garrulax pectoralis* 29 cm

ADULT Resident from west-central areas eastwards; local and uncommon in central areas, becoming more frequent farther east; below 1220 m. Larger and bigger-billed than the Lesser Necklaced Laughingthrush. Other useful distinquishing features are blackish primary coverts, broad necklace, pale lores, and complete black moustachial stripe bordering white, black or black-and-white ear-coverts. Also throat is uniform buff or white without two-toned apearance of the Lesser Necklaced Laughingthrush, and legs are slate-grey rather than brownish. Moist broadleaved forest and secondary growth.

Rufous-necked Laughingthrush *Garrulax ruficollis* 23 cm

ADULT Very local resident; mainly at Chitwan, where locally frequent; 275 m. Black face and throat, rufous patch on neck side, and rufous vent. Thick undergrowth in dense broadleaved forest.

Striated Laughingthrush *Garrulax striatus* 28 cm

ADULT Locally common resident; 1200–2850 m. Crested appearance, white streaking on head and body, and stout black bill. Broadleaved forest.

Rufous-chinned Laughingthrush *Garrulax rufogularis* 22 cm

a ADULT *G. r. rufogularis* and **b** ADULT *G. r. occidentalis* Local and frequent resident; 915–1675 m (–2135 m). Blackish cap, rufous chin and throat, black barring on upperparts, bold patterning on wing, and rufous-orange tip and black subterminal band to tail. Two intergrading races occur: eastern *rufogularis* which has grey ear-coverts, and western *occidentalis* with rufous ear-coverts. Undergrowth in broadleaved forest.

Spotted Laughingthrush *Garrulax ocellatus* 32 cm

ADULT Fairly common and widespread resident; chiefly 2135–3660 m. White spotting on chestnut upperparts, black throat and barring on breast, and white tips to chestnut, grey and black tail. Undergrowth in forest and rhododendron shrubberies.

Grey-sided Laughingthrush *Garrulax caerulatus* 25 cm
ADULT Local resident from central areas eastwards; uncommon in the centre and east; 1370–2745 m. Black face with blue orbital skin, black scaling on rufous-brown crown, and white underparts. Undergrowth in moist broadleaved forest and bamboo thickets.

Streaked Laughingthrush *Garrulax lineatus* 20 cm
ADULT Widespread resident; common in east-central Himalayas and westwards, frequent farther east; summers chiefly 2440–3905 m, winters from 1065 m to at least 2745 m. Small, and mainly grey-brown with fine pale streaking. Grey-tipped olive tail, and grey panel in wings. Scrub-covered hills, secondary growth and bushes in cultivation.

Blue-winged Laughingthrush *Garrulax squamatus* 25 cm
ADULT Scarce and local resident from west-central areas eastwards; 1220–2440 m (–700 m). White iris, black supercilium, rufous and bluish wing panels, black rear edge to wing, chestnut uppertail-coverts, and rufous-tipped tail. Undergrowth in moist broadleaved forest and bamboo thickets.

Scaly Laughingthrush *Garrulax subunicolor* 23 cm
ADULT Resident from west-central areas eastwards, local and frequent in west-central and central areas, fairly common in the east; 1500–3450 m. Yellow iris, olive and blue-grey wing panels, olive uppertail-coverts, and white-tipped tail; lacks black supercilium. Undergrowth in moist forest and rhododendron shrubberies.

Variegated Laughingthrush *Garrulax variegatus* 24 cm
ADULT Resident from east-central areas westwards, common in the west and centre, scarce farther east; 2100–4100 m. Black eye patch and throat, rufous-buff forehead, black patches on greyish wings, and grey tip to tail. Forest undergrowth and rhododendron shrubberies.

Black-faced Laughingthrush *Garrulax affinis* 25 cm
ADULT Common resident, mainly from west-central areas eastwards; summers 2750–4000 m (–4600 m), occasionally winters down to 1830 m. Black supercilium and ear-coverts, white malar stripe and neck-side patch, and grey-tipped tail. Bushes in forest and shrubberies above treeline.

Chestnut-crowned Laughingthrush *Garrulax erythrocephalus* 28 cm
ADULT Common and fairly widespread resident; summers chiefly 1800–3000 m, mainly winters 1800 m to at least 2750 m (–900 m). Race from eastern Nepal illustrated; in this race crown is grey and streaked with black, and has some chestnut on forehead and nape. Birds from central and western Nepal have chestnut crown. Other features include dark scaling/spotting on mantle and breast, olive-yellow wings, and olive-yellow tail sides. Undergrowth in broadleaved forest.

1 Abbott's Babbler *Malacocincla abbotti* 17 cm

ADULT Very local resident in the centre and east, common in the far east, rare farther west; below 275 m. Top heavy, with large bill. Unspotted white throat and breast, grey lores and supercilium, rufous uppertail-coverts and tail, and rufous-buff flanks and vent. Gives three to four whistled notes, *three cheers for me*, with the last note highest. Thickets in moist forest.

2 Puff-throated Babbler *Pellorneum ruficeps* 15 cm

ADULT Resident; locally fairly common below 915 m in the centre and east, rare up to 1675 m. Rufous crown, prominent buff supercilium, white throat (often puffed out), and bold brown spotting/streaking on breast and sides of neck. Song is a halting, impulsive *swee ti-ti-hwee hwee hwee ti swee-u,* rambling up and down the scale. Undergrowth in broadleaved forest and secondary growth.

3 Rusty-cheeked Scimitar Babbler *Pomatorhinus erythrogenys* 25 cm

ADULT Common and fairly widespread resident; 305–2440 m. Rufous sides of head and neck, and rufous sides of breast and flanks contrasting with white of rest of underparts. Forest undergrowth and thick scrub.

4 White-browed Scimitar Babbler *Pomatorhinus schisticeps* 22 cm

ADULT Frequent resident; mainly 245–915 m, rare up to 1500 m. Yellow bill and white supercilium. White centre to breast and belly, and chestnut sides to neck and breast; usually has slate-grey crown. Forest undergrowth and thick scrub.

5 Streak-breasted Scimitar Babbler *Pomatorhinus ruficollis* 19 cm

ADULT Fairly common resident; 1500–2590 m. Yellow bill and white supercilium. Smaller and smaller-billed than White-browed Scimitar Babbler, with olive-brown crown. Also has olive-brown streaking on breast and belly, and distinct rufous neck patch extending diffusely across nape. Forest undergrowth and dense scrub.

6 Coral-billed Scimitar Babbler *Pomatorhinus ferruginosus* 22 cm

ADULT Possibly resident; only one record in twentieth century, from Arun Valley. Stout red bill and white supercilium. Blackish crown. White malar stripe and upper throat contrast with rufous underparts. Undergrowth in moist forest and bamboo thickets.

7 Slender-billed Scimitar Babbler *Xiphirhynchus superciliaris* 20 cm

ADULT Scarce resident from west-central areas eastwards; 1500–3350 m. Long, down-curved black bill, feathery white supercilium, deep rufous underparts. Undergrowth in moist broadleaved forest and bamboo thickets.

Scaly-breasted Wren Babbler *Pnoepyga albiventer* 10 cm

a ADULT WHITE and **b** FULVOUS MORPH Fairly common and quite widespread resident; summers chiefly 2440–4000 m, winters 275–2285 m. Larger than the Winter Wren. Usually has buff spotting on crown and sides of neck, occasionally extending on to mantle. Song is a strong warble *tze-tze-zit tzu-stu-tzit* rising and ending abruptly. Tall herbage in moist forest.

Nepal Wren Babbler *Pnoepyga immaculata* 10 cm

a ADULT WHITE and **b** FULVOUS MORPH Local and fairly common resident from west-central areas eastwards; recorded mainly 1730–3100 m from April to July, just one sighting at 250 m in March. Narrow black centres to underpart feathers; lack of buff spotting on crown, neck sides and wings. Eight high-pitched piercing notes, fairly quickly delivered *si-su-si-si-swi-si-si-si*. Tall herbage at forest edges or in open forest near running water.

Pygmy Wren Babbler *Pnoepyga pusilla* 9 cm

a ADULT WHITE and **b** FULVOUS MORPH Frequent and quite widespread resident; summers chiefly 1500–2590 m, winters 915–1770 m (–275 m). Similar in size to the Winter Wren. Lacks buff spotting on crown and neck sides (spotting confined to lower back and wing coverts). Song is a loud, slowly drawn-out *see-saw*. Tall herbage in moist forest.

Rufous-throated Wren Babbler *Spelaeornis caudatus* 9 cm

ADULT Very rare resident in the east; 2135–2440 m. Rufous-orange throat and breast, and barring on flanks; grey ear-coverts. Song is a sudden outburst, each phrase consisting of three to five rapidly-repeated *swediddy* notes. Mossy rocks and ferns in dense broadleaved forest.

Spotted Wren Babbler *Spelaeornis formosus* 10 cm

ADULT Rare and very local resident; only recorded in the Barun Valley; 1785 m (November). Broad, dark-brown barring on rufous-brown wings and tail, irregular white flecking on grey-brown upperparts. Call is a spluttering *put-put-put* trill; quite different from the hard *chick* of the Pygmy Wren Babbler. Song is a high-pitched faltering whistle *did-did-did-dit, did-di-di-did*. Dense undergrowth in moist forest.

Wedge-billed Wren Babbler *Sphenocichla humei* 18 cm

ADULT Rare and very local resident; only recorded in Dharan forests in the east; 500 m. Large size and conical bill. Diffuse grey supercilium, blackish underparts with white streaking, and finely barred wings and tail. Dense streamside vegetation in moist broadleaved forest.

1 Rufous-capped Babbler *Stachyris ruficeps* 12 cm
ADULT Fairly common resident in the far east; 1220–2745 m. Rufous cap. Yellowish-buff ear-coverts that contrast with nape, pale yellow throat, and yellowish-buff underparts. Dense undergrowth in moist broadleaved forest.

2 Black-chinned Babbler *Stachyris pyrrhops* 10 cm
ADULT Quite widespread resident; fairly common east to east-central areas, rare farther east; 245–2440 m. Black chin and lores, and orange-buff underparts. Undergrowth in open forest and secondary growth.

3 Golden Babbler *Stachyris chrysaea* 10 cm
ADULT Rare and local resident in west-central and eastern areas; 1800–2440 m. Yellow crown with black streaking, black mask, and yellow underparts. Dense undergrowth in moist broadleaved forest.

4 Grey-throated Babbler *Stachyris nigriceps* 12 cm
ADULT Local resident from west-central areas eastwards, frequent east of Kathmandu Valley, rare farther west; summers chiefly 1220–2000 m, winters 245–1830 m. Blackish crown with white streaking, whitish supercilium, and grey and black throat. Undergrowth in moist broadleaved forest.

5 Tawny-bellied Babbler *Dumetia hyperythra* 13 cm
ADULT Scarce and local resident, mainly in the west; below 305 m. Rufous-brown forehead and forecrown and orange-buff underparts. Thorny scrub and tall grass.

6 Striped Tit Babbler *Macronous gularis* 11 cm
ADULT Fairly widespread resident, common from central areas eastwards, frequent farther west; 75–760 m. Rufous-brown cap, pale-yellow supercilium, and finely streaked pale-yellow throat and breast. Undergrowth in broadleaved forest.

7 Chestnut-capped Babbler *Timalia pileata* 17 cm
ADULT Resident, common at Chitwan, uncommon elsewhere; below 305 m. Chestnut cap and black mask contrasting with white forehead and supercilium. Tall grass, reedbeds and scrub.

8 Yellow-eyed Babbler *Chrysomma sinense* 18 cm
ADULT Local resident, fairly common at Chitwan and Sukila Phanta, frequent in the west; below 365 m. Yellow iris and orange eye-ring, white lores and supercilium, and white throat and breast. Tall grass, bushes and reeds.

9 Jerdon's Babbler *Chrysomma altirostre* 17 cm
ADULT Rare and very local resident, only recorded at Chitwan and Sukila Phanta; below 250 m. Brown iris, grey lores and supercilium, and grey throat and breast. Stout bill. Reedbeds and tall grassland. Globally threatened.

Spiny Babbler *Turdoides nipalensis* 25 cm

a **b** ADULT Frequent and fairly widespread endemic resident; summers 1500–2135 m, winters 915–1830 m. White patterning on face, and black shaft streaking on white or buff throat and breast. Dense scrub, especially away from cultivation.

Common Babbler *Turdoides caudatus* 23 cm

ADULT Very local, but fairly common resident in the west terai; up to 120 m. Streaked upperparts. Unstreaked whitish throat and breast centre. Legs and feet are yellowish. Dry cultivation and scrub.

Striated Babbler *Turdoides earlei* 21 cm

ADULT Fairly widespread resident; locally common in the east, uncommon elsewhere; below 305 m. Streaked upperparts. Brown mottling on fulvous throat and breast. Legs and feet are greyish to olive-brown. Reedbeds and tall grass in wet habitats.

Slender-billed Babbler *Turdoides longirostris* 23 cm

ADULT Very local resident, recorded only at Chitwan, where locally fairly common; 250 m. Unstreaked dark rufous-brown upperparts, white throat and buff underparts, and curved black bill. Tall grass and reeds. Globally threatened.

Large Grey Babbler *Turdoides malcolmi* 28 cm

ADULT Local and frequent resident in the western terai; up to 105 m. Dull white sides to long, graduated tail; unmottled pinkish-grey throat and breast, pale grey forehead and dark grey lores. Open dry scrub and cultivation.

Jungle Babbler *Turdoides striatus* 25 cm

ADULT Fairly common and widespread resident; below 1220 m (–1500 m). Uniform tail; variable dark mottling and streaking on throat and breast. Cultivation and secondary scrub.

Silver-eared Mesia *Leiothrix argentauris* 15 cm

MALE Local resident; frequent in the far east, rare farther west; mainly 365–1220 m (205–1830 m). Black crown, grey ear-coverts, orange-yellow throat and breast, and crimson wing panel. Male has crimson uppertail-coverts and undertail-coverts. Female has olive-yellow uppertail-coverts and orange-buff undertail-coverts. Bushes in broadleaved evergreen forest.

Red-billed Leiothrix *Leiothrix lutea* 13 cm

MALE Fairly common resident; chiefly 1220–2440 m (915–2745 m). Red bill, yellowish-olive crown, yellow throat and orange breast, and forked black tail. Male has some crimson edgings to flight feathers; in female the crimson is replaced by yellow. Undergrowth in moist broadleaved forest.

Cutia *Cutia nipalensis* 20 cm

a MALE and **b** FEMALE Scarce and very local resident from west-central areas eastwards; favours 2100–2300 m (1095–2745 m). Grey crown and dark mask, blue-grey panel in wings, and black barring on flanks. Female has spotted mantle. Mossy broadleaved forest.

Black-headed Shrike Babbler *Pteruthius rufiventer* 17 cm

a MALE and **b** FEMALE Scarce and local resident from west-central areas eastwards; mainly 2135–2500 m (–3230 m). Male has grey throat and breast, black head without white supercilium, black wings, and rufous-brown mantle. Female has black on nape, and olive mantle and tail. Dense, moist broadleaved forest.

White-browed Shrike Babbler *Pteruthius flaviscapis* 16 cm

a MALE and **b** FEMALE Fairly common and quite widespread resident; summers mainly 1800–2200 m, winters 1500–2135 m (–305 m). Male has rufous tertials, black cap with white supercilium, and grey mantle. Female has grey cap and olive mantle; larger size and rufous tertials best distinguish it from the Green Shrike Babbler. Broadleaved forest, favours oaks.

Green Shrike Babbler *Pteruthius xanthochlorus* 13 cm

MALE Frequent resident; 1980–3355 m. Grey crown and nape, narrow white or yellowish-white wing-bar, greyish-white throat and breast, and yellowish flanks. Broadleaved and coniferous forests.

Black-eared Shrike Babbler *Pteruthius melanotis* 11 cm

a MALE and **b** FEMALE Local and frequent resident from west-central areas eastwards; summers 1800–2440 m, winters 1500–2000 m (–305 m). Black patch on ear-coverts. Male has chestnut throat and breast, and white wing-bars. Female has chestnut reduced to malar stripe, and buff wing-bars. Moist broadleaved forest.

White-hooded Babbler *Gampsorhynchus rufulus* 23 cm

a ADULT and **b** JUVENILE Very rare, possibly resident in far east; below 1400 m. Adult has white head and underparts. Juvenile has rufous-orange crown. Bamboo and other undergrowth in evergreen broadleaved forest.

Rusty-fronted Barwing *Actinodura egertoni* 23 cm

ADULT Rare and local resident from west-central areas eastwards; 1785–2400 m. Rufous front to head, unstreaked grey crown and nape. Has longer tail than Hoary-throated Barwing. Undergrowth in moist broadleaved forest.

Hoary-throated Barwing *Actinodura nipalensis* 20 cm

ADULT Fairly common and quite widespread resident; mainly 1980–3000 m (1500–3500 m). Prominent buffish-white shaft streaking on crown and nape, black moustachial stripe, streaked mantle, and greyish throat and breast. Mossy broadleaved forest.

Blue-winged Minla *Minla cyanouroptera* 15 cm

ADULT Fairly common and quite widespread resident; summers up to 2440 m (–2750 m), winters mainly 1000–1830 m (–2285 m). Blue on crown and on wings and tail; wine-red to grey underparts. Bushes in forest.

Chestnut-tailed Minla *Minla strigula* 14 cm

ADULT Common and widespread resident; summers chiefly 2440–3750 m, winters mainly 1400–2745 m (–1035 m). Orange crown, black-and-white barring on throat, and yellow sides to tail. Mainly broadleaved forest.

Red-tailed Minla *Minla ignotincta* 14 cm

a MALE and **b** FEMALE Resident from west-central areas eastwards, fairly common in the far east, frequent farther west; summers mainly 1830–3400 m, winters 760 m to at least 2285 m. White supercilium contrasting with dark crown and ear-coverts. Male has maroon-brown mantle (olive-brown in female), and bright red panel in wings and tail (more orange in female). Moist broadleaved forest.

Golden-breasted Fulvetta *Alcippe chrysotis* 11 cm

ADULT Very local resident in west-central and far eastern areas; 2435–3050 m. Blue-grey and yellow fulvetta with silvery-grey ear-coverts. Bamboo.

Rufous-winged Fulvetta *Alcippe castaneceps* 10 cm

ADULT Common resident from west-central areas eastwards; summers 1825–2745 m (–3505 m), winters from 1525 m to at least 2745 m. Chestnut crown streaked with buffish-white, black wing-bar, white supercilium and black eye-stripe. Undergrowth in moist broadleaved forest.

White-browed Fulvetta *Alcippe vinipectus* 11 cm

a ADULT *A. v. vinipectus* from centre and west; **b** ADULT *A. v. chumbiensis* from east Common and widespread resident; summers 1825–2745 m (–3505 m), winters from 1525 m to at least 2745 m. Broad white supercilium, dark ear-coverts, and black panel in flight feathers. *Chumbiensis* has streaked throat. Subalpine shrubberies and bushes in temperate and subalpine forest.

Nepal Fulvetta *Alcippe nipalensis* 12 cm

ADULT Locally common resident; winters chiefly 245–1830 m, summers up to 2285 m. Grey head with black lateral crown stripes. Undergrowth in moist forest.

White-naped Yuhina *Yuhina bakeri* 13 cm

ADULT Very rare and local resident in far east; 1525 m, 2200 m. Rufous crest, white nape, and white streaking on ear-coverts. Broadleaved evergreen forest.

Whiskered Yuhina *Yuhina flavicollis* 13 cm

ADULT Common and widespread resident; summers chiefly 1830–2745 m, winters 800–2745 m. Pale orange hindcollar, and black moustachial stripe. Broadleaved forest and secondary growth.

Stripe-throated Yuhina *Yuhina gularis* 14 cm

ADULT Common and widespread resident; summers mainly 2435–3700 m, winters 1700–3050 m (–1400 m). Large size, streaked throat, and black and orange wing panels. Broadleaved and broadleaved/coniferous forests.

Rufous-vented Yuhina *Yuhina occipitalis* 13 cm

ADULT Common resident from west-central areas eastwards; summers 2400–3600 m, winters from 1830 m to at least 2745 m. Grey crest, rufous lores and nape patch, and rufous vent. Broadleaved forest.

Black-chinned Yuhina *Yuhina nigrimenta* 11 cm

ADULT Rare resident; 500–1500 m. Black lores and chin, black crest with grey streaking, and red lower mandible. Moist broadleaved forest.

White-bellied Yuhina *Yuhina zantholeuca* 11 cm

ADULT Local and frequent resident, locally fairly common; 150–2285 m, mainly below 1600 m. Olive-yellow upperparts and white underparts. Broadleaved forest.

Fire-tailed Myzornis *Myzornis pyrrhoura* 12 cm

a MALE and **b** FEMALE Uncommon and local resident from west-central areas eastwards; recorded 2000–3950 m, up to at least 2745 m in winter. Emerald-green, with black mask. Male has red breast-patch, and brighter red sides to tail than female. Subalpine shrubberies, mossy forest and bamboo.

Rufous-backed Sibia *Heterophasia annectans* 18 cm

ADULT Rare and local resident in the far east; 1450–2650 m. Black cap, white throat and breast, rufous back and rump, and black tail with white tips. Broadleaved evergreen forest.

Rufous Sibia *Heterophasia capistrata* 21 cm

ADULT Common and widespread resident; summers chiefly 1980–3000 m, winters 1050–2750 m (–850 m). Black cap, and rufous collar and underparts; black and grey bands on rufous tail. Mainly broadleaved forest, especially oak.

Long-tailed Sibia *Heterophasia picaoides* 30 cm

ADULT Recorded in nineteenth century; also several recent unconfirmed reports from the Churia hills, Chitwan. Mainly grey, with long tail with whitish tips, and white patch on secondaries. Broadleaved forest.

Great Parrotbill *Conostoma oemodium* 28 cm

ADULT Uncommon and quite widespread resident; 2700–3660 m. Huge conical yellow bill, greyish-white forehead, and dark brown lores. Bamboo stands in forest.

Brown Parrotbill *Paradoxornis unicolor* 21 cm

ADULT Uncommon and very local resident from west-central areas eastwards; 2590–3300 m. Stout yellowish bill, blackish lateral crown stripes, and dusky grey underparts. Bamboo stands and bushes.

Fulvous Parrotbill *Paradoxornis fulvifrons* 12 cm

ADULT Uncommon and local resident from west-central areas eastwards; 2745–3505 m. Fulvous and olive-brown head markings, and fulvous throat and breast. Bamboo stands.

Black-throated Parrotbill *Paradoxornis nipalensis* 10 cm

a ADULT *P. n. nipalensis* from west and centre; **b** ADULT *P. n. humii* from far east Frequent resident; 2000–3000 m (–1050 m). Grey or orange crown and ear-coverts, blackish lateral crown stripes and throat, white malar patch. Bamboo and dense forest undergrowth.

Singing Bushlark *Mirafra cantillans*   14 cm
ADULT Scarce, probably resident, only recorded at Sukila Phanta; 100 m. Stout bill, and rufous on wing; white outer tail feathers, weak and rather restricted spotting on upper breast, and whitish throat with brownish to rufous-buff breast-band. Song, delivered in flight, is sweet and full with much mimicry. Grassland.

Bengal Bushlark *Mirafra assamica*   15 cm
ADULT Common and widespread resident; below 275 m. Stout bill, short tail with rufous-buff on outer tail feathers, and rufous on wing. Upperparts are brownish-grey, and underparts are dirty rufous with paler throat. Has pronounced dark spotting on breast. Song is a repetition of a series of thin, high-pitched disyllabic notes, usually delivered in prolonged song flight. Fallow cultivation, short grassland.

Ashy-crowned Sparrow Lark *Eremopterix grisea*   12 cm
a MALE and **b   c** FEMALE Fairly common and widespread resident; below 305 m (–730 m). Male has grey crown and nape, and brownish-black underparts. Female has stout greyish bill, rather uniform head and upperparts, and dark grey underwing-coverts. Open dry scrub, dry cultivation.

Rufous-tailed Lark *Ammomanes phoenicurus*   16 cm
ADULT Rare and local resident in the western terai; 75 m. Dusky grey-brown upperparts, rufous-orange underparts, prominent dark streaking on throat and breast, and rufous orange uppertail-coverts and tail, with dark terminal bar. Open dry scrub, cultivation.

Greater Short-toed Lark *Calandrella brachydactyla*   14 cm
a ADULT *C. b. dukhunensis* and **b** ADULT *C. b. longipennis* Frequent, mainly a passage migrant, also a winter visitor; 75–4575 m (–5000 m). Stouter bill than Hume's Short-toed Lark, with more prominent supercilium and eye-stripe; upperparts warmer, with more prominent streaking; dark breast-side patches often apparent. Breast of *dukhunensis* has warm rufous-buff wash, especially at sides. Open stony and short grass areas, fallow cultivation.

Hume's Short-toed Lark *Calandrella acutirostris*   14 cm
ADULT Common in summer in the north-west, uncommon in winter and on passage; 75–4800 m. Greyer and less heavily streaked upperparts than the Greater Short-toed Lark, with pinkish uppertail-coverts; dark breast-side patch usually apparent, with greyish-buff breast-band. Head pattern less pronounced than that of the Greater Short-toed Lark, with rather uniform ear-coverts. Breeds in high-altitude semi-desert; winters in fallow cultivation.

Sand Lark *Calandrella raytal*   12 cm
ADULT Locally common and fairly widespread resident; below 305 m. Small size, short tail, cold sandy-grey upperparts, and whitish underparts with fine sparse streaking on breast. Sandy river banks.

Crested Lark *Galerida cristata*   18 cm
ADULT Widespread resident, fairly common in the west, rare in the east; below 275 m. Large size and very prominent crest. Sandy upperparts and well-streaked breast; broad, rounded wings, rufous-buff underwing-coverts and outer tail feathers. Dry cultivation.

Oriental Skylark *Alauda gulgula*   16 cm
ADULT Widespread, fairly common resident and winter visitor; resident below 150 m, also breeds up to at least 3600 m, and winters 1280–1700 m. Fine bill, buffish-white outer tail feathers, and indistinct rufous wing panel. Grassland, cultivation.

Horned Lark *Eremophila alpestris*   18 cm
a MALE and **b** FEMALE Fairly common resident; 3965–5490 m (2600–5900 m). Black-and-white head pattern and black breast-band. Stony ground, pastures.

Thick-billed Flowerpecker *Dicaeum agile* 10 cm

ADULT Frequent and widespread resident; below 800 m all year, summers up to 2135 m. Thick bill; diffuse malar stripe, streaking on breast, and indistinct white tip to tail. Broadleaved forest and well-wooded country.

Yellow-vented Flowerpecker *Dicaeum chrysorrheum* 10 cm

ADULT Rare and very local resident in the centre and east; 245 m. Fine, down-curved bill; dark malar stripe and breast streaking, and orange-yellow vent. Open forest and forest edges.

Yellow-bellied Flowerpecker *Dicaeum melanoxanthum* 13 cm

a MALE and **b** FEMALE Local and frequent resident from west-central areas eastwards; summers 2350–3000 m, winters from 1050 m to at least 1550 m. Large size and stout bill; white centre of throat and breast, dark breast sides, and yellow belly and vent. Broadleaved forest.

Pale-billed Flowerpecker *Dicaeum erythrorynchos* 8 cm

ADULT Frequent and widespread resident; below 305 m. Pale bill. Greyish-olive upperparts, and pale-grey underparts. Open broadleaved forest and well-wooded areas.

Plain Flowerpecker *Dicaeum concolor* 9 cm

ADULT Locally fairly common resident from central areas eastwards; 305–1525 m (150–2500 m). Dark bill. Olive-green upperparts and dusky greyish-olive underparts. Edges of broadleaved forest and well-wooded areas.

Fire-breasted Flowerpecker *Dicaeum ignipectus* 9 cm

a MALE and **b** FEMALE Common and widespread resident; summers mainly 1830–2700 m, winters 915–2285 m. Male has metallic blue/green upperparts, and buff underparts with red breast. Female has olive-green upperparts, and orange-buff throat and breast. Broadleaved forest and secondary growth.

Scarlet-backed Flowerpecker *Dicaeum cruentatum* 9 cm

a MALE and **b** FEMALE Rare and very local in the east, probably resident; 305 m, 2135 m. Male has scarlet upperparts and black 'sides'. Female has scarlet rump. Broadleaved forest.

Ruby-cheeked Sunbird *Anthreptes singalensis* 11 cm

a MALE, **b** FEMALE and **c** JUVENILE Very local and rare resident in central and eastern areas; below 455 m. Rufous-orange throat and yellow underparts. Male has metallic green upperparts and 'ruby' cheeks. Juvenile is uniform yellow below. Open broadleaved forest and forest edges, favours evergreens.

Purple Sunbird *Nectarinia asiatica* 10 cm
a MALE, **b** FEMALE and **c** ECLIPSE MALE Widespread and common resident below 365 m; mainly a summer visitor 900–2135 m. Male metallic purple. Female has uniform yellowish underparts, with faint supercilium and darker mask; can have greyer upperparts and whiter underparts. Eclipse plumage male is similar to female but with dark stripe down centre of throat. Open forest and gardens.

Mrs Gould's Sunbird *Aethopyga gouldiae* 10 cm
a MALE and **b** FEMALE Widespread and uncommon resident; summers chiefly 2500–3655 m, winters from 1830 m up to at least 2700 m. Male has metallic purplish-blue crown, ear-coverts and throat, crimson mantle and back (reaching yellow rump), yellow belly, and blue tail. Female has pale yellow rump, yellow belly, short bill, and prominent white on tail. Rhododendron and other flowering trees and shrubs in forest.

Green-tailed Sunbird *Aethopyga nipalensis* 11 cm
a MALE and **b** FEMALE Widespread and common resident; summers chiefly 1830–3000 m (–3505 m), winters 915–2745 m (–305 m). Male has metallic blue-green crown, throat and tail; mantle is maroon but has olive-green back. Lack of well-defined yellow rump-band (although rump can be a slightly paler yellowish-green), and longer, graduated tail help separate from female Mrs Gould's Sunbird. Oak/rhododendron and mixed forests and secondary growth.

Black-throated Sunbird *Aethopyga saturata* 11 cm
a MALE and **b** FEMALE Widespread and frequent resident; mainly 1000–1830 m (305–2200 m). Male has black throat and breast, greyish-olive underparts, and crimson mantle. Combination of dusky olive-green underparts, yellow rump, and long, dark and noticeably down-curved bill, are useful features from other female sunbirds. Bushes in forest and secondary growth.

Crimson Sunbird *Aethopyga siparaja* 11 cm
a MALE and **b** FEMALE Widespread resident; fairly common below 915 m, frequent up to 1200 m (–2100 m). Male has crimson mantle, scarlet throat and breast, and grey belly. Female lacks yellow rump; most similar to the female Green-tailed Sunbird but has shorter and squarer tail with only indistinct pale tips to outertail feathers, and shorter and broader-based bill with paler lower mandible. Light forest, groves and gardens.

Fire-tailed Sunbird *Aethopyga ignicauda* 12 cm
a MALE, **b** ECLIPSE MALE and **c** FEMALE Widespread and fairly common resident; summers mainly 3000–4000 m, winters 1050–2135 m (610–2895 m). Male has red uppertail-coverts and red on tail. Female has yellowish belly, yellowish wash to rump, and brownish-orange tail sides (which lack white at tip). Breeds in rhododendron shrubberies; winters in broadleaved and mixed forest.

Little Spiderhunter *Arachnothera longirostra* 16 cm
ADULT Rare and very local resident in central and eastern areas; below 305 m. Very long down-curved bill, unstreaked upperparts, yellowish underparts. Wild bananas in moist broadleaved forest.

Streaked Spiderhunter *Arachnothera magna* 19 cm
ADULT Patchily distributed and locally fairly common resident in central and eastern areas; below 450 m (–2135 m). Very long down-curved bill, and boldly streaked upperparts and underparts. Moist broadleaved forest, favours bananas.

House Sparrow *Passer domesticus* 15 cm
a MALE and **b** FEMALE Common and widespread resident; below 1600 m, occasionally up to 2135 m (–4350 m). Male has grey crown, black throat and upper breast, chestnut nape, and brownish mantle. Female has buffish supercilium and unstreaked greyish-white underparts. *See* Appendix 1 for comparison with Spanish Sparrow. Habitation, also nearby cultivation,

Russet Sparrow *Passer rutilans* 14.5 cm
a MALE and **b** FEMALE Resident, fairly common from west-central areas westwards, uncommon farther east; mainly 915–2900 m, also common at 4270 m (75–4350 m). Male lacks black cheek patch; has bright chestnut mantle, and yellowish wash to underparts. Female has prominent supercilium and dark eye-stripe, rufous-brown scapulars and rump, and yellowish wash to underparts. Open forest, forest edges and cultivation.

Eurasian Tree Sparrow *Passer montanus* 14 cm
ADULT Common and widespread resident; summers chiefly 610–4270 m, up to 3795 m in winter, also breeds at 75 m. Chestnut crown, and black spot on ear-coverts. Sexes similar. Habitation and nearby cultivation.

Chestnut-shouldered Petronia *Petronia xanthocollis* 13.5 cm
a MALE and **b** FEMALE Fairly widespread resident, frequent in the far west and at Chitwan, uncommon elsewhere; mainly below 305 m (–650 m). Unstreaked brownish-grey head and upperparts, and prominent wing-bars. Male and some females have yellow on throat. Male with chestnut lesser coverts and white wing-bars; lesser coverts brown and wing-bars buff in female. Open dry forest and scrub.

Tibetan Snowfinch *Montifringilla adamsi* 17 cm
a ADULT and **b** JUVENILE Common resident in the Tibetan plateau region in the north-west; summers 4200–5100 m, winters 2530–3445 m. Largely white or buffish-white wing coverts. Adult has black throat, but head otherwise rather plain grey-brown. Open stony hillsides, plateaux and near upland villages.

White-rumped Snowfinch *Pyrgilauda taczanowskii* 17 cm
ADULT Status uncertain, possibly a rare resident; one collected in June at 4815 m in Mustang, in the north-west. White rump, black lores, white supercilium and throat, and streaked greyish upperparts. Open stony Tibetan steppe habitat.

Rufous-necked Snowfinch *Pyrgilauda ruficollis* 15 cm
ADULT Status uncertain; possibly a rare resident, several records June–November; 3290–4850 m. Cinnamon nape and neck sides, rufous patch at rear of ear-coverts, black malar stripe and white throat, and prominent wing-bars. Open stony areas and short grassland in Tibetan steppe country.

Plain-backed Snowfinch *Pyrgilauda blanfordi* 15 cm
ADULT Status uncertain, possibly a rare resident; one collected in June at 4815 m in Mustang, in the north-west. Cinnamon nape and neck sides, black 'spur' dividing white supercilium, black throat; lacks wing-bars. Tibetan steppe country.

1 White Wagtail *Motacilla alba* 19 cm

a MALE BREEDING, **b** MALE NON-BREEDING and **c** JUVENILE *M. a. alboides*; **d** MALE BREEDING and **e** 1ST-WINTER *M. a. personata*; **f** MALE *M. a. leucopsis*; **g** MALE *M. a. ocularis*; **h** MALE *M. a. baicalensis*; **i** MALE *M. a. dukhunensis* Common and widespread passage migrant, winter visitor and resident; summers 2400–4800 m, winters mainly below 1500 m (–5000 m on passage). Extremely variable. Head pattern, and grey or black mantle, indicate racial identification of breeding males. Non-breeding and first-winter birds often not racially distinguishable. Never has head pattern of the White-browed Wagtail. Breeds by running waters in open country; winters near water in open country.

2 White-browed Wagtail *Motacilla maderaspatensis* 21 cm

a ADULT and **b** JUVENILE Fairly common and widespread resident; mainly below 915 m, uncommon up to 1700 m, a summer visitor at higher altitudes. Large black-and-white wagtail. Head black with white supercilium, and black mantle. Juvenile has brownish-grey head, mantle and breast, with white supercilium. Banks of rivers, pools and lakes.

3 Citrine Wagtail *Motacilla citreola* 19 cm

a MALE BREEDING, **b** ADULT FEMALE, **c** JUVENILE and **d** **e** 1ST-WINTER, *M. c. calcarata*; **f** MALE BREEDING *M. c. citreola* Mainly a winter visitor below 250 m, also a passage migrant up to 5200 m; fairly common at Chitwan and Koshi, scattered records from elsewhere. Broad white wing-bars in all plumages. Male breeding has yellow head and underparts, and black or grey mantle. Female breeding and adult non-breeding have broad yellow supercilium continuing around ear-coverts, grey upperparts, and mainly yellow underparts. Juvenile lacks yellow, and has brownish upperparts, buffish supercilium (with dark upper edge) and ear-covert surround, and spotted black gorget. First-winter has grey upperparts; distinguished from the Yellow Wagtail by white surround to ear-coverts, dark border to supercilium, pale brown forehead, pale lores, all-dark bill, and white undertail-coverts; by early November, has yellowish supercilium, ear-covert surround and throat. Marshes and wet fields.

4 Yellow Wagtail *Motacilla flava* 18 cm

a MALE BREEDING, **b** ADULT FEMALE, **c** JUVENILE and **d** 1ST-WINTER *M. f. beema*; **e** MALE *M. f. leucocephala*; **f** MALE and **g** 1ST-WINTER *M. f. lutea*; **h** MALE *M. f. melanogrisea*; **i** MALE *M. f. taivana*; **j** MALE and **k** 1ST-WINTER *M. f. thunbergi* Frequent and widespread; mainly a winter visitor below 1350 m, also a passage migrant up to 3800 m. Five races have been recorded, and *lutea* is likely to occur. Male breeding has olive-green upperparts and yellow underparts, with considerable variation in coloration of head depending on race. Female extremely variable, but often has some features of breeding male. First-winter birds typically have brownish-olive upperparts, and whitish underparts with variable yellowish wash; in some races can closely resemble the Citrine Wagtail, but have narrower white supercilium that does not continue around ear-coverts. Damp grasslands and marshes.

5 Grey Wagtail *Motacilla cinerea* 19 cm

a MALE BREEDING and **b** ADULT FEMALE Common and widespread resident; breeds mainly 1110–3550 m (–4115 m), winters below 365 m, occasionally up to 1550 m. Longer-tailed than other wagtails. In all plumages, shows white supercilium, grey upperparts, and yellow vent and undertail-coverts. Male has black throat when breeding. Fast-flowing rocky streams in summer, slower streams in winter.

Richard's Pipit *Anthus richardi* 17 cm

ADULT Frequent winter visitor and passage migrant; below 1500 m. Large size and loud *schreep* call. Well-streaked upperparts and breast, pale lores, long and stout bill, and long hindclaw. When flushed, typically gains height with deep undulations (compared with Paddyfield Pipit). Moist grassland and cultivation.

Paddyfield Pipit *Anthus rufulus* 15 cm

ADULT Common and widespread resident; below 1830 m (–2440 m in summer). Smaller than Richard's Pipit, with *chip-chip-chip* call. Well-streaked breast; lores usually look pale. When flushed, has comparatively weak, rather fluttering flight. Short grassland and cultivation.

Tawny Pipit *Anthus campestris* 16 cm

a ADULT, **b** 1ST-WINTER and **c** JUVENILE Rare winter visitor below 305 m, and passage migrant. Loud *tchilip* or *chep* call. Adult and first-winter have plain or faintly streaked upperparts and breast. Juvenile more heavily streaked. Useful features are dark lores, comparatively fine bill, rather horizontal stance, and wagtail-like behaviour.

Blyth's Pipit *Anthus godlewskii* 16.5 cm

ADULT Passage migrant in the east; up to 4250 m. Call a wheezy *spzeeu*. Smaller than Richard's Pipit, with shorter tail and shorter and more pointed bill. Shape of centres to adult median coverts distinctive if seen well, but this feature is of no use in first-winter and juvenile plumage; these feathers have square-shaped, well-defined black centres with broad, pale tips; centres to median coverts more triangular in shape, and more diffuse, in the adult Richard's Pipit. Pale lores and well-streaked breast useful distinctions from the Tawny Pipit. Grassland and cultivation.

Long-billed Pipit *Anthus similis* 20 cm

ADULT Rare breeder, possibly resident, found mainly in the west; below 1700 m. Considerably larger than the Tawny Pipit, with very large bill and shorter-looking legs. Dark lores. Greyish upperparts and warm buff colour to unstreaked or only lightly streaked underparts. Call is a deep *chup* and a loud ringing *che-vlee*. Breeds on rocky or scrubby slopes; winters in dry cultivation and scrub.

Upland Pipit *Anthus sylvanus* 17 cm

a **b** ADULT Widespread and locally fairly common resident; summers 1830–2900 m, winters 1350–2000 m. Large, heavily streaked pipit with short and broad bill, and rather narrow, pointed tail feathers. Fine black streaking on underparts, whitish supercilium; ground colour of underparts varies from warm buff to rather cold and grey. Call is a sparrow-like *chirp*. Rocky and grassy slopes.

Tree Pipit *Anthus trivialis* 15 cm

a ADULT *A. t. trivialis* and **b** ADULT *A. t. haringtoni* Uncommon and widespread winter visitor and passage migrant; up to 3050 m. *Haringtoni* has not been recorded but probably occurs. Buffish-brown to greyish ground colour to upperparts (lacking greenish-olive cast), and buffish fringes to greater coverts, tertials and secondaries. Fallow cultivation and open country with scattered trees.

Olive-backed Pipit *Anthus hodgsoni* 15 cm

a ADULT FRESH and **b** WORN *A. h. hodgsoni*; **c** ADULT *A. h. yunnanensis* Common and widespread resident; summers mainly 2200–4000 m (–1800 m), winters below 2560 m. Greenish-olive cast to upperparts, and greenish-olive fringes to greater coverts, tertials and secondaries. Typically, has more striking head pattern than the Tree Pipit. *A. h. yunnanensis*, which is a winter visitor, is much less heavily streaked on upperparts than nominate race. Open forest and shrubberies.

Red-throated Pipit *Anthus cervinus* 15 cm

a ADULT MALE BREEDING and **b** 1ST-YEAR Uncommon winter visitor and passage migrant; up to 5180 m. Adult has reddish throat and upper breast, which tend to be paler on female and on autumn/winter birds. First-year has heavily streaked upperparts, pale 'braces', well-defined white wing bars, strongly contrasting blackish centres and whitish fringes to tertials, pronounced dark malar patch, and more boldly streaked breast and (especially) flanks. Call a drawn-out *seeeeee*. Marshes, grassland and stubble.

Rosy Pipit *Anthus roseatus* 15 cm

a b ADULT BREEDING and **c** NON-BREEDING Fairly common and widespread resident; summers mainly 4000–5050 m, winters 760–1500 m (–75 m). Always has boldly streaked upperparts, olive cast to mantle, and olive to olive-green edges to greater coverts, secondaries and tertials. Adult breeding has mauve-pink wash to underparts. Non-breeding plumage has heavily streaked underparts and dark lores. Call a weak *seep-seep*. Breeds above tree-line; winters in marshes, damp grassland, cultivation.

Water Pipit *Anthus spinoletta* 15 cm

a ADULT BREEDING and **b** NON-BREEDING Probably a rare winter visitor and passage migrant; below 915 m. In all plumages, has lightly streaked upperparts, lacks olive-green on wing, has dark legs, and usually has pale lores; underparts less heavily marked than on Rosy and Buff-bellied Pipits. Orange-buff wash to supercilium and underparts in breeding plumage. Marshes, cultivation.

Buff-bellied Pipit *Anthus rubescens* 15 cm

a ADULT BREEDING and **b** NON-BREEDING Probably a rare winter visitor and passage migrant; below 2715 m. In all plumages, has lightly streaked upperparts, lacks olive-green on wing, and has pale lores; underparts more heavily streaked, upperparts darker and legs paler compared with the Water Pipit. Marshes, damp cultivation.

Alpine Accentor *Prunella collaris* 15.5–17 cm
ADULT Frequent resident; summers chiefly 4200–5500 m (–7900 m), winters from 2440 m to at least 3795 m. Black barring on throat, grey breast and belly, and black band across greater coverts. Open stony slopes, rocky pastures.

Altai Accentor *Prunella himalayana* 15–15.5 cm
ADULT Fairly common winter visitor; 2135–4300 m (–1200 m). White throat, with black gorget and spotting in malar region; white underparts, with rufous mottling on breast and flanks. Grassy and stony slopes.

Robin Accentor *Prunella rubeculoides* 16–17 cm
ADULT Fairly common resident; summers mainly 4200–5000 m, winters from 2655 m up to at least 3960 m. Uniform grey head, rusty-orange band across breast, and whitish belly. Breeds in dwarf scrub near streams and pools, winters in dry stony areas.

Rufous-breasted Accentor *Prunella strophiata* 15 cm
a ADULT and **b** 1ST-WINTER? Fairly common resident; summers chiefly 3500–4930 m, winters from 1600 m up to at least 3650 m. Rufous band across breast, white-and-rufous supercilium, blackish ear-coverts, and streaking on neck sides and underparts. Breeds on high-altitude slopes; winters in bushes in cultivation and scrub.

Brown Accentor *Prunella fulvescens* 14.5–15 cm
ADULT Common resident in the Tibetan plateau region in the north-west; summers up to 4880 m, winters from 2300 m up to at least 3800 m. White supercilium, faintly streaked upperparts, and pale orange-buff underparts. Dry scrubby and rocky slopes.

Black-throated Accentor *Prunella atrogularis* 14.5–15 cm
a ADULT and **b** 1ST-WINTER FEMALE Fairly common winter visitor to the far north-west; 2440–3050 m. Orange-buff supercilium and submoustachial stripe, and black throat. Some have indistinct (or lack) black on throat, which instead is whitish; note heavily streaked mantle. Bushes near cultivation, dry scrub.

Maroon-backed Accentor *Prunella immaculata* 16 cm
ADULT Frequent winter visitor to west-central areas and eastwards; 1830–2700 m (3600–4400 m in September). Grey head and breast, maroon-brown mantle, yellow iris, and grey panel across wing. Moist forest.

Plain Mountain Finch *Leucosticte nemoricola* 15 cm
a ADULT BREEDING and **b** JUVENILE Common and widespread resident; summers chiefly 4200–5200 m, winters from 2000 m up to at least 3650 m. Distinguished from Brandt's Mountain Finch by boldly streaked mantle with pale 'braces', and distinct patterning on wing coverts (dark-centred, with well-defined wing-bars). Juvenile warmer rufous-buff than adult. Breeds on alpine slopes; winters in open forest and upland cultivation.

Brandt's Mountain Finch *Leucosticte brandti* 16.5–19 cm
a MALE BREEDING and **b** 1ST-SUMMER Fairly common resident; summers mainly 4200–5250 m (–6000 m), usually winters above 3500 m (–2350 m). Unstreaked to lightly streaked mantle, and rather uniform wing coverts. More striking white panel on wing and more prominent white edges to tail compared with Plain Mountain Finch. Adult breeding has sooty-black head and nape, and brownish-grey mantle with poorly defined streaking. Male has pink on rump. Stony slopes and alpine meadows

Black-breasted Weaver *Ploceus benghalensis* 14 cm

a MALE BREEDING and **b** **c** NON-BREEDING Local and fairly common resident; below 245 m. Breeding male has yellow crown and black breast-band. In female and non-breeding plumages, breast-band can be broken by whitish fringes or restricted to small patches at sides, and may show indistinct, diffuse streaking on lower breast and flanks; head pattern as on female/non-breeding Streaked Weaver, except crown, nape and ear-coverts more uniform; rump also indistinctly streaked and, like nape, contrasts with heavily streaked mantle/back. Tall moist grassland, reedy marshes.

Streaked Weaver *Ploceus manyar* 14 cm

a MALE BREEDING and **b** NON-BREEDING Rare and very local migrant, mainly found at Koshi; below 150 m. Breeding male has yellow crown, dark brown head sides and throat, and heavily streaked breast and flanks. Other plumages typically show boldly streaked underparts; can be only lightly streaked on underparts, when best differentiated from the Baya Weaver by combination of yellow supercilium and neck patch, heavily streaked crown, dark or heavily streaked ear-coverts, and pronounced dark malar and moustachial stripes. Reedbeds.

Baya Weaver *Ploceus philippinus* 15 cm

a MALE BREEDING and **b** NON-BREEDING *P. p. philippinus* in west; **c** MALE BREEDING *P. p. burmanicus* in east Common and widespread, resident in lowlands, mainly a summer visitor in Himalayas; below 1370 m. Breeding male *P. p. philippinus* has yellow crown, dark-brown ear-coverts and throat, unstreaked yellow breast, and yellow on mantle and scapulars. Breeding male *burmanicus* has buff breast, and buff or pale grey throat. Female/non-breeding birds usually have unstreaked buff to pale yellowish underparts; can show streaking as prominent as on some poorly marked Streaked Weavers, but generally has less distinct and buffish supercilium, lacks yellow neck patch, and lacks pronounced dark moustachial and malar stripes. Head pattern of some (non-breeding males?) can, however, be rather similar to the Streaked Weaver. Female *burmanicus* more rufous-buff on supercilium and underparts. Cultivation and grassland.

Finn's Weaver *Ploceus megarhynchus* 17 cm

a MALE BREEDING and **b** NON-BREEDING Frequent and very local summer visitor or resident; found at Sukila Phanta in March and May at 100 m. Large size and bill. Breeding male has yellow underparts and rump, and dark patches on breast (can show as complete breast-band). Breeding female has pale yellow to yellowish-brown head, and pale yellow to buffish-white underparts. Adult non-breeding and immature very similar to the non-breeding Baya Weaver. Grassland. Globally threatened.

Red Avadavat *Amandava amandava* 10 cm

a MALE BREEDING, **b** FEMALE and **c** JUVENILE Local and frequent resident; below 305 m (–670 m). Breeding male mainly red with white spotting. Non-breeding male and female have red bill, red rump and uppertail-coverts, and white tips to wing coverts and tertials. Juvenile lacks red in plumage; has buff wing-bars, pink bill-base, and pink legs and feet. Tall wet grassland, reedbeds.

Indian Silverbill *Lonchura malabarica* 11–11.5 cm

ADULT Uncommon resident; below 305 m. Adult has white rump and uppertail-coverts, black tail with elongated central feathers, and rufous-buff barring on flanks. Dry cultivation, grassland, thorn scrub.

White-rumped Munia *Lonchura striata* 10–11 cm

ADULT Local resident below 1220 m; mainly a summer visitor up to 2135 m. Dark breast and white rump. Pale streaking on ear-coverts, rufous-brown to whitish fringes to brown breast, and dingy underparts with faint streaking. Open wooded areas, scrub.

Scaly-breasted Munia *Lonchura punctulata* 10.7–12 cm
a ADULT and **b** JUVENILE Fairly common and widespread resident; below 1525 m (–2680 m in summer). Adult has chestnut throat and upper breast, and whitish underparts with dark scaling. Juvenile has brown upperparts and buffish underparts; bill black. Open forest, bushes, cultivation.

Black-headed Munia *Lonchura malacca* 11.5 cm
ADULT Local and frequent resident; mainly below 1220 m (–1370 m). Black head, neck and upper breast, rufous-brown upperparts, chestnut lower breast and flanks, and black belly centre and undertail-coverts. Juvenile has uniform brown upperparts and buff to whitish underparts; bill blue-grey. Cultivation, grassland.

Chaffinch *Fringilla coelebs* 16 cm
a MALE NON-BREEDING and **b** FEMALE Uncommon winter visitor; 2000–2750 m (1555–3050 m). White wing-bars; lacks white rump. Male has blue-grey crown and nape, orange-pink face and underparts, and maroon-brown mantle. Female dull, with greyish-brown mantle and greyish-buff underparts. Upland fields with nearby bushes and coniferous forest.

Brambling *Fringilla montifringilla* 16 cm
a MALE BREEDING, **b** MALE NON-BREEDING and **c** FEMALE Erratic winter visitor, mainly in the north and north-west; 2135-3050 m (–1500 m). White rump and belly, and orange scapulars, breast and flanks. Patterning of head and mantle varying with sex and feather wear. Upland fields and nearby bushes and coniferous forest.

Fire-fronted Serin *Serinus pusillus* 12.5 cm
a MALE, **b** FEMALE and **c** JUVENILE Fairly common resident, mainly from west-central areas westwards; summers 2440–4575 m, occasionally winters down to 2100 m. Adult has blackish head with scarlet forehead. Juvenile has cinnamon-brown head. Breeds in Tibetan steppe; winters on stony and bushy slopes.

Tibetan Siskin *Carduelis thibetana* 12 cm
a MALE and **b** FEMALE Winter visitor, possibly breeds; local, regularly recorded in the Kathmandu Valley, uncommon elsewhere; 1050–3500 m. Lacks large yellow patches on wing. Male mainly olive-green, with yellowish supercilium and underparts. Female heavily streaked, with indistinct yellowish wing-bars. Summers in mixed forest; winters in alders.

Yellow-breasted Greenfinch *Carduelis spinoides* 14 cm
a MALE, **b** FEMALE and **c** JUVENILE Common and widespread resident; summers chiefly 2440–3700 m (–4400 m), winters 915–1850 m (–75 m). Yellow supercilium and underparts, dark ear-coverts and malar stripe, and yellow patches on wing. Juvenile heavily streaked. Open forest, shrubberies and cultivation with nearby trees.

European Goldfinch *Carduelis carduelis* 13–15.5 cm
a MALE and **b** JUVENILE Uncommon resident from east-central areas westwards; summers mainly 2450–4250 m, winters 1920–2440 m (–75 m). Red face (lacking on juvenile), and black-and-yellow wings with white tertial markings. Upland cultivation, shrubberies and open coniferous forest.

Twite *Carduelis flavirostris* 13–13.5 cm
a MALE and **b** FEMALE Probably resident, fairly common in Dolpo and Mustang in the north-west, uncommon farther east; 3965–4575 m. Rather plain and heavily streaked, with small yellowish bill, buff wing-bars, and white edges to remiges and rectrices. Male has pinkish rump. Boulder-strewn alpine meadows and stony hills.

Spectacled Finch *Callacanthis burtoni* 17–18 cm
a MALE and **b** FEMALE Chiefly a local and erratic winter visitor; one summer record; 2135–3355 m. Black wings with white tips to feathers. Blackish head with red (male) or orange-yellow (female) 'spectacles'. Juvenile has browner head with buff eye patch, and buffish wing-bars. Open mixed forest.

Red Crossbill *Loxia curvirostra* 16–17 cm
a MALE, **b** FEMALE and **c** JUVENILE Frequent; movements are poorly understood, probably resident; mainly 2590–3660 m (–2100 m). Dark bill with crossed mandibles. Male rusty-red. Female olive-green, with brighter rump. Juvenile heavily streaked; mandibles are initially not crossed. Coniferous forest, favours hemlocks.

Blanford's Rosefinch *Carpodacus rubescens* 15 cm
a MALE and **b** FEMALE Rare, possibly resident; 2950 m in May, 2745–3050 m in August and September, 2135–3050 m in winter. Slimmer bill than the Common Rosefinch; male has more uniform head, duller crimson crown, and often distinct greyish cast to underparts. Female plain, lacks supercilium, has uniform wings and upperparts, and reddish or bright olive cast to rump and uppertail-coverts. Glades in coniferous and mixed forest.

Dark-breasted Rosefinch *Carpodacus nipalensis* 15–16 cm
a MALE and **b** FEMALE Fairly common resident; summers mainly 3050–3900 m (–4270 m), winters 1830–2745 m (–1370 m). Slim, with slender bill. Male has maroon-brown breast-band, dark eye-stripe, and maroon-brown upperparts with indistinct dark streaking. Female has unstreaked underparts, lacks supercilium, and has streaked mantle, buffish wing-bars and tips to tertials, and olive-brown rump and uppertail-coverts. Breeds in high-altitude shrubberies; winters in forest clearings.

Common Rosefinch *Carpodacus erythrinus* 14.5–15 cm
a MALE and **b** FEMALE *C. e. roseatus*; **c** MALE and **d** FEMALE *C. e. erythrinus* Fairly common and widespread resident and winter visitor; summers mainly 3350–4000 m, winters 275–2000 m. Compact, with short, stout bill. Male has red head, breast and rump. Female has streaked upperparts and underparts, and double wing-bar. Migrant nominate race has less red in male, and female is less heavily-streaked, compared with *roseatus* which is a resident race. Breeds in high-altitude shrubberies and open forest; winters in cultivation with bushes.

Beautiful Rosefinch *Carpodacus pulcherrimus* 15 cm
a MALE and **b** FEMALE Common and widespread resident; summers mainly 3600–4650 m, winters from 2100 m up to at least 3300 m. Male has pale lilac-pink supercilium, rump and underparts; upperparts grey-brown and heavily streaked. Female has poorly defined supercilium and heavily streaked underparts. Breeds in high-altitude shrubberies; winters on bush-covered slopes and cultivation with bushes.

Pink-browed Rosefinch *Carpodacus rodochrous* 14–15 cm
a MALE and **b** FEMALE Fairly common and widespread resident; summers mainly 3050–3965 m, winters 915–3000 m. Male has deep pink supercilium and underparts, and crimson crown. Female has buff supercilium and fulvous ground colour to rump, belly and flanks. Breeds in high-altitude shrubberies and open forest; winters in oak forest and on bushy slopes.

Vinaceous Rosefinch *Carpodacus vinaceus* 13–16 cm

a MALE and **b** FEMALE Scarce, probably resident; 3050–3200 m in probable breeding season, 1065–3050 m in winter. Male dark crimson, with pink supercilium and pinkish-white tips to tertials. Female lacks supercilium; has whitish tips to tertials, and streaked underparts. Understorey in moist forest.

Dark-rumped Rosefinch *Carpodacus edwardsii* 16–17 cm

a MALE and **b** FEMALE Scarce and local, status uncertain; recorded only in Langtang National Park and upper Mai Valley in March and May; 2440–3635 m. Male has pink supercilium and dark rump; maroon breast and flanks contrast with pink throat and belly. Female has narrow buff supercilium, pale tips to tertials, and brownish-buff underparts with lightly streaked throat and breast. High-altitude shrubberies and open forest; favours rhododendron.

Spot-winged Rosefinch *Carpodacus rodopeplus* 15 cm

a MALE and **b** FEMALE Local and fairly common resident; summers mainly 3050–4000 m, winters 2000–3050 m. Male has pink supercilium and underparts, maroon upperparts, and pinkish tips to wing coverts and tertials. Female has prominent buff supercilium, buff tips to tertials, and fulvous underparts with bold streaking on throat and breast. Supercilium more prominent than in the female Dark-rumped Rosefinch, with dark ear-coverts, paler and more heavily-steaked throat, and more prominent wing-bars. Breeds in rhododendron shrubberies; winters in forest understorey.

White-browed Rosefinch *Carpodacus thura* 17 cm

a MALE and **b** FEMALE Fairly common resident from west-central areas eastwards; summers mainly 3800–4200 m, winters 2440–3660 m (–1830 m). Large size. Male has pink-and-white supercilium, pink rump and underparts, and heavily streaked brown upperparts. Female has prominent supercilium with dark eye-stripe, ginger-brown throat and breast, and olive-yellow rump. Breeds in high-altitude shrubberies and open forest; winters on bushy hills.

Streaked Rosefinch *Carpodacus rubicilloides* 19 cm

a MALE and **b** FEMALE Frequent resident; summers up to 4700 m, winters 2800–3660 m (–2440 m). Large size and long tail. Male has crimson-pink head and underparts and heavily streaked upperparts. Female lacks supercilium and has streaked upperparts. Open stony ground with sparse dry scrub.

Great Rosefinch *Carpodacus rubicilla* 19–20 cm

a MALE and **b** FEMALE Frequent resident; chiefly 3660–5000 m (–2650 m). Large size and long tail. Male has pale pink head and underparts, and pale sandy-grey and lightly streaked upperparts. Female lacks supercilium, and has lightly streaked pale sandy-brown upperparts; centres to wing coverts and tertials pale grey-brown (much darker brownish-black on the female Streaked Rosefinch). Open stony ground with sparse dry scrub.

Red-fronted Rosefinch *Carpodacus puniceus* 20 cm

a MALE and **b** FEMALE Frequent resident; summers mainly 4265–5490 m, winters from 2745 m up to at least 4575 m. Large size, conical bill and short tail. On male, red of plumage contrasts with brown crown, eye-stripe and upperparts. Female lacks supercilium, is heavily streaked, and may show yellow-to-olive rump. High-altitude rocky slopes.

Crimson-browed Finch *Propyrrhula subhimachala* 19–20 cm

a MALE and **b** FEMALE Uncommon resident from west-central areas eastwards; summers mainly 3500–4000 m, winters from 2590 m up to at least 3050 m. Short, stubby bill. Male has red forehead, throat and upper breast, greenish coloration to upperparts, and greyish underparts. Female has olive-yellow forehead and supercilium, greyish belly and greenish-olive upperparts. Breeds in high-altitude shrubberies, favours junipers; winters in forest undergrowth.

Scarlet Finch *Haematospiza sipahi* 18 cm
a MALE, **b** FEMALE and **c** IMMATURE MALE Uncommon and local resident from west-central areas eastwards; 2135–3100 m in May, winters from 1220 m up to at least 2560 m (–520 m). Male scarlet. Female olive-green, with yellow rump. First-summer male has orange rump. Broadleaved forest.

Brown Bullfinch *Pyrrhula nipalensis* 16–17 cm
ADULT Local and frequent resident; winters 1600–3050 m, summers up to 3200 m. Adult has grey-brown mantle, grey underparts, narrow white rump, and long tail. Juvenile has brownish-buff upperparts and warm buff underparts, and lacks adult head pattern. Dense moist broadleaved forest.

Red-headed Bullfinch *Pyrrhula erythrocephala* 17 cm
a MALE, **b** FEMALE and **c** 1ST-SUMMER MALE Fairly common and widespread resident; summers mainly 3050–4000 m, winters 1830–3865 m. Male has orange crown, nape and breast, and grey mantle. Female has yellow crown and nape. First-summer male has yellow breast. Mainly broadleaved forest.

Black-and-yellow Grosbeak *Mycerobas icterioides* 22 cm
a MALE and **b** FEMALE Very rare and local; possibly breeds, seen collecting nest material at Rara Lake in the north-west; 3050 m. Male usually lacks orange cast to mantle and rump; black of plumage duller than on the Collared Grosbeak, and has black thighs. Female has pale grey head, mantle and breast, and peachy-orange rump and belly. Coniferous forest.

Collared Grosbeak *Mycerobas affinis* 22 cm
a MALE and **b** FEMALE Widespread resident, fairly common from east-central areas westwards, uncommon farther east; summers mainly 3000–3900 m, winters down to 2440 m (–1065 m). Male has orange cast to mantle; black of plumage strongly glossed, and thighs yellow. Female has olive-yellow underparts and rump and greyish-olive mantle. Coniferous and coniferous/broadleaved forests.

Spot-winged Grosbeak *Mycerobas melanozanthos* 22 cm
a MALE and **b** FEMALE Uncommon resident; winters 1400–2135 m, summers up to 3355 m. Male has black rump and white markings on wings. Female yellow, boldly streaked with black; wing pattern similar to male's. Breeds in mixed forest; winters in broadleaved forest.

White-winged Grosbeak *Mycerobas carnipes* 22 cm
a MALE and **b** FEMALE Fairly common resident; summers mainly 3050–4270 m (–4600 m), winters down to 2745 m. White patch in wing. Male dull black and olive-yellow, with yellowish tips to greater coverts and tertials. Female similar, but black of plumage replaced by sooty-grey. Juniper shrubberies, and forest with junipers.

Gold-naped Finch *Pyrrhoplectes epauletta* 15 cm
a MALE and **b** FEMALE Uncommon resident subject to poorly understood altitudinal movements; 3260–3355 m in May, 1525–3000 m in winter. Small, with fine bill. White 'stripe' down tertials. Male black, with orange crown and nape. Female has olive-green on head, grey mantle, and rufous-brown wing coverts and underparts. Undergrowth in oak–rhododendron forest and rhododendron shrubberies.

Crested Bunting *Melophus lathami* 17 cm

a MALE, **b** FEMALE and **c** 1ST-WINTER MALE Fairly common and widespread resident; summers 2440–1220 m and possibly lower, winters 75–1460 m. Always has crest and chestnut on wing and tail; tail lacks white. Dry rocky and grassy hillsides, terraced cultivation.

Yellowhammer *Emberiza citrinella* 16.5 cm

a MALE BREEDING, **b** MALE NON-BREEDING and **c** FEMALE Rare, local and irregular winter visitor; 1100–2745 m. Chestnut rump and long tail. Most show yellow on head and underparts. (Note that hybrids with the Pine Bunting can show a variety of intermediate characters.) Upland cultivation.

Pine Bunting *Emberiza leucocephalos* 17 cm

a MALE BREEDING, **b** MALE NON-BREEDING and **c** FEMALE Irregular winter visitor, usually fairly common in upper Kali Gandaki Valley and in north-west; mainly 2440–3050 m (–915 m). Chestnut rump and long tail. Male has chestnut supercilium and throat, and whitish crown and ear-covert spot; pattern obscured in winter. Female has greyish-supercilium and nape/neck sides, dark border to ear-coverts, usually some rufous on breast/flanks, and white belly. Upland cultivation, grassy areas with bushes.

Rock Bunting *Emberiza cia* 16 cm

a MALE and **b** FEMALE Common and widespread resident in west-central areas and westwards; summers mainly 2440–4600 m, occasionally winters down to 1800 m. Male has grey head, black crown sides and border to ear-coverts, and rufous underparts. Female duller. Open dry grassy and rocky slopes.

Chestnut-eared Bunting *Emberiza fucata* 16 cm

a MALE, **b** FEMALE and **c** 1ST-WINTER Uncommon, probably resident, mainly in the west; has poorly understood altitudinal movements; 2135–2300 m in breeding season, below 915 m in winter (–5000 m, presumably on passage). Adult has chestnut ear-coverts, black breast streaking, and chestnut on breast sides. Some nondescript; plain head with warm brown ear-coverts and pale eye-ring distinctive. Dry rocky and bushy hills.

Little Bunting *Emberiza pusilla* 13 cm

1ST-WINTER Fairly common and widespread winter visitor; mainly below 2000 m (–3560 m). Small size. Chestnut ear-coverts (and often supercilium and crown stripe), and lacks dark moustachial stripe. Fallow cultivation, meadows.

Yellow-breasted Bunting *Emberiza aureola* 15 cm

a MALE BREEDING, **b** MALE NON-BREEDING, **c** FEMALE and **d** JUVENILE Common, mainly a passage migrant, some birds overwinter; below 1370 m. Male has black face and chestnut breast-band, and white inner wing coverts. Female has strikingly patterned head and mantle, and white median-covert bar. Juvenile streaked on underparts. Cultivation and grassland.

Black-headed Bunting *Emberiza melanocephala* 16–18 cm

a MALE BREEDING, **b** MALE NON-BREEDING, **c** WORN FEMALE and **d** IMMATURE Scarce winter visitor, recorded mainly from the east; below 105 m (–1340 m). Male has black on head and chestnut on mantle. Female when worn may show ghost pattern of male; fresh female almost identical to Red-headed Bunting (*see* Appendix 1), but indicative features include rufous fringes to mantle and/or back, slight contrast between throat and greyish ear-coverts, and more uniform yellowish underparts. Immature has buff underparts and yellow undertail coverts. Cultivation, bushes at field edges.

Black-faced Bunting *Emberiza spodocephala* 15 cm

a MALE BREEDING, **b** MALE NON-BREEDING and **c** FEMALE Uncommon and local winter visitor; below 1280 m. Male has greenish-grey head with blackish lores, and yellow underparts; non-breeding with yellow submoustachial stripe and throat. Female has yellowish supercilium, yellow throat, olive rump, and white on tail. Long grass, paddy-fields, marsh edges.

APPENDIX 1: VAGRANTS TO NEPAL

Vagrants (very irregular visitors that have only been recorded once or on few occasions) and extirpated species are listed below.

Jungle Bush Quail *Perdicula asiatica*
Extirpated; only recorded in 19th century. Male has barred underparts, rufous-orange throat and supercilium (with supercilium edged above and below with white), white moustachial stripe, and brown ear-coverts. Female has vinous-buff underparts, with head pattern similar to male. Dry grass and scrub.

Rain Quail *Coturnix coromandelica*
Vagrant. Male has strongly patterned head and neck (recalling Common Quail). Best told from that species by black breast, and black streaking on flanks. Female very similar to female Common Quail, but is smaller and has unbarred primaries. Cultivation, grass and scrub.

Fulvous Whistling-duck *Dendrocygna bicolor*
Vagrant. Larger than Lesser Whistling-duck, with bigger, squarer head and larger bill. Shows white uppertail-coverts in flight. Adult and juvenile show rufous-brown crown and blackish line down hindneck. Lakes and large rivers.

Whooper Swan *Cygnus cygnus*
Vagrant; only recorded in 19th century. Adult is white with black-and-yellow bill; has yellow of bill extending as wedge towards tip. Juvenile is smoky-grey, with pinkish bill. Longer neck and more angular head shape than Tundra Swan. Lakes and large rivers.

Tundra Swan *Cygnus columbianus*
Vagrant. Adult is white with black-and-yellow bill; has yellow of bill typically as oval-shaped patch. Juvenile is smoky-grey, with pinkish bill. Smaller in size, and with shorter neck and more rounded head, compared with Whooper Swan. Lakes and large rivers.

Bean Goose *Anser fabalis*
Vagrant. Black bill with orange band, and orange legs. Has slimmer neck and smaller, more angular head than Greylag Goose; head, neck and upperparts are darker and browner. In flight, lacks pale grey forewing of Greylag. Open country.

Mandarin Duck *Aix galericulata*
Vagrant. Male is spectacular. Most striking features are reddish bill, orange 'mane' and 'sails', white stripe behind eye, and black-and-white stripes on sides of breast. Female and eclipse male are mainly greyish with white 'spectacles' and white spotting on breast and flanks. In flight, shows dark upperwing and underwing, with white trailing edge, and white belly. Large rivers.

Pink-headed Duck *Rhodonessa caryophyllacea*
Extinct; only recorded in 19th century. Male has pink head and bill and dark brown body. Female has greyish-pink head and duller brown body. Pools and marshes.

Greater Scaup *Aythya marila*
Vagrant. Larger and stockier than Tufted Duck, and lacking any sign of crest. Male is superficially similar to Tufted but has grey upperparts contrasting with black rear end. Female is very similar in plumage to Tufted but has broad white face patch, which is less extensive on juvenile/immature. Lakes and large rivers.

Baikal Teal *Anas formosa*
Vagrant. Grey forewing and broad white trailing edge to wing in flight in both sexes (recalling Northern Pintail). Male has striking head pattern of black, yellow, bottle-green and white; also black-spotted pinkish breast, black undertail-coverts, and chestnut-edged scapulars. Female superficially resembles female Common Teal; has dark-bordered white loral spot and buff supercilium that is broken above eye by dark crown; some females have white half-crescent on cheeks. Lakes and large rivers.

Long-tailed Duck *Clangula hyemalis*
Vagrant. Small, stocky duck with stubby bill and pointed tail. Swims low in water and partly opens wings before diving. Both sexes show dark upperwing and underwing in flight. Winter male is mainly white; has dark cheek patch and breast, and long tail. Female and immature male variable; usually with dark crown, and pale face with dark cheek patch. Lakes and large rivers.

Smew *Mergellus albellus*
Vagrant. Small size. Male is mainly white, with black markings. Immature male and female are mainly grey; have chestnut cap, with white throat and lower ear-coverts. Lakes and large rivers.

Red-breasted Merganser *Mergus serrator*

Vagrant. Superficially resembles Common Merganser. Male has spiky crest, white collar, ginger breast, and grey flanks. Female and immature male have chestnut head that merges with grey of neck. Slimmer than Common Merganser, and with finer bill; chestnut of head and upper neck contrasts less with grey lower neck than in that species. Large rivers.

Rufous-necked Hornbill *Aceros nipalensis*

Extirpated; only recorded in 19th century. Mainly black with white terminal band to tail and white wing-tips. Red pouch. Male and immature have rufous head and neck. Female has black head and neck. Mature broadleaved evergreen forest.

Hodgson's Hawk Cuckoo *Hierococcyx fugax*

Vagrant. Stouter bill and shorter-looking tail than Common Hawk Cuckoo; typically darker slate-grey above, and underparts are more rufous and lack barring. Juvenile also similar to juvenile Common Hawk Cuckoo; underparts have broad spotting. Song is a shrill, thin *gee-whiz...gee-whiz*. Broadleaved evergreen and moist deciduous forest.

Long-eared Owl *Asio otus*

Vagrant; only recorded in 19th century. Superficially resembles Short-eared Owl. Has heavily streaked underparts and long ear-tufts. Orange-brown facial discs and orange eyes. Forest and groves.

Black-necked Crane *Grus nigricollis*

Vagrant. Adult is pale grey with contrasting black head, upper neck and bunched tertials; shows more contrast between black flight feathers and pale grey coverts than Common Crane, and has black tail-band. Immature has buff or brownish head, neck, mantle and mottling to wing coverts. Fallow fields and marshes.

Slaty-legged Crake *Rallina eurizonoides*

Vagrant. Broad black-and-white barring on underparts. Adult told from Red-legged (not recorded in Nepal) by greenish or grey legs, lack of white barring on wings, olive-brown mantle contrasting with rufous neck and breast, narrower and more numerous white barring on underparts, and prominent white throat. Juvenile from juvenile Red-legged by leg colour and lack of barring on wings. Marshes.

Slaty-breasted Rail *Gallirallus striatus*

Vagrant. Straight, longish bill with red at base. Legs olive-grey. Adult has chestnut crown and nape, slate-grey foreneck and breast, white barring and spotting on upperparts, and barred undertail-coverts. Juvenile has rufous-brown crown and nape, and white barring on wing coverts. Marshes.

Spotted Crake *Porzana porzana*

Vagrant. Profuse white spotting on head, neck and breast. Stout bill, barred flanks, and unmarked buff undertail-coverts. Adult has yellowish bill with red at base, and grey head and breast. Juvenile has buffish-brown head and breast, and bill is brown. Marshes.

Swinhoe's Snipe *Gallinago megala*

Vagrant. Very similar to Pintail Snipe. In flight, is heavier, with longer bill and more pointed wings, and feet only just project beyond tail. Some birds quite dusky on neck, breast and flanks, unlike Pintail. Wet fields.

Terek Sandpiper *Xenus cinereus*

Vagrant. Stocky, mainly greyish wader. Longish, upturned bill and short yellowish legs. In flight, shows prominent white trailing edge to secondaries and grey rump and tail. Adult breeding has blackish scapular lines. River banks.

Ruddy Turnstone *Arenaria interpres*

Vagrant. Short bill and orange legs. In flight, shows white stripes on wings and back and black tail. In breeding plumage, has complex black-and-white neck and breast pattern and much chestnut-red on upperparts; duller and less strikingly patterned in non-breeding and juvenile plumage. River banks.

Sanderling *Calidris alba*

Vagrant. Stocky, with short bill. Very broad white wing-bar. Adult breeding usually shows some rufous on sides of head, breast and upperparts. Non-breeding is pale grey above and very white below. Juvenile chequered black-and-white above. River banks.

Long-toed Stint *Calidris subminuta*

Vagrant. Long and yellowish legs, longish neck, and upright stance. In all plumages, has prominent supercilium and heavily streaked foreneck and breast. Adult breeding and juvenile have prominent rufous fringes to upperparts; juvenile has very striking mantle V. In winter, upperparts more heavily marked than Little Stint. Call is a soft *prit* or *chirrup*. Marshes and river banks.

Red-necked Phalarope *Phalaropus lobatus*

Vagrant. Typically seen swimming. Delicately built with fine bill. Adult breeding has white throat and red stripe down side of grey neck. Adult non-breeding has dark mask, and grey upperparts with white edges to mantle and scapular feathers forming fairly distinct lines. Juvenile also has dark mask; upperparts are dark grey and has orange-buff mantle and scapular lines. Lakes.

Eurasian Oystercatcher *Haematopus ostralegus*

Vagrant. Black-and-white, with broad white wing-bar. Bill reddish. White collar in non-breeding plumage. River banks.

Grey Plover *Pluvialis squatarola*

Vagrant. Greyish coloration to upperparts, white underwing, and black axillaries. Stockier, with stouter bill and shorter legs, than Pacific Golden Plover. Whitish rump and prominent white wing-bar. In breeding plumage, has black face, foreneck, breast and belly, with striking white border to sides of face and neck. Banks of rivers and lakes.

Greater Sand Plover *Charadrius leschenaultii*

Vagrant. Larger and lankier than Lesser Sand Plover, with longer and larger bill, usually with pronounced gonys and more pointed tip. Longer legs are paler, with distinct yellowish or greenish tinge. In flight, feet project beyond tail and has broader white wing-bar across primaries. Otherwise very similar to Lesser in all plumages. River banks.

White-tailed Lapwing *Vanellus leucurus*

Vagrant. Mainly sandy-brown with plain head. Blackish bill, and very long yellow legs. Tail all white, lacking black band of other *Vanellus* lapwings. Marshes.

Mew Gull *Larus canus*

Vagrant. Smaller and daintier than Yellow-legged Gull, with shorter and finer bill. Adult has darker grey mantle than Yellow-legged, with more black on wing-tips; bill yellowish-green, with dark subterminal band in non-breeding plumage, and dark iris. Head and hindneck heavily marked in non-breeding (unlike adult non-breeding Yellow-legged). First-winter/first-summer have uniform grey mantle. Distinctions from second-year Yellow-legged (which also has grey mantle) include unbarred greyish greater coverts forming mid-wing panel, narrow black subterminal tail-band, and well-defined dark tip to greyish/pinkish bill. Lakes and large rivers.

Red Kite *Milvus milvus*

Vagrant. Long and deeply forked rufous-orange tail. Wings long, and usually sharply angled. Rufous underparts and underwing-coverts, whitish head, pale band across upperwing-coverts, and striking whitish patches at base of primaries on underwing. Lightly wooded semi-desert.

White-bellied Heron *Ardea insignis*

Extirpated; only recorded in 19th century. Large size and very long neck. Bill blackish, and legs and feet grey. Grey foreneck and breast contrast with white belly. In flight, has uniform dark-grey upperwing, and white underwing-coverts contrasting with dark-grey flight feathers. Rivers in broadleaved foothill forests.

Malayan Night Heron *Gorsachius melanolophus*

Vagrant. Stocky, with stout bill and short neck. Adult has black crown and crest and rufous-brown upperparts. Immature finely vermiculated with white, grey and rufous-buff, and with bold white spotting on crown and crest. Streams and marshes in dense forest.

Greater Flamingo *Phoenicopterus ruber*

Vagrant. Only confusable with Lesser Flamingo (not recorded in Nepal), but is larger with longer and thinner neck. Bill larger and less prominently kinked. Adult has pale pink bill with prominent dark tip, and variable pinkish coloration to head, neck and body; in flight, crimson-pink upperwing-coverts contrast with whitish body. Immature has greyish-white head and neck, and white body lacking any pink; pink on bill develops with increasing age. Juvenile brownish-grey, with white on coverts; bill grey, tipped with black, and legs grey. Wetlands.

Glossy Ibis *Plegadis falcinellus*

Vagrant. Small, dark ibis with rather fine down-curved bill. Adult breeding deep chestnut, glossed with purple and green, with metallic green-and-purple wings; has narrow white surround to bare lores. Adult non-breeding duller, with white streaking on dark-brown head and neck. Juvenile similar to adult non-breeding, but is dark brown with white mottling on head, and only faint greenish gloss to upperparts. Wetlands.

Great White Pelican *Pelecanus onocrotalus*

Vagrant. Larger than Spot-billed Pelican; best told by black underside to primaries and secondaries which contrast strongly with underwing-coverts (except in juvenile – *see* below). Adult breeding has white body and wing coverts tinged with pink, bright-yellow pouch and pinkish skin around eye. Adult non-breeding has duller bare parts and lacks pink tinge and white crest. Immature has variable amounts of brown on wing coverts and scapulars. Juvenile has largely brown head, neck and upperparts, including upperwing-coverts, and brown flight feathers; upperwing appears more uniform brown, and underwing shows pale central panel contrasting with dark inner coverts and flight feathers; greyish pouch becomes yellower with age. Lakes and large rivers.

Silver-breasted Broadbill *Serilophus lunatus*
Extirpated; only recorded in 19th century. Mainly greyish with stout bluish bill, crested appearance, dusky supercilium, large eye with yellow eye-ring, pale chestnut tertials, and white-and-blue on wing. Broadleaved evergreen forest.

Black-naped Oriole *Oriolus chinensis*
Vagrant. Large stout bill; nasal call. Male has yellow mantle and wing coverts concolorous with underparts (brighter in Slender-billed). Female and immature probably not safely separated from Slender-billed on plumage.

White-bellied Minivet *Pericrocotus erythropygius*
Vagrant. Both sexes have white wing patch and orange rump. Male has black head and upperparts, and white underparts with orange breast. Female has brown upperparts and white underparts. Open dry deciduous forest and scattered dry scrub.

Bohemian Waxwing *Bombycilla garrulus*
Vagrant. Mainly fawn-brown in coloration. Prominent crest, black throat, and waxy red and yellow markings on wings. Open country with fruiting trees and bushes.

Brown-breasted Flycatcher *Muscicapa muttui*
Vagrant. Compared with Asian Brown Flycatcher has larger bill with entirely pale lower mandible, pale legs and feet, rufous-buff edges to greater coverts and tertials, and slightly rufescent tone to rump and tail. Dense undergrowth in broadleaved forest.

Siberian Blue Robin *Luscinia cyane*
Vagrant. Short tail, which is constantly quivered, horizontal stance, and pinkish legs and feet. Male has dark-blue upperparts, black sides to throat and breast, and white underparts. Female has olive-brown upperparts and pale-buff throat and breast; usually has blue on uppertail-coverts and tail. First-winter male similar to female, but with blue on mantle. Dense bushes.

Green Cochoa *Cochoa viridis*
Extirpated; only recorded in 19th century. Mainly green, with bluish head, and blue tail with black band. Male has blue wing panelling. Female has green in blue wing panels. Broadleaved evergreen forest.

Northern Wheatear *Oenanthe oenanthe*
Vagrant. Breeding male has blue-grey upperparts, black mask, and pale-orange breast. Breeding female greyish to olive-brown above. Compared with Isabelline Wheatear, adult winter and first-winter have blackish centres to wing-coverts and tertials and show more white at sides of tail. Open stony ground and cultivation.

Pied Wheatear *Oenanthe pleschanka*
Vagrant. Different tail pattern than Variable Wheatear; always shows black edge to outer feathers (lacking in Variable) and often has only a narrow and broken terminal black band (broad and even on Variable). Finer features of breeding male are white of nape extends to mantle, black of throat does not extend to upper breast, and breast is washed with buff. Non-breeding and first-winter male and female have pale fringes to upperparts and wings (not apparent on fresh-plumaged Variable). Open stony ground.

Rufous-tailed Wheatear *Oenanthe xanthoprymna*
Vagrant. Similar in appearance to Isabelline Wheatear but has rufous-orange lower back and rump, and rufous tail sides. Male has black lores. Semi-desert with rocky ground and scattered bushes.

Rosy Starling *Sturnus roseus*
Vagrant. Adult has blackish head with shaggy crest, pinkish mantle and underparts, and blue-green gloss to wings. Juvenile mainly sandy-brown, with stout yellowish bill, and broad pale fringes to wing feathers. Cultivation, damp grassland and thorn scrub.

Asian Stubtail *Urosphena squameiceps*
Vagrant. Very short tail. Otherwise similar in appearance to Pale-footed Bush Warbler with long supercilium, rufous-brown upperparts, white underparts, and pale pinkish legs and feet. Broadleaved forest.

Brown Bush Warbler *Bradypterus luteoventris*

Extirpated; only recorded in 19th century. Told from Chinese Bush Warbler by rufescent-brown upperparts, rufous-buff breast sides and flanks, rufous-buff supercilium, and lack of prominent pale tips to undertail-coverts. Lacks spotting on throat and breast. Undergrowth of bushes and grass in pine forest.

Lanceolated Warbler *Locustella lanceolata*

Vagrant. Heavily-streaked upperparts. Best told from Grasshopper Warbler by heavy streaking on throat, breast and flanks. Streaking on underparts can be weak on some, and can be very similar in appearance to some Grasshopper Warblers; subtle differences are patterning of undertail-coverts (streaking less extensive but blacker and more clear-cut) and patterning of tertials (darker with clearer-cut pale edges). Tall grass.

Grasshopper Warbler *Locustella naevia*

Vagrant. Diffusely-streaked, olive-brown upperparts, indistinct supercilium, and (usually) unmarked or only lightly streaked throat and breast. *See* account for Lanceolated Warbler for further differences from that species. Tall grass and reeds.

Rusty-rumped Warbler *Locustella certhiola*

Vagrant. Streaked upperparts. Distinct supercilium, greyish crown, rufous rump and uppertail-coverts, and rather dark tail with white tips. Juvenile has yellowish wash to underparts and light spotting on breast. Reedbeds.

Black-browed Reed Warbler *Acrocephalus bistrigiceps*

Vagrant. Similar in appearance to Paddyfield Warbler, and like that species has broad supercilium. Features from Paddyfield are blackish lateral crown stripes (much more pronounced than on Paddyfield), shorter tail, long primary projection, and dark grey legs. Tall grass and reedbeds.

Blunt-winged Warbler *Acrocephalus concinens*

Longer and stouter bill than Paddyfield, with pale lower mandible. Supercilium indistinct behind eye. Lacks dark edge to supercilium and eye-stripe is less striking than in Paddyfield. Reedbeds, and tall grass near water.

Oriental Reed Warbler *Acrocephalus orientalis*

Vagrant. Smaller than Clamorous Reed, with shorter, squarer tail. Often has streaking on sides of neck and breast, and well-defined whitish tips to outer rectrices. Reedbeds and wet paddy-fields.

Radde's Warbler *Phylloscopus schwarzi*

Vagrant. Similar to Dusky with long buffish-white supercilium contrasting with dark eye-stripe. Has stout bill, and orangish legs and feet; call different from Dusky's, a nervous *prit-prit*. In fresh plumage, can show pronounced greenish-olive cast to upperparts and buffish-yellow cast to supercilium and underparts which are distinctive features from Dusky. Undergrowth and bushes.

Red-faced Liocichla *Liocichla phoenicea*

Extirpated; only recorded in 19th century. Mainly brown laughingthrush. Has crimson ear-coverts and neck sides, crimson and orange on wing, and rufous-orange tip to black tail. Broadleaved evergreen forest.

Black-breasted Parrotbill *Paradoxornis flavirostris*

Only recorded in 19th century in the terai. Rufous-brown head and olive-brown upperparts. Has black patch on breast, and rufous-buff underparts. Dense thickets of reeds, high grass and bamboo.

Orphean Warbler *Sylvia hortensis*

Vagrant. Larger and bigger-billed than Lesser Whitethroat; more ponderous movements, and heavier appearance in flight. Adult has blackish crown, pale grey mantle, blackish tail, and pale iris. First-year has crown concolorous with mantle, with darker grey ear-coverts, and dark iris; very similar to Lesser Whitethroat. Orphean Warbler often shows darker-looking uppertail, eye-ring is absent or indistinct, and has greyish centres and pale fringes to undertail-coverts; these features variable and difficult to observe in the field. Bushes and forest edges.

Spanish Sparrow *Passer hispaniolensis*

Vagrant. Male has chestnut crown, black breast and streaking on flanks, and blackish mantle with pale 'braces'; pattern obscured by pale fringes in non-breeding season. Female very similar to female House Sparrow; subtle differences are longer whitish supercilium, fine streaking on underparts, and pale 'braces'. Reedbeds and marshes.

Forest Wagtail *Dendronanthus indicus*

Vagrant. Broad yellowish-white wing-bars, double black breast-band, olive upperparts, white supercilium, and whitish underparts. Clearings in broadleaved forest.

Eurasian Siskin *Carduelis spinus*

Vagrant. Male has black crown and chin, and black-and-yellow wings. Female differs from female Tibetan Siskin in wing pattern (with yellowish patches at base of secondaries and primaries) and brighter yellow rump; bill is marginally longer and slimmer. Conifers.

Eurasian Linnet *Carduelis cannabina*

Vagrant. Told from Twite by greyish crown and nape contrasting with browner mantle, whitish lower rump and uppertail-coverts, and larger greyish bill. Forehead and breast crimson on breeding male. Cultivation and meadows.

Mongolian Finch *Rhodopechys mongolica*

Vagrant. Sandy coloration with whitish panels at bases of greater coverts and secondaries (which can be rather indistinct), whitish outer edges to tail. Shows some pink coloration to head and underparts, except juvenile. Dry rocky areas.

Grey-headed Bullfinch *Pyrrhula erythaca*

Vagrant. Male has grey crown and nape (concolorous with mantle) and orange-red underparts. Female has grey crown and nape and brown mantle. Conifer/rhododendron forest and thickets.

White-capped Bunting *Emberiza stewarti*

Vagrant. Male has grey head, black supercilium and throat, and chestnut breast-band; pattern obscured in winter. Female has rather plain head with pale supercilium; crown and mantle uniformly and diffusely streaked, and underparts finely streaked and washed with buff. Cultivation, grass and scrub.

Rustic Bunting *Emberiza rustica*

Vagrant. Striking head pattern (broad supercilium, dark sides to crown and border to ear-coverts), rufous streaking on breast, white belly, rufous on nape, and prominent white median-covert bar. Crown feathers are frequently raised, resulting in crested appearance. Damp habitats.

Chestnut Bunting *Emberiza rutila*

Vagrant. Small size. Male has chestnut head and breast, which may be barely apparent due to pale fringes in first-winter plumage. Female from female Black-faced Bunting by buff throat and brighter yellow underparts (lacking bold dark flank streaking of that species), chestnut rump, and little or no white on tail. Head pattern less striking than on Yellow-breasted Bunting. Bushes in cultivation, forest clearings.

Red-headed Bunting *Emberiza bruniceps*

Vagrant. Smaller than Black-headed Bunting, with shorter and more conical bill. Male has rufous on head and yellowish-green mantle. Female when worn may show rufous on head and breast, and/or yellowish to crown and mantle, and are then distinguishable from Black-headed. Fresh female has throat paler than breast, with suggestion of buffish breast-band; forehead and crown often virtually unstreaked (indicative features from Black-headed). Immature with buff underparts and yellow undertail coverts often not separable from Black-headed but may exhibit some of the features mentioned above for female. Cultivation.

Reed Bunting *Emberiza schoeniclus*

Vagrant. Male has black head and white submoustachial stripe; head pattern obscured by fringes in fresh plumage. Female resembles Little Bunting but lacks warm chestnut on ear-coverts, and black moustachial stripe and malar stripe reach bill; further, has more boldly-streaked mantle (often with pale braces), less prominent (rufous-brown) wing-bars, bolder and more diffuse breast streaking, and stouter bill with convex culmen. *See* account below for Pallas's Bunting. Marshes.

Pallas's Bunting *Emberiza pallasi*

Vagrant. Very similar in all plumages to Reed Bunting, but always has grey lesser coverts (rufous in Reed). Indicative features are two-toned bill (dark grey upper mandible and pinkish lower mandible) which is small and with straight culmen, and pale rump. Indicative features of fresh-plumage male and female are rather uniform crown (lacking prominent dark sides to crown), less distinct supercilium, prominent buff wing-bars (indistinct and rufous in Reed), and sparse streaking on underparts. Some eastern races of Reed can be very similar in appearance, however. Marshes.

APPENDIX 2: SPECIES COLLECTED BY HODGSON

The following species were collected by Brian Hodgson in the nineteenth century and formerly listed as coming from Nepal, but may well have originated in India close to the Nepalese border. *See* the Introduction, p.16.

Oriental Dwarf Kingfisher *Ceyx erithacus*
Tiny kingfisher. Orange head with violet iridescence, and black upperparts with variable blue streaking. Juvenile duller, with whitish underparts and orange-yellow bill.

Dark-rumped Swift *Apus acuticauda*
Similar in shape and appearance to Fork-tailed Swift, but has blackish rump, and lacks distinct pale throat.

Oriental Bay Owl *Phodilus badius*
Oblong-shaped, vinaceous-pinkish facial discs. Underparts vinaceous-pink, spotted with black; upperparts chestnut and buff, spotted and barred with black. Call is a series of eerie, upward-inflected whistles.

Indian Bustard *Ardeotis nigriceps*
Very large bustard. In all plumages, has greyish or white neck, black crown and crest, uniform brown upperparts, and white-spotted black wing-coverts. Upperwing lacks extensive area of white.

Chestnut-bellied Sandgrouse *Pterocles exustus*
Pin-tailed, with dark underwing and blackish-chestnut belly. Female has buff banding across upperwing-coverts and lacks black gorget across throat, which are useful distinctions at rest from Black-bellied Sandgrouse.

Black-bellied Sandgrouse *Pterocles orientalis*
Large, stocky and short-tailed. Has black belly, and white underwing-coverts contrast with black flight feathers.

Painted Sandgrouse *Pterocles indicus*
Small, stocky, and heavily barred. Underwing dark grey. Male has chestnut, buff and black bands across breast, and unbarred orange-buff neck and inner-wing coverts. Female heavily barred all over, with yellowish face and throat.

Collared Treepie *Dendrocitta frontalis*
Black face and throat, grey nape and underparts, rufous lower belly and vent, rufous rump, and black tail.

Blue-fronted Robin *Cinclidium frontale*
Long, graduated tail, lacking any white or rufous. Male deep blue, with glistening blue forehead. Female has dark brown tail and uniform pale-brown underparts.

Rufescent Prinia *Prinia rufescens*
Large bill with paler lower mandible. Grey cast to crown, nape and ear-coverts in summer. In non-breeding plumage has more rufescent mantle and edgings to tertials, and has stronger buffish wash to throat and breast, compared with Grey-breasted Prinia. Buzzing call.

Mountain Tailorbird *Orthotomus cuculatus*
Long bill, yellowish supercilium, greyish throat and breast, and yellow belly. Juvenile has olive green crown and nape.

White-spectacled Warbler *Seicercus affinis*
White eye-ring, grey crown and supercilium, well-defined blackish lateral crown stripes; greenish lower ear-coverts, and yellow lores and chin.

Long-billed Wren Babbler *Rimator malacoptilus*
Down-curved bill, dark moustachial stripe, fine buff shaft streaking on upperparts, broad buff streaking on underparts.

Greater Rufous-headed Parrotbill *Paradoxornis ruficeps*
Rufous head, white underparts. Larger and longer-billed than Lesser Rufous-headed Parrotbill. Lores and ear-coverts deep rufous-orange (lores whitish in Lesser).

Yellow-throated Fulvetta *Alcippe cinerea*
Yellow supercilium, black lateral crown-stripes, greyish crown, and yellow throat and breast.

TABLES

SMALL TO MEDIUM-SIZED *PHYLLOSCOPUS* WARBLERS, LACKING WING-BARS AND CROWN STRIPE (+ = vagrant)

Species	Head pattern	Upperparts including wings	Underparts	Call	Additional features
Common Chiffchaff	Whitish or buffish supercilium, and prominent crescent below eye	Greyish to brownish with olive-green cast to rump and edges of remiges and rectrices	Whitish with variable buffish or greyish cast to breast sides and flanks	Plaintive *peu*, more disyllabic *sie-u*	Blackish bill and legs (compare with Greenish, and Dusky)
Dusky Warbler	Broad, buffish-white supercilium with strong dark eye-stripe	Dark brown to paler greyish-brown; never shows any greenish in plumage	White with buff to sides of breast and flanks	Hard *chack chack*	Pale brown legs, and orangish base to lower mandible. Typically skulking
Smoky Warbler	Comparatively short and indistinct yellowish supercilium with prominent white eye-crescent	Dark sooty-olive, with greenish tinge in fresh plumage	Mainly dusky-olive, almost concolorous with upperparts, with oily yellow centre to throat, breast and belly	Throaty *thrup thrup*	Skulking
Tickell's Leaf Warbler	Prominent yellow supercilium concolorous with throat, well-defined eye-stripe	Dark greenish to greenish-brown upperparts, with greenish edges to remiges	Bright lemon-yellow underparts, lacking strong buff tones	A *chit*, or *sit*; not so hard as Dusky	
Sulphur-bellied Warbler	Prominent, bright sulphur-yellow supercilium, distinctly brighter than throat	Cold brown to brownish-grey lacking greenish tones, and with greyish edges to remiges	Yellowish-buff with strong buff tones to breast and flanks, and sulphur-yellow belly	Soft *quip* or *dip*	Climbs about rocks, or nuthatch-like on tree trunks
Radde's Warbler+	Long buffish-white supercilium, contrasting with dark eye-stripe. In fresh plumage, supercilium is buffish-yellow	Olive-brown. In fresh plumage can have pronounced greenish-olive cast	Whitish with buff wash to breast sides and flanks. In fresh plumage, can have buffish-yellow wash to entire underparts	A nervous *twit-twit*, and sharp *chuck chuck*	Long tail, sometimes cocked; stout and rather pale bill; thick and strong-looking orangish legs and feet
Tytler's Leaf Warbler	Prominent, fine white to yellowish-white supercilium, with broad dark olive eye-stripe	Greenish, becoming greyer when worn	Whitish, with variable yellowish wash when fresh	A double *y-it*	Long, slender mainly dark bill; shortish tail

MEDIUM-SIZED TO LARGE *PHYLLOSCOPUS* WARBLERS, WITH NARROW WING-BARS, AND LACKING CROWN STRIPE

Note wing-bars may be missing when plumage is worn (when confusion possible with species in table on p.273)

Species	Head pattern	Upperparts including wings	Underparts	Bill	Call	Other features
Greenish Warbler *P. t. viridanus*	Prominent yellowish-white supercilium, usually wide in front of eye and extends to forehead; eye-stripe, usually falls short of base of bill	Olive-green, becoming duller and greyer when worn; generally lacking darker crown. Single narrow but well-defined white wing-bar	Whitish with faint yellowish suffusion	Lower mandible orangish, usually lacking prominent dark tip	Loud, slurred *chit-wee*	
Greenish Warbler *P. t. nitidus*	Prominent yellowish supercilium, and yellow wash to cheeks	Upperparts brighter and purer green than those of *viridanus*, with one or two slightly broader and yellower wing-bars	Strongly suffused with yellow, which can still be apparent in worn plumage	As *viridanus*	More trisyllabic than that of *viridanus*, a *chis-ru-weet*	
Greenish Warbler *P. t. trochiloides*	Prominent whitish or yellowish-white supercilium, broad, dark eye-stripe and dusky mottling to cheeks	Dark oily green upperparts, with darker olive crown; one or two whitish or yellowish-white wing-bars	Greyish cast to underparts. Often with diffuse oily yellow wash to breast, belly and undertail-coverts	Dark bill, with orange at base, or basal two-thirds, of lower mandible	*Chis-weet*	Very similar to Large-billed; best distinguished by call
Large-billed Leaf Warbler	Striking yellowish-white supercilium contrasting with broad, dark eye-stripe, with greyish mottling on ear-coverts	Dark oily green with noticeably darker crown; one or two yellowish-white wing-bars	Dirty, often with diffuse streaking on breast and flanks and oily yellow wash to breast and belly; can, however, appear whitish	Large and mainly dark, with orange at base of lower mandible; often with pronounced hooked tip	Loud, clear whistled, upward-inflected *der-tee*	Large

SMALL *PHYLLOSCOPUS* WARBLERS WITH BROAD, GENERALLY DOUBLE, WING-BARS; MOST HAVING PALE CROWN STRIPE

Species	Head pattern	Wing bars	Rump and tail	Underparts	Call	Other features
Buff-barred Warbler	Poorly defined dull yellowish crown stripe; yellowish supercilium	Double buffish-orange wing-bars, although median-covert wing-bar often not apparent	White on tail; small yellowish rump patch	Sullied with grey and can be washed with yellow	Short, sharp *swit*	
Ashy-throated Warbler	Greyish-white crown stripe, contrasting with dark grey sides to crown; greyish-white supercilium	Double yellowish wing-bars	White on tail; prominent yellow rump	Greyish throat and breast and yellow belly, flanks and undertail-coverts	Short *swit*	
Lemon-rumped Warbler	Yellowish crown stripe contrasting with dark olive sides to crown; yellowish-white supercilium	Double yellowish-white wing-bars	No white on tail; well-defined yellowish (sometimes almost whitish) rump	Uniform whitish or yellowish-white	High-pitched *uist*	
Yellow-browed Warbler	Lacks well-defined crown stripe, although can show diffuse paler line; broad yellowish-white supercilium and cheeks	Broad, yellowish or whitish wing-bars; median-covert wing-bar is prominent	Lacks pale rump patch and does not have white in tail	White with variable amounts of yellow	A loud *chee-weest*, with distinct rising inflection	Brighter greenish-olive upperparts (in fresh plumage) compared with Hume's. Bill has extensive pale (usually orangish) base to lower mandible, and legs are paler (compared with Hume's)
Hume's Warbler	Lacks well-defined crown stripe, although can show diffuse paler line; broad buffish-white supercilium and cheeks	Broad, buffish or whitish greater-covert wing-bar; median-covert wing-bar tends to be poorly defined, but can be prominent	Lacks pale rump patch and does not have white in tail	White, often sullied with grey	A rolling, disyllabic *whit-hoo* or *visu-visu*, and a flat *chwee*	Greyish-olive upperparts, with variable yellowish-green suffusion, and browner crown. Bill appears all dark and legs are normally blackish-brown

LARGE *PHYLLOSCOPUS* WARBLERS WITH CROWN STRIPE, PROMINENT WING-BARS, AND LARGE BILL WITH ORANGE LOWER MANDIBLE

Species	Head pattern	Upperparts including wings	Underparts	Call	Additional features
Western Crowned Warbler	Greyish-white to pale yellow crown stripe, contrasting with dusky olive sides to crown, which may be darker towards nape; prominent dull yellow supercilium	Generally duller greyish-green compared with Blyth's, with stronger grey cast to nape; wing-bars narrower and less prominent than those of Blyth's, because bases not so dark	Whitish, strongly suffused with grey, especially on throat and breast; can show traces of yellow on breast and belly	A repeated *chit-weei*	Larger and more elongated than Blyth's, with larger and longer bill
Blyth's Leaf Warbler	Tends to be more striking than Western Crowned with yellow supercilium and crown stripe contrasting with darker sides to crown	Usually darker and purer green than those of Western Crowned, although may be similar. Wing-bars are more prominent than those of Western Crowned, being broader and often divided by dark panel across greater coverts	Generally has distinct yellowish wash, especially to cheeks and breast	Constantly repeated *kee-kew-i*	
Yellow-vented Warbler	Brighter yellow crown stripe and supercilium than those of similar species, contrasting with darker sides to crown	Bright yellowish-green with yellow wing-bars	Yellow throat, upper breast and undertail-coverts contrasting with white belly	A double note	

CETTIA BUSH WARBLERS

See plate caption text for description of song

Species	Head pattern	Upperparts	Underparts	Additional features
Pale-footed Bush Warbler	Pale buff supercilium and dark brown eye-stripe; more prominent than that of Brownish-flanked	Rufescent brown	White throat, centre of breast and belly, strongly contrasting with brownish-olive breast sides and flanks	Shorter, square-ended tail compared with Brownish-flanked. Pale pinkish legs and feet
Brownish-flanked Bush Warbler *C. f. pallidus* (W Nepal)	Greyish-white supercilium, less prominent than that of Pale-footed	Olive-brown	Pale buffish-grey with brownish-olive flanks with only a small area of off-white on belly	Longer, rounded tail compared with Pale-footed. Brownish legs and feet
Brownish-flanked Bush Warbler *C. f. fortipes* (E Nepal)	Buffish supercilium, less prominent than that of Pale-footed	Warmer, rufous-brown upperparts compared with *C. f. pallidus* and close to coloration of Pale-footed. First-year? with olive cast	Brownish-buff coloration to throat and breast; olive-buff flanks; duskier underparts than those of Pale-footed. First-year? with yellow wash to belly	As *C. f. pallidus*
Chestnut-crowned Bush Warbler	Chestnut on forehead and crown; supercilium indistinct and rufous-buff in front of eye and buffish-white behind	Dark brown	Whitish with greyish-olive sides to breast and brownish-olive flanks; whiter, particularly on throat and centre of breast, than Grey-sided	Larger than Grey-sided
Aberrant Bush Warbler	Yellowish supercilium	Yellowish-green cast to olive upperparts	Buffish-yellow to olive-yellow, becoming darker olive on sides of breast and flanks. Some worn? birds have less yellow on throat and upper breast and are duller on rest of underparts	
Yellowish-bellied Bush Warbler	Crown is rufous-brown, as mantle; buffish-white supercilium	Pale rufous-brown with strong olive cast, especially to lower back and rump; noticeable rufous fringes to remiges (especially tertials)	Yellowish belly and flanks	Small with small, fine bill
Grey-sided Bush Warbler	Chestnut forehead and crown; short, whitish-buff supercilium is well defined in front of eye (compared with Chestnut-crowned)	Dark brown	Greyish-white with grey sides to breast and brownish-olive flanks	Smaller than Chestnut-crowned

BRADYPTERUS BUSH WARBLERS

Note none of the following species has streaked upperparts; *see* plate caption text for description of song
(+ = vagrant)

Species	Head	Bill	Throat and breast	Undertail-coverts	General appearance
Spotted Bush Warbler	Greyish supercilium	Dark	Usually has bold spotting; some only show fine spotting	Boldly patterned with dark brown centres and sharply-defined white tips	Dark olive-brown with rufescent cast grey ear-coverts and sides of breast, and olive-brown flanks
Chinese Bush Warbler	Yellowish-white to buffish-white supercilium	Whitish-horn lower mandible	Unspotted or with fine spotting on lower throat	Pale tips	Greyer-brown upperparts than those of Brown with olive cast; olive grey-brown ear-coverts and sides of breast, and olive-buff flanks; often with yellowish wash to underparts
Brown Bush Warbler+	Indistinct rufous-buff supercilium, which barely extends beyond eye and is concolorous with the lores	Pale pinkish-orange lower mandible	Lacks spotting	Lack of prominent pale tips	Warm brown upperparts with slight rufescent cast warm rufous-buff ear-coverts, sides of neck and breast, and flanks, contrasting with silky-white of rest of underparts

SMALL UNSTREAKED *ACROCEPHALUS* WARBLERS AND BOOTED WARBLER (+ = vagrant)

Species	Bill/feet	Head pattern	Upperparts	Underparts	Additional features
Black-browed Reed Warbler+	Dark grey legs and feet	Square-ended buffish-white supercilium, broader and more prominent than that of Paddyfield; broad black lateral crown stripes	Rufous-brown in fresh plumage; more olive-brown when worn	Warm buff sides to breast and flanks when fresh	Shorter-looking tail, and longer projection of primaries beyond tertials, compared with Paddyfield
Paddyfield Warbler	Shorter bill than that of Blyth's Reed, usually with well-defined dark tip to pale lower mandible. Yellowish-brown to pinkish-brown legs and feet	Prominent white supercilium, often broadening behind eye, becoming almost square-ended, with dark eye-stripe; supercilium can appear to be bordered above by diffuse dark line. Supercilium less distinct on some	More rufescent than those of Blyth's Reed. Typically shows dark centres and pale fringes to tertials. Greyer or sandier when worn but usually retains rufous cast to rump	Warm buff flanks; underparts whiter when worn. Often shows whitish sides to neck	Typically looks longer-tailed than Blyth's Reed, with tail often held cocked
Blyth's Reed Warbler	Bill longer than that of Paddyfield. Lower mandible either entirely pale or has diffuse dark tip	Comparatively indistinct supercilium; often does not extend beyond eye, or barely does so, and never reaches rear of ear-coverts. Lacks dark upper border to supercilium and dark eye-stripe	Generally colder olive-grey to olive-brown than Paddyfield. Noticeable warm olive cast to upperparts when fresh (more rufescent in first-winter). Tertials rather uniform	Can have light buffish wash to flanks when fresh; otherwise cold whitish	Shorter looking, more rounded tail than that of Booted, and longer upper- and undertail-coverts; more skulking and lethargic than that species
Booted Warbler *H. c. caligata*	Comparatively short and fine bill	Supercilium rather prominent; can appear to have dark border	Warm brown. Fine whitish fringes to remiges and edges of outer tail feathers often apparent	Off-white	Rather *Phylloscopus*-like in appearance, often feeding on ground. Squarer tail and short undertail-coverts compared with *Acrocephalus*

WHITE WAGTAILS (BREEDING MALES ONLY)

Subspecies	Mantle coloration	Head pattern
M. a. dukhunensis	Grey	Black chin; white forehead and face
M. a. personata	Grey	Black chin; white forehead and mask
M. a. alboides	Black	Black chin; white forehead and mask
M. a. leucopsis	Black	White chin and throat; white forehead and face
M. a. ocularis	Grey	As *dukhunensis*, but with black eye-stripe
M. a. baicalensis	Grey	White chin, forehead and face

YELLOW WAGTAILS (BREEDING MALES ONLY)

Subspecies	Head pattern
M. f. beema	Pale bluish-grey head, complete and distinct white supercilium, white chin, and usually a white sub-moustachial stripe contrasting with yellow throat; ear-coverts are grey or brown, usually with some white feathers
M. f. leucocephala	Whole head to nape white, with a variable blue-grey cast on the ear-coverts and rear crown; chin is white, and throat yellow as is rest of underparts
M. f. melanogrisea	Black head, lacking any supercilium, and white chin and poorly defined submoustachial stripe contrasting with yellow throat.
M. f. taivana	Differs from all other races in having olive-green crown, concolorous with mantle, and broad yellow supercilium contrasting with blackish lores and ear-coverts
M. f. thunbergi	Dark slate-grey crown with darker ear-coverts, lacking supercilium (although may show faint trace behind eye)
M. f. lutea	Mainly yellow head, with variable amounts of yellowish-green on crown and nape and ear-coverts (concolorous with mantle)

IDENTIFICATION OF FEMALE ROSEFINCHES

Species	Most likely confusion species	Size/structure	Supercilium	Wing-coverts and tertials	Underparts	Upperparts	Other features
Blanford's	Dark-breasted and Vinaceous	Small and compact	Lacking	Relatively uniform, with indistinct pale fringing	Unstreaked, pale greyish-brown	Uniform grey-brown, unstreaked but for indistinct crown streaking	Reddish or bright olive cast to rump and uppertail-coverts
Dark-breasted	Blanford's and Vinaceous	Relatively small, slim-bodied, with slender bill	Lacking	Variable, broad buffish wing-bars and tips to tertials	Unstreaked, dark greyish-brown	Relatively uniform dark greyish-brown, with diffuse mantle streaking	Dark greyish olive-brown rump
Common	Beautiful	Small and compact, with stout, stubby bill	Lacking	Narrow, whitish or buff tips to coverts, forming narrow double wing-bar	Whitish, with variable, bold, dark streaking	Grey-brown with some dark streaking	Beady-eyed appearance
Beautiful	Common	Small and compact	Whitish, but very poorly defined	Indistinct pale tips to median and greater coverts	Whitish, quite heavily streaked	Buffish-grey, heavily-streaked darker	
Pink-browed	Dark-rumped, Spot-winged and White-browed	Relatively small and compact	Prominent buff supercilium, contrasting with dark ear-coverts	Relatively uniform, lacking wing-barred effect	Heavily streaked, with strong fulvous wash from breast to undertail-coverts	Warm brownish-buff with heavy dark streaking	Fulvous coloration on rump
Vinaceous	Blanford's and Dark-breasted	Relatively small and compact	Lacking	Uniform wing-coverts, but conspicuous whitish tips to tertials	Warm brownish-buff, lightly streaked	Warm brown, almost concolorous with underparts, with diffuse streaking	Plain-faced appearance
Dark-rumped	Pink-browed, Spot-winged and White-browed	Medium-sized	Prominent buff supercilium	Buffish tips to greater coverts and outer edge of tertials	Brownish-fulvous, heavily streaked	Rather dark brown with heavy dark streaking	Lacks well-defined dark ear-coverts
Spot-winged	Pink-browed, Dark-rumped and White-browed	Medium-sized and rather stocky	Prominent, very broad, buff, supercilium	Prominent pale buff tips to greater coverts and outer edge of tertials	Brownish-fulvous, very heavily streaked, including on throat	Rather dark brown with heavy dark streaking	Well-defined dark ear-coverts contrasting with supercilium
White-browed	Pink-browed, Dark-rumped and Spot-winged	Medium-large	Prominent, long, white supercilium, contrasting with dark lower border and rear of ear-coverts	Whitish to buff tips to median and greater coverts, forming narrow double wing-bar	White, heavily streaked, with racially variable ginger-buff wash to throat and breast	Mid to dark brown with heavy dark streaking	Deep olive-yellow rump, heavily streaked
Streaked	Great	Large, with stout bill	Lacking	Lacks prominent wing-bars but has dark centres to median and greater coverts and tertials	Whitish underparts, heavily streaked	Dark grey, rather heavily streaked	
Great	Streaked	Large, with stout bill	Lacking	Relatively uniform, pale grey-brown	Whitish, heavily streaked	Sandy-brown with faint streaking	
Red-fronted	Streaked	Very large, with rather long, conical bill	Lacking	Lacks wing-bars	Greyish, very heavily streaked, with variable pale yellow wash on breast	Very dark grey with bold, heavy dark streaking	Rump and uppertail-coverts more olive than black, or yellow
Crimson-browed Finch	Unmistakable	Large grosbeak-like shape with heavy, stout, stubby bill	Bright olive-yellow, extending across forehead	Relatively uniform	Grey, with olive-yellow breast	Greenish-olive with some diffuse streaking	Often shows olive-yellow rump

IDENTIFICATION OF MALE ROSEFINCHES

Species	Most likely confusion species	Size/structure	General coloration	Supercilium	Wing-coverts and tertials	Underparts	Upperparts	Rump
Blanford's	Common	Small and compact, with relatively slender bill	Pinkish-crimson	Lacking	Lacks wing-bars and contrasting tertial fringes	Dull pinkish-crimson, unstreaked, often with greyish cast	Unstreaked, dull crimson	Unstreaked, dull crimson
Dark-breasted	Dark-rumped	Relatively small, slim-bodied, with long, slender bill	Dark maroon-pink and brown	Quite prominent, reddish-pink, contrasting with dark maroon eye-stripe	Uniform; lacks wing-bars and contrasting tertial fringes	Maroon-brown breast band contrasting with rosy-pink throat and belly	Maroon-brown, with indistinct darker streaks, and reddish-brown forecrown	Maroon-brown, concolorous with rest of upperparts
Common	Blanford's	Small and compact, with short, stubby bill	Bright geranium-red	Lacking	Rather indistinct bright red fringes to wing-coverts and tertials	Bright geranium-red, especially on throat and breast	Diffusely streaked bright geranium-red	Unstreaked, bright red
Beautiful	Pink-browed	Small and compact	Cold greyish-pink	Rather indistinct, pale lilac-pink	Indistinct paler fringes to wing-coverts and tertials	Cold greyish-pink with pronounced dark crown streaks, especially on flanks	Cold pinkish-grey, with conspicuous dark crown and mantle streaking	Contrasting, unstreaked pale lilac-pink
Pink-browed	Beautiful	Smallish and compact	Deep, warm pink	Prominent, deep pink, contrasting with dark maroon-pink eye-stripe	Rather uniform; lacks prominent paler fringing to wing-coverts and tertials	Unstreaked, warm pink	Pinkish-brown mantle and back streaked darker; unstreaked or lightly streaked maroon-pink crown	Unstreaked, deep pink
Vinaceous	Unmistakable	Relatively small and compact	Dark crimson	Prominent, pale pink	Uniform coverts; lacks wing-bars but has prominent pinkish-white tertial tips	Uniform dark crimson	Dark crimson, with diffuse dark mantle streaking	Paler, dull crimson, contrasting with rest of upperparts
Dark-rumped	Dark-breasted and Spot-winged	Medium-sized	Brownish-maroon	Prominent, bright pink, contrasting with pinkish-maroon	Rather indistinct pinkish tips to coverts and buffish tips to tertials	Indistinctly streaked, with brownish-maroon breast and flanks	Pink-tinged brown and broad diffuse streaks	Pinkish-brown, concolorous with rest of upperparts
Spot-winged	Dark-rumped	Medium-sized and rather stocky	Maroon and pink	Prominent, pale pink, contrasting with crown and ear-coverts	Very prominent pink tips to median and greater coverts and tertials	Rather uniform pink, with some darker mottling	Rather uniform maroon, indistinctly streaked, with irregular pink splashes	Maroon, prominently splashed with pink
White-browed	Pink-browed	Medium-large	Brownish and pale pink	Prominent, long, pinkish with splashes of white, extends across forehead	Pronounced pale tips to greater and median coverts forming narrow wing-bars	Pink, with some white streaking	Brown, with conspicuous darker streaking	Pink, well defined contrasting with rest of upperparts
Streaked	Great	Large, with stout bill	Crimson-pink	Lacking	Very indistinct paler fringing	Crimson-pink, with clearly defined white spotting	Grey-brown, washed pink, and with conspicuous darker streaking	Uniform deep pink
Great	Streaked	Large with stout bill	Rose-pink and sandy-grey	Lacking	Very indistinct paler fringing	Rose-pink, with large diffuse white spots	Sandy-grey, washed pink, with narrow streaking	Uniform rose-pink
Red-fronted	Streaked	Very large, with rather long, conical bill	Red and dark grey-brown	Short and red, extending across forehead	Very indistinct paler fringing	Red throat and breast, contrasting with dark-streaked grey-brown remainder of underside	Grey-brown, with bold dark streaks	Deep pink, contrasting with rest of upperparts
Crimson-browed Finch	Confusion very unlikely	Crossbeak-like shape with large, stout, stubby bill	Red and brownish-green	Red, extending across forehead	Very indistinct paler fringing	Red throat and upper breast, contrasting with pale olive-grey remainder of underparts	Warm olive-brown, tinged with red, and diffusely streaked	Quite bright red, uniform

INDEX

Figures in **bold** are plate numbers; * = vagrant to Nepal; (H) = collected by Hodgson (Appendix 2)

English Names

Scientific Names